THE SIGNIFIER POINTING AT THE MOON

THE SIGNIFIER POINTING AT THE MOON
Psychoanalysis and Zen Buddhism

Raul Moncayo

KARNAC

Masao Abe, *Zen and Western Thought*, 1999, University of Hawaii Press, reproduced with permission of Palgrave Macmillan.

Ekaku Hakuin (1685–1788). Daruma, 18th century. Hanging scroll, ink on paper © 2012 Museum Associates/LACMA. Licensed by Art Resource, NY.

First published in 2012 by
Karnac Books Ltd
118 Finchley Road
London NW3 5HT

British Library Cataloguing in Publication Data

A C.I.P. for this book is available from the British Library

ISBN-13: 978-1-85575-476-8

Typeset by V Publishing Solutions Pvt Ltd., Chennai, India

Printed in Great Britain

www.karnacbooks.com

In Zen, the positive and creative aspects of human thinking have been neglected and only its dualistic and discriminative aspects have been clearly realized as something to be overcome. Reason in Buddhism was only grasped as a negative principle .... The Zen position of non-thinking always harbors the danger of degenerating into not-thinking .... Essentially, the standpoint of non-thinking should also be able to be said to have the possibility of giving life to the positive aspects of human thinking that have been developed in the West. But this possibility has not yet been actualized. Precisely the actualization and existentialization of this possibility must be the theme of the future for the standpoint of the true emptiness of the Eastern tradition.

Masao Abe,
Zen and Western Thought (1999, p. 112)

CONTENTS

ACKNOWLEDGEMENTS

I wish to dedicate this book to my Zen teacher Sojun Mel Weitsman Roshi to thank him for his teaching over several decades of practice and study of Soto Zen, for transmitting Suzuki Roshi's teaching of beginner's mind, and for having supported me despite his misgivings about psychoanalysis, intellectual pursuits, and doing more than One main thing in one's life. This book represents my One purposeful or "senseless" mistake of proposing a non-dual relationship between Zen and psychoanalysis. Are they one or are they two? The relationship between Zen and psychoanalysis is best described by the Zen principle of "Not-one, not-two". Only the mistake is One; neither the two nor me are. Do you understand? This book will neither mix them up nor leave psychoanalysis and Zen unrelated and isolated from one another.

Sections of Chapter One were previously published in the *Journal for the Psychoanalysis of Culture and Society* under the title "Psychoanalysis and postmodern spirituality" (1998). Chapter Two began as a response to Michael Thompson's commentary on a chapter that was published in Safran's edited collection on *Psychoanalysis and Buddhism* (Wisdom Books, 2003). Chapter Nine is an expanded and revised version of the chapter in Safran's book. Chapter Three is an expanded version of a chapter that appeared in Molino's edited collection: *Tra Sogni Del Buddha E Risvegli Di Freud* ("From the Dreams of the Buddha to the Awakenings of Freud", Milan: Arpanet, 2010). Sections of Chapter Four appeared under a different title in the journal *Psychoanalysis and Contemporary Thought* (Autumn 1998). Finally, Chapter Five is a revised and updated version of a paper that was published in the *International Journal for the Psychology of Religion* (Autumn 1998).

Last but not least, I want to thank Andre Patsalides for being one of the few Lacanian analysts who openly supported my interest in Zen and psychoanalysis, and for believing that my understanding and elaboration of Lacanian psychoanalysis were significantly enhanced and made possible by Zen practice. Patsalides' stance is entirely consistent, of course, with what Roudinesco called Lacan's desire for the Far East.

The first and third paragraphs of this page point to a polarity between Zen and psychoanalysis that is not always easily negotiated. Despite D. T. Suzuki's and Fromm's introduction of Zen to the West as a form of spirituality highly compatible with Western Enlightenment values, tensions between Western and Eastern approaches to enlightenment still remain. Many psychoanalysts, intellectuals, and scientists, especially in Europe, remain highly suspicious of any religion or spirituality, including Buddhism, and there are Buddhists who reject many of the values associated with the modern and postmodern worlds.

The latter has become a tension internal to Buddhism itself, and one that has a long history within the Buddhist tradition extending all the way back to councils before the Common Era. Monasticism may reject the modern ordinary world and promote a life consistent with the monastic or ascetic rules that existed during the Middle Ages whether in Europe or Asia (China and Japan). Lay Zen Buddhists, by contrast, emphasise the importance of living and testing/tasting the Dharma and meditation practice in ordinary activities of life in the contemporary world. Both of these "sides" over time have struggled for the control of the legitimate or authentic manifestation of the tradition. Sometimes monks refer to lay practice as "Zen Lite" (as lightweight and "laid-back" or lazy illumination). These kinds of expected disagreements diminish the non-duality of the teaching of Big mind or beginners' mind whether in its monastic or lay aspects. Most Buddhists interested in psychoanalysis have come from the lay manifestation of meditation practice, although not exclusively. Several monasteries or residential communities in the West have enlisted the help of psychoanalysts or psychotherapists to help them with the mental health problems of community members or to facilitate issues and scandals within community residential life.

Finally, internal tensions and divisions, not unlike those of Buddhism, also exist within psychoanalysis and psychology, but for different reasons. My personal way of working through these tensions is by creation, rather than by ignoring or holding grudges against different perspectives. The importance of creativity highlights the value of scholarship and the free exercise of reason/intuition (the sun of the Real) and language (evocative and communicative) in providing a venue for differences to be aired out. It is very important to address differences in a Way that bypasses the restrictions and bitterness that group dynamics and hierarchies place upon open and empty speech. May this book be of some help in building a bridge across the various schools and perspectives.

ABOUT THE AUTHOR

Raul Moncayo is a Zen teacher at the Berkeley Zen Center in the lineage of Shunryo Suzuki Roshi, supervising analyst of the Lacanian School of Psychoanalysis of the San Francisco Bay Area, and Training Director for Mission Mental Health in San Francisco. He has a private practice of psychoanalysis and psychotherapy.

INTRODUCTION

This book is intended as a contribution to the growing field of psychoanalysis and Buddhism and reviews most of what has been published on the subject. This book differs from books that are written "as if" this was the first book on the subject.

Unfortunately, books are often marketed in this way. Whether in psychoanalysis or Buddhism, many books ignore or don't mention other authors who have written books on the same topic. This is an aspect of power and capitalism (master's discourse) that creeps into the ideology of the social sciences and spiritual literature. Without critical theory or a metalevel analysis that can take various social, cultural, and ideological factors into account, market forces and the ego will continue to rule the production and diffusion of knowledge even in the universities. The natural sciences may be in a better position because of the agreement on the scientific method and established channels for funding and publication.

The social sciences need different levels/types of logic and therefore the exclusive appeal to the empirical method and the limitations of university discourse only fragments the field among different cultural and national manifestations. The lack or paucity of critical theory leaves people with pragmatic or technical procedures that become more rigid and fragmented over time and applicable to limited situations, circumstances, and populations. Authors come up with their own pet theories, however deficient these may be in the light of the broader stream of knowledge that has been transmitted over the generations. At the other end, sophisticated theories can become dogmatic statements by forcing adherence to principles of faith that ignore other schools of thought and practice.

In the case of Zen in China, the five original schools, of which two survived (Soto and Rinzai), were somewhat unified by the common practice of zazen or Zen meditation. In addition, Zen is related to the larger movement of Mahayana Buddhism, which includes Tibetan Buddhism, and that owes its inner coherence to the scholarly writings of Nagarjuna and Vasubhandu. The latter were two major theorists/practitioners/ancestors of the Mahayana who were inspired by magnificent Mahayana sutras (Heart sutra, Lankavatara sutra, Surangama sutra, Vimalakirti sutra, and others).

The element of tradition is important because it constitutes the reference for considerations of legitimacy and authenticity in both psychoanalysis and Buddhism. New generations imbue the tradition with new meaning and develop criteria by which to transform the tradition over time. Here there is a difference between Kohut and Lacan, for example. Kohut was against Freud and Oedipal theory. Lacan was not against Freud, he studied him closely, and then proceeded to place Freudian theory in a new framework that to a large degree preserves Freud's insights and logic while amplifying the range and meaning of the theory. The Other has to be carefully used in order to realise the self or the subject and generate enduring permutations/corrections within the theory/teaching.

The first chapter of this book reviews the literature on the psychology of religion as well as the literature on religion and psychoanalysis. The more specific literature on Zen and psychoanalysis will be considered throughout the book. Although the foreground focus of the book is the relationship between Zen Buddhism and Lacanian psychoanalysis, its content matter will be examined and elucidated against the cultural background of the relationships among tradition, modernity, and postmodernity, and within the larger context of the psychology of religion (which Freud considered an important sister science of psychoanalysis), and the similarities and differences among various psychoanalytic schools. Finally, differences among different forms of Buddhism will also be considered wherever relevant.

The dialogue between psychoanalysis and Buddhism, which begun with Erich Fromm, has become quite popular within English-American culture. It is important to remember that Fromm was a member of the Frankfurt School of critical theory which itself was a basis for the later development of postmodernism and poststructuralism in France. Fromm had a background in Marxism, social theory, and Talmudic studies, in addition to being a psychoanalyst and having a keen interest in Zen Buddhism. Unfortunately, his humanistic tendencies, and his successful attempt to reach larger audiences (for example, with his book on the art of love), resulted in an unintended watering down of psychoanalysis that may have affected the fate of his work in one or two generations.

Much has been written about the relationship between psychoanalysis and Judaism, and some even criticise psychoanalysis for being a Jewish science. On the other hand, many of the greatest modern scientists and secular intellectuals have been Jewish in the likes of Freud, Marx, and Einstein. In addition, many of the Western teachers of Buddhism are Jewish, and much has also been said about the relationship between Judaism and Buddhism. There is even a term for Jewish Buddhists: "Jew-Bus". "Jew-Bu" or "Ju-Bu" can be thought of as a neologism or a hermeneutical device built on the homophony between Judah and Buddha (JHBH). Lacan himself was interested in Judaism and Talmudic studies which influenced his work on the Name of the Father despite the Christian history of the concept (as one of the terms of the Trinity). Lacan had a daughter with Sylvia Bataille whose family was Jewish. Roudinesco (1986, p. 147) writes how Lacan went to the police headquarters in occupied Paris and demanded his mistress's family papers. Once he had them in his hands, he quickly ripped them, although he had promised to bring them back. I myself studied Judaism for a period of ten years, and the products of these studies are reflected in Chapters Five and Six as well as throughout the book.

Fromm was interested in the general questions of wellbeing and existential suffering beyond the specific questions posed by clinical suffering and professional expertise. Like in the case of Jungian analysis, this approach would lead people to regard (and critique) psychoanalysis as an alternative or replacement for religion. The questions of wellbeing and existential suffering point to character problems that quickly came to represent the rock that impeded the further progress of psychoanalysis as a treatment method.

On the one hand, psychoanalysis has to become adept at working with ego-syntonic character traits that serve as wellsprings for the development or fixation of symptomatology; on the other hand, the questions posed by character (without clinical symptoms) may be better and less expensively addressed by meditation practice. In some way, these questions lie at the centre of Lacan's interest in what he called the *sinthome*. The *sinthome* is both an aspect of a clinical symptom, a character trait, and at the same time represents what remains of the symptom after analysis or a professional intervention. The *sinthome* lies at the intersection of clinical and existential suffering. Finally, the distinction between clinical and existential suffering is not absolute given that Lacan, for example, used existential questions to define and differentiate the two basic forms of neuroses.

Over the last fifteen years, several books have been published that explore the relationship between Buddhism and psychoanalysis. Epstein (2007), Magid (2002), and Bobrow (2010), focus on psychotherapy rather than psychoanalysis (although the last two are trained psychoanalysts), perhaps in order to broaden the possible reach and interest in their books. Epstein follows ego-psychology, Bobrow could be placed in the object-relations camp, and Magid emerges out of the stream of self-psychology (Kohut). Finally, there are books on Zen and psychotherapy (for example, Rosenbaum, 1999) that are not psychoanalytic in orientation.

Prior to these books, there was a string of edited collections. First was *The Soul on the Couch* (Spezzano, 1997), then came Anthony Molino's (2001) *The Couch and the Tree*, and more recently, *Psychoanalysis and Buddhism: An Unfolding Dialogue* (Safran, 2003) features several authors in dialogue with both psychoanalysts and Buddhist teachers. Although I contributed a chapter to this last work, most prior works have been written mainly from an ego-psychology and object relation's perspective within psychoanalysis (notably Engler, 1981; Epstein, 1995; Rubin, 1996; and Suler, 1993). I decided to write this book not only to offer the Lacanian perspective in which I was formed, but also because I believe that the Lacanian framework offers a fresh perspective from which to consider the internal relations between psychoanalysis and Buddhism.

It is well known that the Lacanian corpus has been linked to a decentring of the ego and a critique of ego-psychology that Lacan believed to be one of the more radical consequences of psychoanalysis and of the Freudian view of the unconscious. Lacan called Zen the religion of the subject and the best of the East. Lacan also interprets psychoanalysis as a radical critique of ego-ideals and identifications. In contrast to this, the object relations (Fairbain, Winnicott, Mahler), ego-psychology, and self-psychology schools all privilege the importance of developing a coherent or integrated ego or self-identity. Prior authors (Engler, 1981; Epstein, 1995; Rubin, 1996; Suler, 1993) have identified this fact as the most salient point of difference or contradiction between contemporary psychoanalysis and the Buddhist doctrine of no-self.

The above authors view the two traditions as holding opposing perspectives with regard to the problem of self and no-self. Buddhism believes in no-self or that the self is a fiction, whereas ego- and self-psychology believe that mental health requires the existence of a coherent and integrated self. Engler and Epstein argue that ego-functions are fundamental for meditation practice.

The Buddhist notion of no-self does not conflict with the Lacanian paradigm given that this is precisely a point where both traditions coincide to a significant degree. The Lacanian perspective offers a view more compatible with Buddhism on the basis of the Lacanian critique of ego-psychology and the related distinction between the ego and the subject. Both converge on the formula that "true subject is no-ego", or on the realisation that the true subject requires the symbolic death or deconstruction of imaginary ego-identifications and representations.

This book attempts to clarify and reframe some of the misunderstandings between psychoanalysis and Buddhism, and between Eastern and Western cultures. Psychoanalysts, as the secular ministers of the soul, classically rejected religion and Buddhism on the basis of considering meditation practice as a kind of primitive hypnotic trance and regression to an archaic pre-rational or irrational fusion with the mother. In prior work (Moncayo, 2008), I proposed various degrees within narcissism, as a contribution to psychoanalysis, but also to help differentiate the emptiness of the subject in meditation experience from the primitive identification with the maternal object.

On the other hand, psychoanalysts do not have the privilege of holding the most prejudice against different perspectives by any means. Within Buddhism, many Buddhists have very negative views and prejudice towards psychoanalysis and towards rational Western thought in general. Masao Abe's quote (1999, p. 2) points to this reality. Rubin has also coined the term "Oriento-centrism" to describe this phenomenon. In Zen, many even reject the value of formal intellectual study. Despite Zen teachings about meditation being the first principle, and scholarly study the second, many Zen practitioners in the past have rejected formal scholarly enquiry even as a second principle. Some forms of Chinese or "Chan" meditation practice were conceived in exclusion of the latter.

In some ways, this is still the legacy of the dualistic conflict between tradition and modernity. Traditional intuition and wisdom suppress the rational ego-intellect, whereas modernity and the latter suppress the former. When neither intuition nor the intellect is suppressed, it is humanity that benefits. Reason, as the sun of the Real, is not based on the ego, and traditional wisdom represents a larger dimension of reason rather than its sheer negation. Thus, although Lacanian psychoanalysis gives a lot of credence to language, and Zen is considered a form of transmission and wisdom beyond the scriptures, Zen is not without words, while Lacanian psychoanalysis stresses the meaningful or senseless letter of the Real or of a *jouissance* written on and with the body.

With this book, I am building a bridge across the cultural and experiential chasm or duality between psychoanalysis and Zen Buddhism, while steering clear of reducing one to the other or creating a simplistic synthesis between the two. In any relationship, both parties have to keep their own place, to be related as well as independent at the same time. Psychoanalysis and Zen Buddhism are related but are not identical. Psychoanalysis addresses the clinical illnesses of humanity whereas Buddhism is the medicine for the larger general existential condition. However, the two traditions should not be collapsed into one another since either one may contain treasures as yet unforeseen and realised by current generations and circumstances.

In addition, both traditions require direct personal insight and emotional catharsis/release as well as scholarly study or investigation. Without personal and direct experience with either psychoanalysis or Zen Buddhism, it is difficult, if not impossible, to transmit either one of them. Book knowledge leads to the practice that then, in turn, illuminates the true experiential meaning of the teaching.

Both psychoanalysis and Buddhism use symbolic forms to access the body–mind relationship and a dimension of experience that lies beyond the reach of ordinary ego-experience (the Real). However, both practices also differ in that what is specific to the analytic path is the use of the Symbolic and language to reach the Real but via the intermediary of the Imaginary. In contrast to this, although Buddhism shares with psychoanalysis a critique of illusions and the imaginary, Buddhism does not explore and track the Oedipal fantasy material that leads to the construction of a false sense of self.

For Lacan, individuality and individuation is not yet. Developmentally, for Lacan, the subject has to separate not only from the mother and the Imaginary via the father and the Symbolic but also from the ideal father and the imaginary use of the Symbolic by realising the non-existence of the Other and of the ego. This paves the way for the real being of the subject, *son être du sujet*. Development seems to consist of a series of progressive and dialectical interactions between non-being or emptiness and the various formations of being and their successive cancellations or negations. The breast is replaced by the internal representation of the object, only to be replaced by the specular image and the ideal ego. The ideal ego then needs to be abandoned in favour of the ego-ideal and the identification with the imaginary father. Finally, following Lacan, and Zen Buddhism, I argue that the imaginary father and the ego-ideal need to be abandoned in the direction of the symbolic father and the empty subject of the Real. It is only in this final form of subjectivity that the ego can become the subject in the strict sense outlined by Lacan.

Thus, within the Lacanian paradigm, the lack in the Other, or the destitution of the imaginary father, represents a source of creativity and inventiveness. Desire does not conflict with emptiness because a desire for emptiness or the emptiness at the root of desire regenerates rather than negates or ends desire. This "middle way" perspective, as a meeting point between the Mahayana teaching of Nagarjuna and Lacanian psychoanalysis, reframes the alleged opposition between Buddhist asceticism and psychoanalytic hedonism.

Lacan writes about desire in such a way that sometimes refers to the Freudian concept of wish and sometimes to a different notion emergent in his work. I argue that in one of the implicit Lacanian notions of desire, desire is not finding an object for a forbidden wish but the simple manifestation of infinite emptiness. It is this notion of desire that is pivotal for the understanding of the desire of the analyst. Strictly speaking, whether in Zen or psychoanalysis, there is no liberation from desire itself because such would imply another desire. What becomes possible is to leave the object of desire unfixed and mutable and thereby access the opening of being into emptiness.

Finally, contrary to delusion or psychosis, the empty subject of the Real or the non-ego is precisely what establishes, forges, and supports the link between two signifiers and weaves together the net of the symbolic order and the symbolic and cohesive functioning of the subject. In psychosis, the opposite is true: the severing of the link between subjects and signifiers renders the subject prey to the tyranny of the Imaginary.

The notion of the Real as emptiness needs to be distinguished from how the Real appears within the Imaginary in the image of the phallic mother. This is what has led many within psychiatry and psychoanalysis to confuse so-called mystical experience with psychosis and the "oceanic feeling" characteristic of the mother–infant symbiosis.

It is the Real as a vacuum plenum that turns the wheel of interpretation and begets/releases the sparks and light of new poetic significations. Poetry, just like dreams, has a navel that opens out on to the unknown, on to the empty kernel of being or para-being. Both in Zen and psychoanalysis, playing with words opens up a dimension of experience (the empty Real) that escapes the closure and circularity of ordinary discourse. Turning words in Zen or key Lacanian signifiers, with antithetical or non-dual meaning, gather significations under a unifying principle that generates and transcends meaning at the same time. From the wellsprings of the Real, words are reorganised to generate a new incomprehensible meaning beyond the conventional meaning of words.

Throughout the length of his work, Freud struggled with the concept of sublimation as an independent vicissitude of the drive. He oscillated between linking sublimation with the vicissitudes of aim-inhibited drives (and with defences such as reaction-formation) and thinking of sublimation as a way of producing a direct satisfaction of the drive without involving repression. At stake is whether sublimation conceals or reveals the object of the drive. By defining sublimation as what elevates an object to the dignity of *das Ding* (the Thing or No-thing), Lacan stressed the revelatory dimension of sublimation. But the deconstruction of the Name of the Father at the end of analysis cannot signify a return to the omnipotence of the maternal object because this would represent an actual undoing of sublimation. I argue that Lacan's concept of *das Ding* has more than one meaning and cannot solely represent the archaic maternal object as usually discussed within Lacanian theory.

I propose that the two meanings of the concept of sublimation depend on two different ways of conceiving *das Ding* and the function of the Real. There is the Real of the *objet a* in relation to the Imaginary and then there is the Real of the subject in relation to the signifier. The Name of the Father as ego-ideal represents the defensive function of sublimation. It is what serves as defence and a barrier against the desire of the mother. *Das Ding* appears as a terrifying presence or absence when it functions as an absolute Other to the ego-ideal not the subject. The "Thing" that appears along the Real–Imaginary axis can be described as the id of the Real, the traumatic and anxiety-producing primeval object.

In contradistinction to the id, when *das Ding* is revealed along the Real–Symbolic axis, it is better represented by the It of Zen Buddhism. The It of Zen differs from the It in the work of Buber (1923) or some forms of humanism or existentialism. In the latter, the It represents a form of objectification of others and the world which would be more consistent with the Freudian id, where the object is perceived as an object of the drive and/or of the ego. "It" in Zen represents the no-thing beyond the dual subject–object relationship, or where the object is not there to complete or close the gap in the subject. What is the Other beyond the ego, and "What" the subject beyond the object? Subject and object arise together as a function of the Other-dependent nature, although the Thou or the Other can also be found in the subject in the form of "This" or the It of the Real.

The primitive *das Ding* appears when the ego comes close to the discovery that its most cherished image (ego) is merely an object (*a*) of the *jouissance* of the (m)Other. The ideal father, or the imaginary use of the Name of the Father, functions as a defence against the discovery of this malevolent form of depersonalisation. The ideal father is placed in lieu of rather than elevated to the dignity of the *objet a* (*das Ding*). Finally, the ancient dignity of the object, what gives the object the quality of "the no-thing" (*das Ding*), is not so much the presence of a fixed imaginary object but rather the emptiness at the core of the object and the subject. In addition, the emptiness of the object does not only allude to the absence of the object but to emptiness as a benevolent presence and to a presence within absence. As the love poem of Pablo Neruda (1924) goes: "I like it when you are still and quiet because it is as if you were absent." It looks like you are absent but in reality you are only sitting still. When we sit still and quiet, we are like the *objet a*: although it is there, it is empty, and although it is not there, it is.

CHAPTER ONE

The cultural context: contemporary psychoanalysis and postmodern spirituality

The historical context

It is well known that since the eighteenth century, the most optimistic proponents of the Enlightenment and the scientific paradigm had predicted the demise of spirituality and religion. This has proven to be only partially true. Statistical studies (Wuthnow, 1992) have shown that the scientific mindset has succeeded in establishing itself as an alternative paradigm in the thinking of most people. However, people also tend to mix scientific and spiritual views in varying proportions. Thus, science has succeeded; but on the other hand, the empirical evidence points largely to the survival of spirituality in the post-secular era.

Thus, spirituality has become a growing focus of interest in contemporary Western culture. After a couple of centuries that witnessed the rapid growth of science and modernity, it is now plausible to assume that postmodern-world people are interested in legitimising and re appropriating the truths embedded in traditional cross-cultural ways and practices. Sociological studies (Roof et al., 1995) have reported an unmistakable trend in the baby-boom generation that describes how in Europe and the United States disenchantment with traditional Western religion has led to a search for spiritual alternatives such as Westernised versions of Hinduism and Buddhism. Moreover, it is interesting to note that, with the exception of fundamentalists, most people appear to be retaining the values of a modern secular society as well.

Political developments initiated by the Enlightenment have also helped to make the contemporary landscape possible. The democratic pluralism emerging from the Enlightenment not only undermined the dominant position of the Judaeo-Christian religious tradition but unwittingly also curtailed the possible ideological hegemony of the scientific paradigm. The modern values of tolerance and pluralism, combined with migration patterns associated with post-colonialism, plus the development of technologies of mass communication and transportation within a global economy, have led to a convergence of many traditional models nervously co-existing in the midst of scientific modernity.

Furthermore, it is likewise important to remember that trends towards the transformation of religion have co-existed for two centuries in the West alongside the rejection of religion advocated by the scientific paradigm. The Enlightenment of humanity promised by the natural and social sciences sought not only the elimination of religion but also a more evolved form of spirituality and/or religiosity. Current trends of spiritual renewal and negative theology within Buddhism, Judaism, and Christianity are the heirs apparent of spiritual tendencies within the Enlightenment. The goal of the Enlightenment was to transform and not simply to eliminate religion. In this historical context or juncture, Buddhism has been introduced in the West.

The psychology of religion

Psychology, and psychoanalysis in particular, has been regarded by many as the instrument required for a radical cleansing of religion from dogma, intolerance, prejudice, and bigotry. Thus, although the majority of psychologists reject conventional expressions of religion, and both psychoanalysis and behaviourism have considered religion as antithetical to a scientific or materialistic point of view, within psychoanalysis and its offshoots the views regarding religion have extensively fallen into two camps. The first represented by Freud follows the tendencies of the Enlightenment to completely replace religion with science and a rational approach to ethical principles. The second camp described below follows the aspects of "the enlightenment" that sought to transform religion. Mahayana Buddhism (Zen Buddhism, Tibetan Buddhism, and *Vipassana* meditation in the United States) looks very much like the kind of transformed religion that the Enlightenment envisioned and that potentially stands in a very compatible relationship to a renewed psychoanalytic perspective regarding the psychology of religion.

A long list of distinguished psychologists and social scientists has developed concepts and theories in search of a purified religion compatible with scientific rationality. They all accept the modern and liberal climate of opinion contained within Freud's psychological analysis and critique of religion, yet at the same time most of these authors reject the Freudian view as applicable or accurate to describe the non-defensive and non-pathological aspects of religious experience.

William James (1902) sought the conceptual basis for a true religion based on experience rather than on chronic institutional affiliation. Jean Piaget (1932) in his developmental psychology of morality and cognition differentiated between a morality of obedience, heteronomy, and unilateral respect and a morality of autonomy, equality, and reciprocity. Oscar Pfister (1944), a Protestant minister and a personal friend of Freud, advocated a psychoanalytic profilaxis to rid religion of infantile fixations. Adorno and colleagues (1950) distinguished between institutionalised practice that relates to religion as a means to a socio-economic end and genuinely interiorised religion that is an end-in-itself.

Allport (1950) followed Adorno in developing scales to separate empirically extrinsic from intrinsic religion. Fromm (1950) developed a similar approach with his humanistic versus authoritarian approach to religion. Carl Jung (1962) was critical of religious beliefs not based on understanding and experience and sought to discover a new form of religiosity based on the numinosity of the archetypes in the collective unconscious. The school of humanistic psychology also joined this rising chorus to emphasise the importance of human potential as the aim of spiritual and religious practice. Maslow (1964) made a distinction between those self-actualised types who have peak experiences and those who are not and do not. Finally, also within humanistic psychology, May (1957a) differentiated dogmatic faith from genuine inner conviction, mature from immature dependence, and defensive from non-defensive religion. As far as forms of religious practice are concerned, liberal and psychologically oriented spirituality has advocated meditation and meditative prayer as paragons of authentic spirituality over what is seen as the more archaic practice of petitionary prayers to parent-like figures and representations.

The scientific method has been used to both delegitimise religion as well as to give it a pseudoscientific dignity. In the first case, empirical research or scientific empiricism has added support to the Enlightenment's and Freud's theoretical critique of the negative side of conventional religion. Galton was the first to employ the method of statistical correlation to investigate the efficacy of petitionary or supplicative prayer. He found no discernible advantage or subjective gain associated with petitionary prayer. Studies by Vetter (1958), Gorsuch and Aleshire (1974), among others, have all shown positive correlations between conventional religion and negative attitudes such as bigotry, prejudice, racism, indifference to social problems, and even dishonesty.

On the other hand, neither do such studies lend support to the kind of non-sympathetic attitude towards religion that led many scientists (including Freud) to choose its worst part or aspects in order to dismiss it altogether. Bellah (1970) has referred to this attitude as a form of scientific or Enlightenment fundamentalism. Successive studies (Feagin, 1964) have argued that it is only extrinsic and conventional religion that is negatively correlated with ethical attitudes and mental health or wellbeing. However, still other studies (Altemayer, 1988; Bock & Warren, 1972) have yielded no difference between the intrinsic and extrinsic scales in terms of a positive correlation with prejudice, racism, and so on. But researchers have also been able to separate confounding variables such as low levels of education (Feagin, 1964), intelligence (Brand, 1981), and frequency of spiritual practice (Shinert & Ford, 1958) that go a long way in accounting for the positive correlations mentioned.

Nonetheless, the problem with empirical research is that all findings completely depend on the content of the measuring instrument, its construction or design, and the characteristics of the sampling population used. This book is in agreement with David Wulff (1991) when he argues that the intrinsic scale still partakes of what Fromm (1976) has called the having as opposed to the being mode. Such spirituality measured on an intrinsic scale is still directed towards some future purpose or goal. At this level, although the aim may be spiritual and go beyond a simple interest in institutional affiliation and the social benefits thereof, practice is still conceived as a means to obtain something (a new experience or self, etc.) and thus remains within the grip of an ideological, utilitarian, or imaginary effect. This work will argue that in order to find the authentic spirituality that would go beyond small-minded prejudices and discriminations, it becomes necessary to access a realm and a dimension of subjectivity beyond beliefs and ego-based ideals.

Psychoanalysis and religion: classical and contemporary perspectives

In the materialistic and behaviourist critique of religion, the world of mystery is a way for priests to hold on to social and political control/power. To this effect, religion fosters illusions and dogmas that are unverifiable in principle. Nevertheless, more than as dogmas, symbolic or spiritual forms of Being need to be understood as mythical evocations of that which lies at the limit of the visible and invisible, as prismatic perspectives on truths that are enigmatic by their very definition. Truth within the Real can never be completely or exhaustively formulated by logic or language, and this is to be contrasted to the postmodern, deconstructionist, or constructivist stance whereby truth as such does not exist. In addition, postmodernism and existentialism, as forms of hyper-modernism, preserve and maintain a materialistic and empiricist notion of myth (as ideology or false knowledge) identical to that found in behaviourism, Marxism, and certain positivistic aspects of the Freudian corpus.

In this respect, Freud's views as outlined in *Totem and Taboo* (1913) and *Moses and Monotheism* (1939) are inaccurate only in so far as they are presented to be positivistic, objective, and scientific historical facts. I follow Lacan in his conception of these Freudian works as modern mythological structures. Employing a term elaborated by Freud (1901) himself, one could call this area of the Freudian corpus a true "psychomythology". The two works aforementioned contain truths not as facts but as myths and metaphors.

In line with this, Lacan followed Lévi-Strauss in rejecting the notion that mythical thought is somehow less rigorous and demanding than scientific thought. In this area of his work, Freud's texts ironically become akin to narrative biblical or traditional stories which describe events that need to be interpreted symbolically and hermeneutically, as opposed to literally or objectively. Although Lacan declared he was more interested in the literal letter of the law rather than its spirit, his declared literalism has to be understood as a literary and linguistic interest and not as a fundamentalist interpretation of scripture.

Finally, with regard to the notion of myth, although Lacan followed Lévi-Strauss rather than Jung, his views are not far removed from Jung's where the latter refers to his work as a circumambulation of unknown factors that constantly requires new definitions and perspectives. Jung considered his opus a new mythical statement and a re-embodiment and permutation of timeless factors. Both Lacan and Bion have formulated ideas similar to Jung, while remaining much more Freudian and true to Freud's work than Jung ever was.

Lacan questioned the notion of progress or of lineal development according to which anything that comes after is necessarily better or more evolved than what came before. Thus, the work of Lacan provides a postmodern interpretation of Freud that allows for a more sympathetic understanding of traditional culture. Traditional culture contained a relationship to a dimension of experience and reality that is lost to the secular, scientific mentality. This work uses the terms "traditional", "modern", and "postmodern" not merely as words but to designate specific conceptual structures. The common use of these terms merely designates a temporal reference: modern is synonymous with contemporary, new, or current, whereas traditional refers to the old and the past (that is, the often mentioned reference to "traditional" psychotherapy or psychoanalysis).

Within the present postmodern paradigm, modern refers to modernity as the secular scientific paradigm with all of its accompanying aesthetic and ethical values, whereas tradition or traditional refers to cultural traditions existing before and outside the Western scientific paradigm. From my perspective, postmodern ideas point in the direction of a new cross-cultural paradigm that permutates and combines, without necessarily integrating or synthesising, traditional and modern, Western and Eastern, European and American, conceptual structures. As mentioned above, this definition of the postmodern begs to differ from mainstream postmodern thought where the latter adopts hyper-modern views and loses the sense of a Real beyond a purely discursive social reality.

This work accepts the modern Enlightenment critique of the dark or pathological side of religion and views Freud's work on the subject as a necessary psychology of such phenomena. It is well known that

Freud (1907) labelled religion the obsessive neurosis of humanity and that he was inclined to interpret spirituality as a defence against sexual and aggressive drives. Freud's materialistic stance follows from the eighteenth-century scientific paradigm that had mistakenly predicted the demise of religion and spirituality. Freud (1927) dismissed the consolations provided by religion as either infantile symbiosis with the mother or infantile dependence on a providential father.

Unlike Freud who judged spirituality to serve only defensive functions and to be in opposition to reality, Lacan has pointed out that metaphor or myth (the Oedipus myth, for example) may be a preferable medium for accessing a dimension of reality and of human experience that cannot be entirely grasped by reason or scientific method. In addition, metaphor always leaves us with the echo and evocation of something that is beyond words and logic.

Lacan's work differs from the school of hermeneutics in that his theory also includes a register of experience that is beyond words and the symbolic order (the Real). I would also argue that the Real differs from the traditional notion of the supernatural and of an extrinsic God by being intrinsic to human experience although outside language and the *a priori* categories of reason. Finally, the concept of the Real also differs from Western metaphysics because metaphysics in philosophy represents abstract ideas underlying the world of appearances.

My interpretation of Lacanian ideas as applied to the psychoanalysis of spirituality also converges with the intellectual tradition in the psychology of religion which accepts Freud's psychological critique of religion as only applicable to the extrinsic and institutionalised traditional religion but not to the non-defensive, non-illusory, and non-pathological aspects of authentic and intrinsic religious experience. Such evolving Lacanian interpretation of religious experience becomes akin to that of William James (1902) who sought the conceptual basis for a true religion based on experience and not on a chronic institutional affiliation passed on by imitation and dull habit and contaminated by dogmatic domination. In extrinsic or institutionalised religiosity, spiritual practice is reduced to external ritualism geared towards placating a childishly conceived god. This is the god that was the target or object of the Freudian and modernist critique of religion.

Furthermore, Freud's explanation of religion in terms of a desire for protection and longing for a father only refers to what Lacan called the imaginary father. Lacan distinguished between the Imaginary and Symbolic in both mother and father. The absent mother points to the symbolic mother and to the father in their function of separating and severing the attachment to the imaginary mother as the root of desire and the first self-object (ideal ego).

The imaginary father is the father that is both idealised and hated, that constitutes the ideal father without faults and inadequacies, while at the same time the father is hated for representing what the boy and girl do not have (imaginary castration). The idealised father is the all-good God of fundamentalism that requires its split-off opposite in the figure of the great Satan. But Gautama the Buddha moves beyond the imaginary father (represented by the figure of his father, the king) whom he renounces and abandons. Such renunciation yields a subjective destitution that led him to the discovery of the symbolic father and mother as a lack and emptiness under girding the symbolic structure of reality.

Finally, as far as forms of spiritual practice are concerned, intrinsic spirituality has advocated meditation and meditative or contemplative prayer as paragons of authentic spirituality over what is seen as the more archaic practice of petitionary prayers to imaginary parental figures and representations. Contemplative prayer is a prayer of aspiration and realisation of the sacred as the emptiness that lies beyond representation.

Empirical research (Batson & Ventis, 1982) has reportedly found that intrinsic spirituality has positive correlations with mental health defined as freedom from guilt and worry, presence of wellbeing and social links, creative productivity, subjective unification and organisation, self-control, flexibility, and open-mindedness. Conversely, extrinsic religiosity has negative correlations to these same mental health conceptions, confirming Freud's ideas on the relationship between psychopathology and religion.

It is well known that Freud associated religion with obsessive and paranoiac phenomena. However, early on, Pfister (1944) noted that Freud selected the weaker aspects of religion, treating them as though they constitute its whole. Since then, many have observed that Freud forced analogy into homology or identity (Meissner, 1996), thus describing only a grotesque caricature of religion. In contradistinction to Freud's and Western psychiatry's linkage of religion with psychopathology, empirical researchers have also reported finding positive correlations between psychopathology and an absence of intrinsic spirituality.

Both psychoanalysts (including Lacan) and empirical researchers have demonstrated how unresolved conflicts with the father and manifestations of psychopathology can be applied not only to theism but to atheism as well.

Overall, mystical experience presumably has a correlation coefficient of 0.52 with measures of psychological wellbeing (Greeley, 1975). Greeley's studies report that 12 million North Americans have frequent mystical or peak experiences. Finally, the difference between extrinsic religiosity and intrinsic spirituality (inaugurated by Adorno) can also be extended to a difference between extrinsic and obsessive ritualism and intrinsic spiritual rites. Erikson (1977) defined such latter rite as marked by "a deepened communality and a timeless quality" and from which all participants emerge with a sense of the sublime and of having undergone a transformational experience. A spiritual rite as an act associated with the meditative experience may result not only in the symbolic overcoming of separation but also in the confirmation of the distinct singularity of a subject.

Spirituality can be distinguished from religion since the first refers to an immediate, intrinsic, and direct experience whereas the second alludes to extrinsic, institutional, and conventional religiosity as a mechanism of social affiliation and control. As a construct, spirituality can also be used to designate a spiritual liberalism or liberation spirituality characterised by an attitude of openness, free of the constraints of orthodoxy, traditional authority, or convention. Spirituality in the case of Zen Buddhism, for example, is also distinguished from the "New Age" phenomenon because it is linked to an ancestral lineage where the direct transmission of the spirit or mind of Buddha has been directly and intrinsically transmitted and confirmed from teacher to disciple for generations (2,500 years to be exact).

Within what is known as the New Age movement, there are many self-proclaimed unauthentic "masters" who, nonetheless, derive substantial profit from the spiritual supermarket. Within Buddhism, this tendency is known as spiritual materialism (Chogyam Trungpa). Furthermore, Suzuki Roshi taught that Zen is neither spiritual nor material, since what we call spirit is actually void or devoid of knowledge and beyond suffering and happiness or pain and pleasure.

In addition, spirituality also needs to be distinguished from a definition of religion solely on the basis of morality. Zen is a form of Mahayana Buddhism that signifies the great, inclusive, and extensive vehicle.

Mahayana designates a place or subjective position that goes beyond the ascetic religious ideal of Hineyana Buddhism (small or narrow vehicle and mind). The latter (which exists in all traditions) is described by what Hegel, Nietzsche, and Freud called the repressive morality of the master, the slave, and the superego. In addition, Mahayana Buddhism is to be found not only beyond the good and evil of morality but also beyond the pursuit of pleasure or the dualistic amorality of modernity. In the example of the Marquis de Sade, as a paradigm of the modern libertine, one observes only an apparent absence of morality. In actuality, as Lacan has noted, there exists a sadistic superego which imposes pleasure and *jouissance* as an obligation. Whoever resists the imperative to enjoy feels guilty not for having enjoyed but for not having enjoyed.

Spirituality as defined in this work also needs to be distinguished from the mere interpretation of texts or a simple socio-historical constructivism. For the school of hermeneutics, there is no self-understanding that is not mediated by signs, symbols, and texts, whereas in Zen there is a transmission of a psychical Real outside all scripture or beyond the bounds of words and the symbolic order. Zen teaching recommends a direct plunge into the Real itself through the experience and practice of meditation. For Zen Buddhism, signs, symbols, and texts do not mediate self-realisation.

In contrast to Zen, Lacan's work lies somewhere in between hermeneutics and Zen Buddhism. On the one hand, Lacan's theory, like Zen, includes a register of experience that is beyond words and the symbolic order (the Real). On the other hand, in contrast to Zen, Lacan considers the beyond language as generated by a deficiency or lack within language itself rather than vice versa (the limitation of language to describe an ontological Real outside language). The same net also filters what goes through the net of language.

I attempt to address the psychoanalytic task as Leavy (1990) put forth "to formulate a concept of reality that need not reduce religious experience to something other than what it claims to be" (p. 48). Both the object relations school and the Lacanian school have developed a much more sympathetic attitude towards religion than Freud ever had. Although for Freud religion was an illusion, according to Winnicott, we cannot enjoy reality without going through a primary illusion with regard to transitional objects. Lacan echoes this when he writes that everybody's opening onto the Real is constituted and derived from a fantasy or phantasm (Marini, 1992, p. 209).

However, despite the anti-reductionist intent, the object relations school does in fact reduce spirituality to object relations and maternal functions and representations (Jones, 1991). Smith (1990), and Leavy, for example, rely on principles of ego-psychology and the object relations school to emphasise that the larger reality of mystical and religious experience may be better accounted for not in terms of Oedipal Freudian theory with its related paternal reality principle, but rather in terms of the pre-Oedipal relationship with the mother.

One of Lacan's major contributions to psychoanalysis is to have postulated human experience as organised by three dimensions: the Symbolic, the Imaginary, and the Real. Within Lacanian theory, at least the experiential dimensions of the Real and the Symbolic do not have to be reduced to maternal and paternal references. The Real includes and surpasses both maternal and paternal aspects. Lacan's symbolic father is not a personal father but a representative figure for a symbolic order. The mother of the Real is not the empirical mother but the mother that occupies the place of what Lacan calls *das Ding*. However, I interpret *das Ding* to signify more than simply the *jouissance* associated with being the imaginary phallus of the mother. I argue that the latter constitutes only the imaginary face of the Real, or the primary process as Freud defined it. In my opinion, *das Ding* also signifies a Real mystery or a gap at the core of the Symbolic. The drive is a push or an intention (internal tension) to realise the emptiness of being.

Following Lacan, I do not limit the Real to an objective reality circumscribed within reason and language. This view is also in contradistinction to that echoed in Vergote (1990) and Spero (1992) when they restrict the field of psychoanalysis and religion to the study of psychical processes that are representational in nature within the scope of an "objective" reality in the lower case (whether social, psychological, or scientific). "In this psychic reality psychoanalysis also recognises the operable references to a divine reality. Concerning that reality it can only maintain silence in its theory as well as its practice" (Vergote, 1990, p. 92). Although, I agree with many in the field of the psychology of religion (Flournoy, 1903; Homans, 1970; James, 1902; and more recently Meissner and Spero), who argue that the higher worlds and levels of religious experience (the God-above of theistic religion) cannot be grasped or apprehended in-itself, in its supra-human dimension, by reason or scientific method, I also do not think that the Real beyond language and reason is entirely outside the field of psychoanalysis. The Kantian noumenon and phenomenon interact like emptiness and form, the absolute and the relative, and the Symbolic and the Real. This would also be consistent with the Hegelian and even Heidegger's way of understanding the relationship between the thing-in-itself and the function of Being in relationship to the Other.

By supra-human or supernatural most writers (Meissner and others) mean a God-realm that if existent (and psychology cannot say anything about this, in their view) would lie outside the so-called natural world. This view of an extrinsic God-realm fails to take into account that the God of Judaism and Christianity (without mentioning the Absolute of Eastern religions) is not only manifest in human form but more importantly in human experience. Here, the distinction between the natural and supernatural is blurred. The beyond nature or experience is the same as the negation of nature and experience.

Contrary to Kant, human experience is not limited to the *a priori* parameters of rational knowledge. The practice of analytic silence and that of sitting and listening without actively doing or saying anything, together with the permutation of speech and sense to encounter the Real of the body and drive, are some of the ways in which the Real of the unconscious appears in the everyday experience of psychoanalysis. Lacan (1973) himself wrote: "No praxis is more oriented towards that which, at the heart of experience, is the kernel of the real than psychoanalysis" (p. 53). I follow Richardson (1990) in his brief mention that religious experience may be rooted in the Lacanian Real but elaborate this theme from a Buddhist perspective and an in-depth exegesis of the Lacanian corpus.

The Real in Lacan includes both Freud's psychical reality and Freud's reality principle. In addition, along these lines, the Real can have negative or positive, pathological or healthy and constructive functions. Rassial (2001) showed how the concept of the Real evolved in Lacan's work and that in the final Lacan, the Real acquired the status of a positive and structural form of negativity. With regard to psychical reality and the primary process, Lacan says that the Real constitutes the impossibility of satisfaction according to the model of hallucinatory wish-fulfilment (primary process). Because reality often bars the access to the objects of desire, we construct our own psychical reality according to our primary wishes. The primary process is after an impossible object of satisfaction, and as such constitutes what Lacan calls an inconvenient *jouissance*. Here, the word *jouissance* describes an intensive experience of pleasure under the primary process that becomes or is intrinsically deadly or painful. In this sense, I argue that the primary process itself is not the Real. Only *what* unconscious desire is seeking under the primary process is Real.

The primary process itself represents how the Real appears within the Imaginary. In the Imaginary, the Real is identified with what Freud called the uncanny and Lacan called *das Ding*. It is in relationship to this imaginary conception of *das Ding* that "the Symbolic is the fundamental screen of the Real". The Symbolic is the screen for what of the Real is perceived through the lens of the Imaginary. The Symbolic is a protective screen against the primary process and the id in the likeness of Freud's secondary process.

There are grounds in Lacan (Seminar VII) to develop two different conceptions of *das Ding* and of the Real. On the one hand, *das Ding* is the absence of the archaic mother and the nothingness or hole around which the *jouissance* of the Other (as a primary process of the id) gravitates. On the other hand, emptiness is a presence or plenitude, an Other *jouissance*, linked to fulfilment and the very act of creation. This emptiness begs to be revealed, whereas the absence of the archaic mother and the primary *jouissance* that ensues needs to be suppressed.

Freud's id represents how the Real appears within the Imaginary, whereas the It of Zen Buddhism better represents how the Real appears within the Symbolic. Two very different versions of the Real appear within the Imaginary and the Symbolic, and the same is true, *mutatis mutandis*, for each one of the registers in relationship to the remaining two. This book will have ample opportunity to use this logical feature of the Borromean knot. Finally, the protection of the Symbolic against the Real itself can only go so far given that the Symbolic itself has a gap and an opening into the Real built into it. This is what Lacan called the lack in the Other. Thus, both the primary process that characterises the Freudian unconscious and the secondary process have respective openings unto the Real.

The primary process does not exclusively define the Imaginary, because in Lacan the Imaginary has certain stability (i.e., the specular image) and language itself has an Imaginary dimension. The primary process is always imaginary but not vice versa. The Imaginary also manifests via the Symbolic and the secondary process. In this sense, both the ideal ego and the ego-ideal are imaginary constructions within the secondary process or imaginary interpretations of the Symbolic. Only in the example of sexual fantasies and dreams can the Imaginary be solely identified with the primary process. Thus, I argue that hallucinatory wish-fulfilment is how the Real appears within the Imaginary.

Lacan comes to identify the name of the father, as a ruling signifier/ organiser of what he called the symbolic order (the Other), with a stop-gap function for the lack within the subject. The father forbids or takes something and at the same time provides the identification (the name) that will plug the hole left in the subject. In addition, within the symbolic order itself, the Name of the Father may function as either a signifier of a lack in the Other or as stopgap for the hole within the Symbolic (to represent the Real). For example, for Lacan, God is a signifier of the Symbolic in the likeness of the Name of the Father. God as a signifier for the Symbolic order can either dignify or delegitimise a symbolic order (the values, laws, or myths of society). For the subject or the Other, the signifier of God can function as either a stopgap and/or as a signifier of a lack or emptiness.

For fundamentalists, God functions as a stopgap for the hole in the Symbolic order. Secular laws, for example, are considered devoid of meaning without the foundation provided by spiritual principles. Conversely, for the secular mentality, God represents the signifier of a lack within the Symbolic order. In this instance, spiritual laws and principles are seen as undermining the secular foundation of society. However, the signifier of a lack (G-d) has more than one meaning/ signified. The absent letter in G-d may represent a deficiency or a lack, but it may also point to a fundamental mystery.

For his theory on the Name of the Father, Lacan turned to the names of God in the Torah or Old Testament. God spoke to Moses in the burning bush and gave him the mission to take the people of Israel out of Egypt. Moses then asks "and whom shall I say sent me?". Lacan regards the name that God then gives to Moses as the signifier of the symbolic father *par excellence*. Why? Because with the mysterious name "I am This I am" or "I am Who I am", the symbolic name appears barred, and the "This" or "Who" or even "I am" remains beyond symbolic nomination and points to the Real through the gap of the Symbolic. The gap is opened rather than closed by the negative function of the name in the form of either a refusal to give a name or the giving of an obscure or mysterious name. Here, the Real of a mystery points to something beyond the Symbolic.

However, the sense of the Real as a mystery or an enigma or as the place of unconscious knowing or the unconscious in the sense of the unknown is very different than the meaning of the Real as the presence of a trauma, an anxiety-provoking object, or the Real of a hallucination or of psychosis. The beyond meaning is very different than a complete absence or a foreclosure of symbolic meaning, as often is the case in psychoses. However, it is also true that most often it is the ego who has many missed encounters with the Real of unconscious knowing and who is duped or mucked up by the formations of the unconscious. I argue that when the subject accepts being cancelled and being made a fool by the Real of unconscious knowing, then a new relationship to the Real is established much closer to the sense of the Real in Buddhism.

Thus, in order to understand the polyvocal meaning of the Real in Lacan, I argue that the Real is *both* an inconvenient/impossible *jouissance* in the sense of the illusory *jouissance* of the (m)Other *and* an *Other jouissance* that women and mystics are said to experience but know nothing of (the experience that knowledge or language cannot describe). These two forms of *jouissance* appear confused and undifferentiated within secular knowledge and within Lacan's work in particular. The *jouissance* of the Other refers to the pleasurable but deadly and painful early childhood experience of being the imaginary phallus of the mother. The Other *jouissance* refers to an ineffable spiritual experience beyond pleasure and pain characterised by the bound energy of the secondary process.

The *jouissance* of the Other is a primary process of unbound energy. The *jouissance* of the Other and the Other *jouissance* hold different positions within the Borromean knot (Lacan's representation of how the three registers are bound up together). The first represents the intersection between the Real and the Imaginary, the second the intersection between the Symbolic and the Real. In the latter, the Real is that which the signifying chain encircles and yet remains inaccessible to language and signification. Therefore, Lacan speaks of a lack or impotence of language to pinpoint the Real. It is this impossibility to symbolise and understand by means of reason and language that lends the Real its essentially traumatic and anxiety-producing quality. Finally, for Lacan, the Real is a plenum without fissures, divisions, oppositions, or differentiations, and this needs to be distinguished from the illusory wholeness ascribed to the Imaginary. When the ego thinks of itself as being whole, in New Age or humanistic fashion, this is a self-image hypercathected with narcissistic energy.

This work will also differ from others in the contemporary field of psychoanalysis and religion in that, following Erich Fromm's (1960) interest in the relationship between psychoanalysis and Zen Buddhism, it will concentrate to a large extent on the understanding of religious experience emanating from Chinese and Japanese Zen Buddhism. Fromm noted that Zen raises the question of existence without contradicting the rationality, realism, and independence of modernity.

Nevertheless, many have already noted a similarity between Eastern forms of religion such as Zen Buddhism and the spiritual teachings of the Kabbalah (Hoffman, 1981) within Judaism and the mystic core of religion in general, including Christianity. In this regard, I disagree with Vergote (1990, p. 76), who ethnocentrically considers that only the Jewish or Christian religion, in their high institutional formats, are worthy of the appellation. In addition, he implies that a religion, in order to deserve the name, must necessarily be theistic as well as be established on the basis of beliefs, morality, and prayer.

A Zen Buddhist-inspired spirituality cannot be categorised as being either theistic or atheistic. Non-duality is best described as a form of nontheism. For non-theism, un-being (*desêtre*), non-being, or non-existence are not the dual opposites of existence. What things are in the Real cannot be defined within these categories, and therefore the judgement of existence or non-existence does not apply to them. Dialectically, non-existence has its own intrinsic existence or constitutes the actual ground of existence. Within social language and logic, things exist, but actually within the Real they do not. The moment we name them, what they are becomes a mere invention of language, and what they are beyond language disappears. Therefore, the existence of things (within language and perception) is their non-existence and their non-existence is their true existence.

Non-existence, or ex-sistence, in this sense, refers to what does in fact exist outside the categories of reason and the signifier, not atheism or nihilism. Another way of putting it is that ex-sistence or non-existence exists within the negative categories of reason and the signifier. Non-existence is contained within negative dialectics and the signifier of a lack. Non-theism or emptiness in Zen Buddhism represents an alternative to both theism (Lacan's "the Other of the Other") and atheism (Lacan's "there is no Other of the Other"). Prior classical psychoanalytic understanding of religion has been restricted to a large extent to theistic forms of spirituality. From this perspective, to say that

God does not exist or that God is dead does not simply imply atheism. As Lacan pointed out with regard to the primal father of *Totem and Taboo*, the more God dies, the more alive God becomes. Although Lacan described Zen as the best of the East and the religion of the subject, he also had a proclivity towards Christianity given his family background and the similarity between the Trinity and his theory of the three registers. Finally, Lacan's concept of the Symbolic has many points of contact with the Western religious tradition and with the Name of the Father in particular. In this regard, this work will not fail to notice the connections between Zen Buddhism, the Judaeo-Christian tradition, and psychoanalysis, while stopping short of endorsing a theistic spirituality that, to a much larger extent than Zen, seems to contain the negative elements that Freud and the Enlightenment critiqued in religion.

According to Jung, God is an archetype that performs a necessary psychological function. But from a Lacanian perspective, God is a signifier of the symbolic father, and it is the latter, or the letter of the Name, that performs a fundamental and necessary symbolic and psychical function. Moreover, the symbolic function can be regarded as either a secular and/or sacred function. G-d is a name not only for the symbolic function but also more importantly for the gap within the Symbolic to represent the Real. The meaning of an enigmatic metaphor or signifier is not found within another symbolic signifier. The meaning of an enigma is a form of knowing contained within the Real. Jung emphasised the nature of an archetype as a category of the imagination but did not realise how a linguistic metaphor can also be used to evoke something beyond language and the Symbolic. Language in Jung was simply reduced to the function of a semiotic sign, while Lacan distinguished between the sign and the signifier.

Knowledge of the world depends on a certain credibility given to words and to the order of language and of the world that they represent. Words such as mother and father, or mama and papa, or even *gugu dada* or *baba wawa*, represent the "worthiness" or value of parental actions with respect to the wellbeing and life of the child. Before children comprehend the meaning of words, they are the recipients and beneficiaries of parental actions such as giving birth, holding, speaking, kissing, and feeding. Children have faith and trust in this experience and the words that flow from it. The alphabet of experience is something that they know with their bodies even though the words, or the combination of letters, are not yet comprehended.

However, words will also have to be used in their negative forms (i.e., no, naught, or *mu* in Chinese) to represent alternating experiences of privation and frustration. Words will now represent the law in its dividing and alienating function, leading to discordance with immediate experience. First words represent experience and the legitimacy of everyday language and the sense of the perceived world that they establish. Second words alienate experience or represent an absence within experience or an absence of experience. Third, experience will seek its revenge from language (so to speak) by questioning the legitimacy and trustworthiness of words. The knowledge conveyed by words is no longer to be trusted. Zen, for example, puts the legitimacy of words into question. Knowledge based on words is put into question. Words cannot give us the Real. The constructed world has to be put in doubt in order to access the unknown and perhaps the unknowable and arrive at new versions and definitions of reality. Not knowing suspends the certainty of words.

Postmodern spirituality

In general, Freudian theory and empiricism do not differentiate between an extrinsic faith as an emotional and naive need to believe in words without experience or understanding (due to an infantile dependence on the father), and a faith in something that is beyond beliefs and language. Authoritarian, extrinsic religion (as Fromm and Adorno defined it) associated with utilitarian, petitionary prayer and with concrete rather than metaphoric beliefs has also been shown to have positive correlations with intolerance of uncertainty, ambiguity, and doubt. In my opinion, doubt needs to be understood as fundamental not as a method, as in Descartes, or as an enemy of faith, but rather as a subjective position wherein knowing emerges from the Real, from a void within the Symbolic, from the non-knowing within knowing.

> *Inscitia* is brute ignorance, whereas *inscientia* is not-knowing as such, as empty, and as call from the void at the center of knowledge.
>
> (Lacan, Seminar VIII. Session 11: 8 February 1961. Translated into Spanish by Ricardo Rodriguez Ponte. English translation is mine.)

In order to access knowing within the Real, the subject has to occupy the place of non-knowing within the Symbolic. Such non-knowing within knowing alludes to an authentic non-speculative intuition which is neither totally rational (as in Hegel), nor irrational (as in Jung), but transrational (a term coined by Wilber, 1984). Within this field, this kind of symbolic intuition rooted within the Real becomes compatible with science. Both science and spirituality converge at that moment of a non-accumulative dialectic (Hopenhayn, 1997), beyond thought but not without thought, and which can be described as subjectivity without attachments to fixed pre-established ideals or beliefs.

A faith based on and limited to religious "beliefs" themselves does not constitute the most specific and intrinsic nature of a religious practice. Jung clarifies that by an archetype, he does not mean a creed but rather an experience of the *numinosom*. Although the numinosom is typically related to a symbolic form, not every symbolic form contains the experience of the Real or the numinosom. Otto (1929) coined the term *numinosom* to describe the reality of the sacred in post-Kantian terms. Kant distinguished between phenomena and noumena. For example, a phenomenon is how we know the things of the natural world according to the categories of time, space, reason, and language. Noumena would be what a thing is in-itself beyond the categories of time, space, reason, and language. For Kant, we cannot know anything about the noumena. The noumena is a transcendent presupposition. In contrast, the *numinosom* is what a spiritual experience can tell us about the noumena beyond the categories of the phenomenal world.

But we only know about infinite time (timeless or synchronic time) or Being within the confines of the passing of time. Within the confines of time and language, there is something or a no-thing that escapes capture or definition within time and language. Faith in a belief, a creed, a doctrine, or a theory is derived from how efficiently the latter can invoke or provoke two things: 1. the articulation of a symbolic structure; and 2. the manifestation or influx of a *jouissance* within a point instant that at the same time momentarily vanishes or erases the structure. Thanks to *jouissance* and the power of the present moment, the structure can be said to be in perpetual change or construction and reconstruction. According to Jung, the "arche" in archetype remains unknowable. The *numinosom* is the a-rche or the *a* or Aleph as the unknowable source of an archetype.

Within Jewish and Islamic monotheism, images have been prohibited because images can be alluring and deceiving; there are no holy images. According to monotheism, the beyond-image aspect of G-d is apprehended either in the holy writ (word or scripture) or in the Sabbath or the experience of rest or meditation. If G-d has a shape, it is akin to the image of a mirror which is devoid of its own image. A clear mirror or looking-glass reflects other images but does not have an image of its own other than the emptiness of images. More than a holy image, emptiness is like two mirrors facing: the emptiness of emptiness. On the other hand, the infinite mirror has to be broken into the thousand pieces of the phenomenal world. In this second moment, the sacred cannot be differentiated from the ordinary or even the profane, as illustrated by the following Zen story.

When Joshu first visited his teacher Nansen, he found him resting, stretched out on his back, on his couch. "Where do you come from?" asked Nansen. Joshu replied, "I come from the holy image monastery." Nansen then asked, "Do you still see the holy image?" Joshu retorted, "No, I only see the sleeping Tatagatha (Buddha)." In this story, Joshu has forgotten all about the holy image and sees Buddha in ordinary perceptions and activities. The *numinosom* is not some special and unique image, but is not some abstract concept either. The *numinosom* has to be perceived within ordinary phenomena. When we look at the world, we see images rather than God; on the other hand, objects are more than visual images produced by the brain. This "more" that things are beyond visual images are the broken pieces that contain the stillness of the infinite mirror. When things are seen from the perspective of infinity, then while being the images that they are, they are also something more.

Freud was right in demanding that assertions regarding religious dogma have to be discovered for oneself in direct experience and cannot be accepted solely on the basis of tradition and dogma. Otherwise religion simply becomes an infantile submission to authority. One believes because our fathers and other significant authority figures have told us that we have to believe, that we should believe. This critique is a fundamental cultural motif of the modern era that runs through the full cultural gamut of the nineteenth and twentieth centuries. But this secular, modern critique of traditional beliefs is also consistent with the teachings of Buddhism.

The Buddha, for example, advised his followers not to rely on what he said, his words, but to discover for themselves what he had already come to realise. This is what makes a religion a living and renewed tradition as opposed to a mere historical record. On his deathbed, the Buddha encouraged his disciples to be a light unto themselves and in the famous parable of the raft (Majjhima Nikaya 22, Alagaddupama

Sutta, Pali Canon), he taught that once the raft of Buddhism had been used to cross from the shore of Samsara to the other shore of Nirvana, the raft itself had to be abandoned. A Buddhist relies on Buddhism only to the extent that it supports a practice of practice/realisation.

Freud was of the opinion that "the truth of religious doctrines is dependent on a rare inner experience" (Freud, 1927c, S.E. 21:28) and that "One cannot erect, on the basis of an experience that exists only for a very few, an obligation that shall apply to everyone" (idem). Freud acknowledges that the truth of religion is based on experience but stresses that it is a very rare experience that very few people have, and that therefore it is unfair, impractical, or unreasonable to establish obligations for everyone on the basis of such experiences.

Although Freud's logic is sound given the premise, there are several problems associated with Freud's conception. First, Freud takes for granted the historical condition of Western religion within which his observation is made. Jung raised this point when he noted that the religion that he and Freud addressed had lost the connection to the living spirit and experience of religion; only the dead and dry obligations remained. Second, followers of Western religion itself are at a disadvantage with respect to experience because, in contrast to Buddhism and Zen Buddhism in particular, the former does not give sufficient importance to direct experience. Western religion in general has relied on beliefs and not on yogic meditation practices. In the case of Zen Buddhism, the obligation is with the experience of meditation itself rather than with rules erected on the basis of someone else's experience. Finally, within monotheism, spiritual experience is too wrapped up in morality to be of interest to the modern secular mentality.

Thus, although Freud and Buddha are saying similar things with respect to the relation between experience and spiritual truth, their arguments move in exactly opposite directions. Buddha emphasises the importance of experience and meditation to reveal an authentic form of spirituality, whereas Freud uses the foundation of spiritual truth on experience to demonstrate its inaccessibility and therefore lack of validity for the majority of the population.

Finally, secular culture also has a role to play in estranging the general public from the living experience of religion. A subject cannot have the allegedly rare inner experience unless they are willing to enter the Real of a traditional symbolic practice. Because Western religion is too laden with beliefs and articles of faith, the majority of the secular public simply does not believe that there exists a rare Real of experience contained within the forms of traditional practice. Even those intellectuals who may be sympathetic towards religion would be weary of immersing their body and mind in the Real of a traditional practice. Such weariness is the operative effect of a prejudice towards religion contained within secular culture.

Thus, one could argue that the fact that "the truth of religious doctrines is dependent on a rare inner experience" (idem) does not undermine religion any more than physics is undermined by its foundation on rarified mathematical formulas (understood only by an Einstein or a Hawking). Nobody today would question the truth-value of science just because they cannot understand quantum physics or the theory of relativity. The majority of people relies and uses modern technology and accepts the validity of the scientific paradigm without understanding its theoretical foundations. Thus, it is difficult to escape the conclusion that faith without understanding and experience may also be operative within the secular scientific paradigm. It is perhaps for these same reasons that some extreme groups within religious fundamentalism completely reject modern technology and refuse to use the advances of modern medicine even at the risk of their own lives. Although this stance may seem extreme and irrational, it operates on the same lack of faith in the scientific paradigm that secular folk have towards religion.

The Frankfurt School (for example, Adorno, 1978; Horkheimer, 1978) earlier articulated a critique that linked scientific modernity to masked forms of oppression and domination. However, this school, being itself an expression of modernity, sought to locate, define, and promote a critical reason that would free modern rationality from the fetters of instrumental scientific rationality. In contrast, the postmodern paradigm questions the superiority and supremacy of reason itself (both critical and instrumental). Science may be as much a socially constructed discourse as other forms of traditional knowledge. Gadamer (1975), Lyotard (1989), Baudrillard (1981), and even Ricoeur (1991), all share an effort to re-appropriate the significance of a traditional understanding that was rejected and ignored by the modern perspective.

While the Frankfurt School distinguished between rational and irrational authority (Fromm, 1966), Gadamer (1975) argues "that tradition has a justification or dimension that is outside the arguments of reason" (p. 249). Moreover, he maintains that human sciences have the continual task of reinterpreting cultural tradition. Nevertheless, a point of clarification needs to be introduced in order to accede to the transrational or post-rational dimension instead of falling right back into emotional, fundamentalist, irrational, or ideological convictions. The Buddha-dharma, the Real, or the dimension that lies outside the arguments of reason, does not constitute a fixed interpretation of a sacred text. The sacred or the holy manifests as the "holeness" or lack of closure or lid of the text itself. The simple, the beautiful, the truthful, *numinous* and luminous, is the void around which the text revolves, permitting its permutation and reinterpretation.

In addition, what distinguishes a postmodern spiritual perspective from more fundamentalist and conservative movements is that nowhere does it advocate that traditional religious institutions, for example, repossess the repressive political and social power they held in the past (before modernity). Such would amount to a renewed attempt to reduce intrinsic spirituality to extrinsic institutional religiosity. Intrinsic spirituality cannot be institutionalised, although by virtue of Buddha-nature, and despite human nature, it has and will be transmitted from one generation to the next. From the postmodern perspective that has been outlined, traditional dogma will not hinder the free expression of reason, nor will reason repress and deny place and merit to traditional wisdom and understanding. Hence, from this vantage point, it becomes possible to consider postmodernism as an all-around triumph for democracy.

Finally, what distinguishes Baudrillard from Lyotard and other postmodern intellectuals is his advocacy, not for revolutionary social-critical practices à la Frankfurt School, but for traditional practices that suspend or transcend, even if temporarily, modern utilitarian or instrumental imperatives. In other words, Baudrillard does not espouse a purely intellectual understanding of tradition but captures its transrational dimension as manifested in practices such as meditation, ritual, and the observance of various holidays and festivals.

CHAPTER TWO

Psychoanalysis as a secular and non-theistic study of the mind

Both Lacan and Zen use language and concepts in a non-dual way to invoke an enigmatic dimension of experience and of the mind that cannot be described by the binary (dual) and lineal characteristic of language and formal logic. Zen koans (stories) and Lacanian aphorisms, like poetry, use the evocative (and perhaps even provocative) more than the explicative or communicative function of language.

At first, the historical Buddha was reluctant to teach out of the concern of being misunderstood due to the perplexing nature of the (non-dual) teaching. He feared that due to not-understanding students might be inclined to disparage or reject him and thereby inadvertently bring on harmful karma upon their own selves.

In a group discussion that followed a meditation session, one of the participants told me that to avoid sleepiness or nodding off during zazen it was better to practise meditation standing up rather than sitting in the cross-legged position. During the meditation, I had nodded off a few times, so her statement could be seen as addressed to me. I responded saying that when the mind is very busy thinking in zazen it is easier not to be sleepy and alert than when the mind is very relaxed and not thinking. Whether thinking or not thinking, being alert or

24

sleepy both are zazen. Furthermore, I said that awakening in Buddhism is not the opposite of sleeping. I quoted Dogen where he teaches that in Zen we awake from a dream within a dream. The participant seemed to be annoyed by this and said, "I'd rather keep things simple" (and dualistic). I kept things simple by not responding to a dualistic statement and letting her have the last word. Another example comes from an online review of a work on Dogen:

> I practice Zen and have always gotten the feeling that I'm supposed to find Dogen's writing poetic and wise, but I've mainly found it to be obtuse, paradoxical gobbledy-gook, and I'm suspicious that many who rave about Dogen don't actually understand him either.

It was not until his students insisted that Shakyamuni agreed to go ahead and teach. Zen and Lacanian teaching can be abstruse and perplexing because of enunciations and statements that seem to advance a knowledge or wisdom with ambiguous meaning. Sometimes, Zen teaching appears to be without or beyond meaning. At other times, it may seem so dense as to be obtuse or downright foolish. Zen appears to be a secret teaching for idiots and fools.

Nonetheless, non-duality is beyond delusion and enlightenment, rationality and irrationality. Lacan (Sem. XXI, 1973–1974) taught that those that do not allow themselves to be duped or fooled by the unconscious may end up making serious mistakes ("the non-duped err"). "Les non-dupes errant" shares a relationship of homophony (similarity in sound) with Le nom-du-père (the Name of the Father). If one can tolerate being duped (symbolic castration) by the father, then one is less likely to make serious mistakes.

Not unlike the experience of analysis, to speak/read what is impossible to speak/read can be quite a frustrating, although ultimately rewarding, experience. In both disciplines, the actual practice (of meditation or analysis) illuminates and facilitates a way through explanation and knowing. Without the practice, the concepts discussed may be more difficult to understand. Moreover, new ideas and perspectives may be preceded by what Lacan and Bion called non-understanding, or non-knowing as Zen would have it. It is this "non understanding" which leads to practice that then may lead to understanding. Having said this, wherever possible, I will make every effort to clarify and unpack the concepts but without compromising the content of what needs to be said.

The enlightenment and the four relations, or quartet, between the secular and the "sacred" (Sesa and Sase)

In this chapter, I will address the differences among spiritual, secular, and non-theistic conceptions of the mind/spirit. As aforementioned, the enlightenment of humanity promised by the natural and social sciences sought not only the elimination of religion but also a more authentic form of spirituality. Thus, I propose four possible ways of conceiving the relationship between psychoanalysis and spirituality under the influence of the rational Enlightenment. First, there is the secular version of spirituality that objectifies and demystifies religious illusions under the guidance and purview of reason and the scientific process. It is well known that Freud thought of the psychoanalyst as a secular minister of the soul. In this category, only the secular perspective remains.

However, what is lost in the process is the evocation of a dimension of human experience that was realised within the experiential field of traditional practices and remains unaccounted for in the secular per-spective. It could be argued that because psychoanalysis, and science in general, historically gave only a partial and biased account of spiritual phenomena and experience, they remain vulnerable or prone to the same dogmatic fundamentalism that they criticised in religion. In fact, many have criticised orthodox psychoanalysis as being tantamount to a secular form of religion in the bad sense of the term. This would hold true despite the contradiction between, say, orthodox psychoanalysis and Orthodox Judaism, for example. Religiosity in this regard, whether in science or spirituality, represents a rigid adherence to concepts or methods that function as basic articles of faith. In addition, because psychoanalysis does in fact attempt to account for spiritual phenom-ena with secular concepts (i.e., the Unconscious instead of the God con-cept), it remains open to the same kind of criticism that science levelled against religion.

A second trend of Enlightenment spirituality, within the Western spir-itual traditions themselves, kept the baby of what is specific and true to the spiritual field, but threw out the bath water of religion by absorb-ing the secular critique of its field. The pastoral-counselling field would be a good example of this trend. By incorporating the techniques of psychotherapy within a religious context (that is, a pastoral relationship between a priest/rabbi and a congregant), religions are able to neutralise the more radical and atheistic expressions of secular knowledge regarding the soul (psyche). In this instance, the secular disappears under the spiritual principle.

Third, it is within the context of the struggle between the secular and the sacred that Buddhism was introduced into the West. Buddhism arrived free of an historical antagonism between science and religion. In addition, Buddhism could be seen either as a religion or as a practical philosophy of life or of Being, and in general spoke of a middle way or a non-dual relation between the secular and the sacred. Here, non-duality represents a both/and rather than an either/or relationship between the two principles. Thus, the transformation of religion under the Enlightenment can also be considered as leading towards a non-theistic spirituality such as that found within the Zen Buddhist tradition.

Non-theistic spirituality stands as a third alternative to traditional and contemporary theism and secular scientific atheism. In Buddhism, the secular remains active within a spiritual perspective (the secular within the sacred), as reflected in Buddha's famous advice (in the Pali Kalama sutra) to not believe in anything unless it is proven true within experience. It is not enough to believe in something simply because Buddha or Lacan said so or on the basis of their sheer authority.

In contrast to this, doctrinal secular dogmatism seems alive and well in some schools of Lacanian psychoanalysis. An example of this is the requirement that before submitting a paper to a conference, the paper not only has to go through peer review, but the speaker has to submit to being tutored by a tutor/preceptor who will ensure that the speaker is in strict adherence to the principles of the "doctrine". In contrast to this, Freud held a view very similar to Buddha's advice. In his paper on a childhood memory of Leonardo da Vinci, Freud (1910) stated that he who argues by appeal to authority works with their memory rather than intelligence. One is simply repeating what the master said rather than articulating the logic and significance of the statement. In this, Freud is truly a child of the Enlightenment: he throws off the yoke of authority and establishes intellectual independence.

Finally, within this framework, a fourth category becomes plausible wherein the spiritual remains implicitly active within the secular paradigm (the sacred within the secular). In other words, the secular mind may also contain unrecognised intrinsic spiritual elements or seeds undestroyed by the secularisation process. Here, some may consider psychoanalysis as a kind of secular form of spirituality rather than as secular knowledge devoid of spirituality. It is in these last two categories (the secular within the sacred and vice versa), where psychoanalysis and Zen Buddhism may have a supplementary rather than a complementary relationship (specific differences still remain).

The non-theistic secular religion/spirituality of the subject

The questions of suffering and happiness/wellbeing, or at least the relief from suffering, are examples of intrinsic spiritual elements within psychoanalysis. Psychoanalysis advocates acceptance of suffering and the capacity to delay gratification. These are two fruits that exemplify the therapeutic effects of psychoanalytic treatment. According to both Buddhism and psychoanalysis, suffering or pain can also be a source of strength and character (not pleasure, as in moral masochism). In psychoanalysis, the analysand has to face or address painful material, and the analyst is a source of frustration in so far as the analyst may not gratify the demands of the analysand. In Buddhist meditation, pain arises from sitting still, paying attention, and stretching the body muscles in the yogic lotus posture. In addition, the practitioner is also instructed to accept painful thoughts and feelings rather than try to avoid them or suppress them.

Intrinsic to the question of the spiritual elements within the secular practice of psychoanalysis are two different definitions of happiness and suffering. Happiness can be thought of as pleasure or as serenity, and suffering can be linked to desire and to the suffering associated with privation, frustration, and renunciation (of the imaginary phallus in the case of symbolic castration). Although serenity and equanimity are pleasant states, unlike seeking pleasure, they do not imply the avoidance of pain or unpleasure. In fact, realising equanimity and composure within pain strengthens serenity. Finally, Buddhism distinguishes between pain and suffering. One can have pain without suffering by making peace with the pain rather than fighting it. There is a difference between relieving suffering and being able to bear it.

Desire has a built-in lack or insatiability, given that we want what we can't have and we don't want what we have, and that *jouissance*, or the drive, always asks for more. Frustration brings this to a stop yet generates its own form of suffering. The suffering that comes with frustration and the delay of gratification is something that needs to be borne in order for a meta level form of pleasure or sublimation to arise (genital pleasure or phallic *jouissance* as well as serenity and equanimity).

In the case of the phases of development, weaning from the breast is an example of a frustration that lays the foundation for the frustration that will come in the form of castration or the necessary loss of the phallus under the phallic function (phase). The latter itself lays the foundation for phallic *jouissance* and beyond.

Zen meditation begins at a point beyond a phallic form of *jouissance* and presupposes that subjects enter meditation as differentiated sexed subjects. Otherwise meditation could be detrimental for subjects who have not gone beyond a fused state with the mother. Contrary to what Freud believed, according to Dogen, the founder of Soto Zen in Japan, the completeness of meditation experience presupposes a state of non-merging. It is well known that Freud linked a "mystical oceanic feeling" with a blissful state of fusion with the mother.

Most meditators are neurotics rather than psychotics or perverts. Perversion implies a disavowal of the law that makes it almost impossible for the perverse structure to enter a discipline such as meditation. By this, I don't mean whatsoever that meditation can be reduced to neurosis. What I do mean, however, is that the psychological problems of practitioners, when present or active, will be mostly of a neurotic kind. Within the Lacanian approach, normality itself is a kind of neurosis or false self in that it implies a mask of normalcy or an imaginary version of the Symbolic rather than the Norm of the symbolic order itself.

The preoccupation with norms or forms can be aspects of an obsessive structure, unless the Law in both Buddhism and psychoanalysis is understood as the Law of emptiness. Ultimately, the Law or forms are themselves empty. The symbolic order or the Other is lacking because emptiness can potentially be perceived as something missing because no thought or image can be said to be "It". Emptiness is itself empty or lacking within words or images, the Symbolic or the Imaginary. Emptiness can be experienced but one cannot "know" anything about it (as Lacan put it in Seminar XX when speaking of the *jouissance* of the mystic). To know something of it implies that one has left the Real and has entered the symbolic register of language. At the same time, the beyond language or the unknown only exists in reference to what is known in language. Emptiness is not ignorance, nor is it exclusively associated with pleasant feelings. Unpleasant feelings are also empty.

Often, the aspect of bearing suffering is contraposed to the impulse to be serene or to obtain relief from suffering. In addition, this distinction can be seen as what separates psychoanalysis from a practice of meditation that seeks to be rid of anxiety or unpleasant states. Within Chinese and Japanese Zen, the Rinzai lineage privileges insight and criticises Soto Zen for quietism or being "quietistic". Insight entails facing one's problems instead of avoiding them. This tension between insight and serenity within Zen was pre-dated by an earlier difference between the Madhyamika and Yogachara Indian schools of Mahayana Buddhism. The Buddha originally spoke about these two aspects of meditation, but they were never construed as opposed to one another.

In the Pali Therevada sutras, the Buddha teaches about two forms of meditation: *Samadhi*, and insight or *Vipassana*. *Samadhi* is the same as calmness, quiescence, or tranquillity and is equivalent to the one-pointedness of the mind. *Vipassana* means seeing beyond the ordinary or seeing things as they are (as form and emptiness). Calmness balances the flurry that comes from the overdoing of analysis. Insight instead balances the indolence that comes from tranquillisation.

Insight gives the serenity to accept things, and serenity supports the function of seeing things clearly and facilitates the development of great insight into the nature or cause of suffering. In Freud, serenity was associated with the secondary process of "quiescent" energy and to ego functioning. Insight, rationality, or sound judgement work well when the turbulence of the primary process dies down.

Psychoanalytic schools also part ways around the question of building or deconstructing defences. Psychoanalysts criticise silent meditation for colluding with defences and underscore the ability of speech to undo defences. After all, psychoanalysis is a talking cure. On the other hand, within the analytical situation analysts make use of silence and do not disclose their own contents of mind to the analysand. Outside the office, psychoanalysts make plenty of use of defences and avoidance of various topics, in order to preserve their own preferred states of mind.

The psychoanalytic situation is also not without cathartic elements despite the fact that Freud abandoned emotional catharsis in favour of insight as a curative factor. Catharsis has to be balanced with insight. "Have a good cry but also put it into words, please." The analyst also plays a gratifying maternal function and not solely a frustrating paternal one. Having an "understanding" person to talk to or cry with provides a modicum of consolation and relief in any form or school of psychoanalysis, or therapy for that matter. This is an aspect of transference love that Freud found unobjectionable: the analyst and the analysand may have feelings of affection towards each other.

On another front, Freud understood the first cause of suffering not as desire but as the reality that the body is doomed to decay and dissolution (impermanence as Buddhism would call it). In addition, Freud accurately cognised that external circumstances and natural disasters could also be causes of suffering. In Buddhism, the story of the Buddha first represents happiness as the life of leisure and pleasure sometimes mistakenly confused, even by me in prior work, as a form of hedonism. For the Greeks, hedonism was understood as pleasure within the context of reason or reasonableness. Gautama's father sheltered the future Buddha from the harsh realities of life. It is only once he left the palace for the first time, and abandoned his wife and son at age 29, that he encountered the reality of old age, illness, and death. Legend has it that upon this encounter, he made a vow to find a path to Nirvana that completely transcends the suffering associated with life. It is this aspect of mythical Buddhism that is commonly misunderstood as idealistic and unrealistic. Freud instead, at the end of his studies on hysteria, more modestly stated that psychoanalysis aimed to transform neurotic misery into ordinary unhappiness.

It is in this sense that psychoanalysis stresses the importance of developing the capacity to bear suffering instead of thinking that one can transcend it. It is foolish to think that one can avoid old age, illness, or death. On the other hand, Buddhism emphasises the dimension of the unageing, the unailing, and the deathless. This is the aspect that appears ridiculous to psychoanalysts and to Western science in general. To say that there is no birth and no death at the same time that there is birth and death appears to be a logical yet ridiculous claim.

Nonetheless, the function of negation is also something that is very close to Western thought and to the understanding of defences. Not this, not that, or neither this nor that, is something that is used in formal logic but only as a method to arrive at a positive determination of what a phenomenon actually is. That an aspect of humans is unageing does not mean that they don't age, but that they can age gracefully or wisely so that old age does not have to be suffering. Also, when you are ill, is there a part of you that is not ill or can bear the illness? This is Nirvana, not the cessation of illness. The acceptance of death or peace in death is Nirvana, not the seeking of annihilation or the denial of death. In fact, this way of understanding Buddhism is very much in consonance or resonance with psychoanalysis.

But in Zen Buddhism, serenity or equanimity do not need to be seen as ego-functions or even healthy defences. They are aspects of the Way of nature or of "It", or of the drive, but not as id or instinct. Serenity and equanimity are there not only in meditation or in joyful or peaceful feelings but also in ordinary life and in pain. Equanimity, as the function of emptiness, functions in pleasant, unpleasant, and neutral feelings. Equanimity is helpful in undoing defences and in developing the capacity to listen to what can't be listened to, or to bear want can't be borne. This is the correct way of understanding meditation. Meditation is not a spiritual bypass to bypass the truths of the ordinary material psyche.

Epstein (2007) has addressed the differences between psychoanalysis and Buddhism, and between different schools of Buddhism, from an ego-psychological perspective. Within Buddhism, Epstein represents the Theravada school of Buddhism that Mahayana Buddhism considers part of the earlier ascetic form of Hinayana Buddhism. In the United States, the Theravada teaching has been secularised and is known mostly as *Vipassana* or insight meditation. They both emphasise mindfulness as one of the two practices mentioned by the Buddha. *Vipassana* and insight meditation consider Zen meditation a quietist concentration practice that emphasises sitting in pain in the lotus posture. In addition, outside *Vipassana*, mindfulness practices have been taken out of the context of Buddhism as well as out of the context of a rigorous form of meditation practice.

On the one hand, it is important to be inclusive in order to make meditation as widely available as possible. On the other hand, mindfulness practices are often presented as improvements over sitting in the lotus posture. The real tiger is also found in a paper tiger, but the paper tiger cannot be a real tiger without the real tiger.

Epstein attributes the repressive or non-psychological aspect of meditation practice to concentration practices that emphasise *Samadhi* practice. These are the practitioners that, according to Epstein, are pursuing the oceanic feeling that Freud considered to be a primitive state of fusion with the mother. Instead, insight meditation is supposed to use the more developed functions of the ego already well known to psychoanalysis. Magid (2002) makes a similar point when he considers concentration practice as a "top-down" koan practice designed to produce an experience of oneness that remains separate from ordinary life or from functioning within social reality. This point had already been made earlier by Welwood (1979) when he critiqued the Jungian way of understanding meditation as a kind of introversion linked to the inner realm of the unconscious. Instead, Welwood emphasised the aspect of enlightenment that represents "a clear and precise way of being and living in the world" (p. 155).

I already mentioned above that for Dogen, *Samadhi*, or the mind of the Buddha, is transmitted or flows in a state of non-merging. The Other *jouissance* differs from the *jouissance* of the Other in the same way that dual unity or the symbiosis with the mother differs from the awakened state that includes separation, differentiation, and the function of the father. *Samadhi* and insight into impermanence, zazen and mindfulness, are two aspects of the Way, of the way things are or go. Nevertheless, different schools of Buddhism want to separate these two or pit them one against the other. Is it One or is it two? Not one, not two!

Magid, like Epstein, rejects the practice of *Samadhi* and the understanding of emptiness as Real experience, in favour of emptiness as impermanence, or emptiness as form. Emptiness as form manifests in ordinary activities, in both delusion and enlightenment, in *Samadhi* and the hindrances that people experience in practice and ordinary life. Impermanence is important because *Samadhi* is not only a still pool but also a violent current, and is not a permanent state. However, the way things are does not simply mean emptiness as form, impermanence, or form is form, but also form is emptiness, and emptiness is emptiness. This is what Jews call the divine light or influx, the radiance that manifests in the ordinary forms and practices of the Sabbath.

Magid quotes pragmatist philosopher Rorty's anti-essentialist position to the effect that there is no Real, only a web of symbolic relations. He equates this argument with the Buddhist teaching of interdependence, but wittingly or unwittingly leaves out that according to Vasubhandu, this is only one of the aspects of the self-nature. Self-nature also includes emptiness and the Real as well as the Imagined or fantasised nature. The teaching of Nagarjuna overcomes the dualism between pro- and anti-essence views by formulating emptiness as wondrous being, and teaching that the essence of being is empty in its own being. Emptiness is the essence of being, the essence of emptiness is empty, and emptiness is the essence of essence. Since emptiness or essence is empty of concept, what can be stated or formulated is always within the realm of form and ordinary experience. But to say that emptiness or the Real is devoid of concept or definition is not the same as stating that emptiness, *Samadhi*, or essence do not exist in a relative sense.

Pragmatist, empirical, and certain postmodern perspectives mistake the fact that nothing can be known about emptiness, or essence, other than its negation, for dualistic non-existence or emptiness as the annihilation of the essence of being. For Dogen, Buddha nature is contained within no-Buddha-nature, true self within no-self, and the great positive is contained within the negative of absolute difference. The positive has to be approached negatively, otherwise it gives rise to the reification of the Real that turns It into an object or fetish. The latter is the imagined nature, or what Lacan calls the Imaginary. Magid confuses the Real with the Imaginary, or dual unity with the One of the Real. On the other hand, he may be precisely criticising the moth-like seekers of enlightenment for confusing the Real with the Imaginary, actual unity for imagined unity. What I am talking about is not intellectual word-play but an actual epistemology that is inseparable from ontology or phenomenology.

Epstein contrasts one-pointed concentration on a single object (breathing, for example) with moment-to-moment awareness of changing objects. However, this distinction may be spurious given that in Zen, awareness of breath is one of the aspects of awareness or of the awarenesses that includes awareness of thinking and non-thinking, awareness of mental formations, awareness of the senses and of the bright luminosity of consciousness, awareness of the body, and in general awareness of the different consciousness that conform our experience. In Zen, the One includes the Other as well as the many. Zazen is an all-inclusive study of Big mind.

Epstein also identifies concentration practice with the ego-ideal because the fixity of mind in a single object leads to stability, serenity, cohesion, and relief of narcissistic anxiety. Epstein, like Freud, associates serenity with a secondary ego-process rather than a primary fusion state. For Epstein, mindfulness is an ego-function that strengthens the ego. However, according to Lacanian theory, this is an imaginary aspect of the ego-ideal and only provides a dual form of unity that reinforces and preserves the division of the subject. The imaginary aspect of the

Name of the Father and of the ego closes the gap or hole within the subject, thus providing the relief or consolation that Epstein is talking about.

True awareness does not have a fixed identity and lives within the emptiness of the Real subject. In mindfulness of breathing, the ego-ideal only appears when there is a clinging to the idea of "mastering" the breath, instead of letting breathing function naturally and spontaneously. According to Lacanian theory, the ideal ego and the ego-ideal are mental formations of the unconscious mind and therefore cannot be identified with awareness. Awareness is not ego-based nor is it an ego-function. Awareness is a mystery beyond consciousness. Who is aware, where does it come from, and where does it go?

Mindfulness or Big mind in zazen includes a panoramic awareness that is not focused on anything in particular. Suzuki Roshi used to say that because in zazen his mind was not focused on anything in particular, he could detect people's movements within the zendo (meditation hall). When the mind is in the awakened state, then it can also wander in free-floating attention, without trying to focus on anything in particular, or trying to attain anything.

In zazen, awareness is resting from pattern or structure and remains unstructured and relaxed. Awareness rests from ego structure by being mindful of the ego but without identification. Concentration practice only leads to building a false sense of self or ego when the ego is trying to use meditation as an end for something else instead of as an end in itself. For this reason, Dogen said that zazen is not a concentration practice. Zazen is the practice of beginners' mind.

Epstein quotes Meissner who associates egolessness with the id and lack of structure. Thus, Epstein identifies ego with structure, and without Mahayana or Lacanian concepts, he is not able to conceive of structure without the ego. What gives structure is the Other-dependent nature, Indra's net (a metaphor developed in the Mahayana Avatamsaka sutra), or what Lacan calls the symbolic order, not the ego. The representational world is not a substructure of the ego. It is actually the other way around: the ego is a formation of the representational world or an imaginary apprehension of the symbolic order.

The notion of ego-adaptation is a misnomer given that what is actually happening is evolution. The organism is not passively adapting to the environment; environment and organism are both arising and evolving together. The environment or the Other changes the subject; and the subject changes the environment and the Other. Mindfulness is as much focused on the subject as it is focused on the environment or the Other. Mindfulness is in fact the recollection of the relationship between the two.

Mindfulness is not a self-conscious awareness or a form of self-consciousness with the ego as a reference. It is more important to strengthen the function or capacity for equanimity without an idea of self or ego. Equanimity still under the ego or as an ego-ideal/ideal ego remains influenced by the ideology of self-improvement and the narcissistic and defensive functions of the ego.

To link equanimity with the ego or with a neutral "objective" stance does a disservice to the very thing that we are trying to help. The ego is always and inevitably bound up with the project of becoming someone or someone important. The analyst is trying to project an image of objectivity in order to be loved and recognised by the Other (of "scientific standards") and in denial of his/her countertransference or the desire for recognition.

Equanimity instead is linked to the open mind of the beginner as a capacity that facilitates the analytic process. Meditation or zazen can be understood as an ally or friend of the analytic process rather than as an obstacle to speech, the talking cure, or self-exploration. The Greeks thought of equanimity as a virtue rather than as an ego-function, although for ego-psychologists, a virtue would be considered an ego-function. Thompson (2004) has pointed out that for Socrates, Plato, and Aristotle, happiness does not come from pleasure but from virtue. In addition, of all the Greeks, "The Stoics were the most preoccupied with obtaining ataraxia or serenity and equanimity" (p. 146).

Thinking of equanimity as a form of virtue has the advantage of not reifying psychical processes that are not linked to or presuppose an ego. On the other hand, the notion of virtue has the disadvantage of invoking a dual moral category that can in fact be a hindrance to the analytical process. Virtue becomes the opposite of vice, and somehow can come to be associated with censoring the open examination of the nature of the latter. Virtue can contain vice, since virtuosity can become egotistical or vain, and vice can contain the virtue of selflessness and even kindness.

Thinking, not thinking, and non-thinking

For Lacan, fantasy or illusion is a window into reality that comes to frame what he calls "objectality". This differs from the notion that fantasy and reality are antithetical to one another. Correctly understood, fantasy can serve the purpose of awakening to the nature of visual reality as illusory or imaginary. On the other hand, fantasy also serves defensive purposes. For Lacan, fantasy and wishful thinking are trying to fill up or close the lack of being that constitutes desire. Freud spoke of wishing as the core of being, but wishing or wishful thinking is actually the activity that attempts to close the gap that constitutes desire and the lack of being. The lack of being is true being or what Nagarjuna called the wondrous emptiness of being. The core of being is non-being and non-being is being. Being without non-being is an example of wishing and fantasising or unconscious thinking.

In Seminar XIV, Lacan (1966–1967) begins from the Cartesian proposition that being is equivalent to the ego, to consciousness, and to a denial of the unconscious: I think, therefore I am. Being here is *not* equivalent to non-being. There is a formal disjunction and a forced choice between being and non-being, being and thinking. The Cartesian ego is like the defensive analysand whose character traits are ego-syntonic: "This is who I am, and what I think", which also implies the opposite: "I am not that, nor do I think that".

The practice of analysis leads Lacan to the disjunction between being and thinking. The ego denies unconscious thought and also denies that that the ego is denying which is how Freud formulated the unconscious ego of unconscious defences. When Lacan writes "I am not thinking", he is referring to the denial of unconscious thinking, not to the fact that the ego may have conscious thoughts or rationalisations. In this formulation, the ego is equivalent to "not thinking" in the sense of a refusal to think beyond the already known. A space not-without thinking or in-between a series of thoughts is an entirely different dimension of "It" that will be considered further on.

What makes Lacan's seminar "On the Logic of Fantasy" (1966–1977) difficult to understand is that he is handling and combining different notions of being stemming from Descartes, Freud, and Heidegger. Of the three, as far as I can tell, only Heidegger has a systematic analysis of Being, and Heidegger's notion of Being is quite different from a notion of an ego or from the notion of being that is implied in Descartes' formula. In his famous declaration "I think, therefore I am", Descartes associates being with conscious ego thinking. Freud (1900) instead defines unconscious wishing and wishful thinking as the core of being. Lacan (1966–1967), on the one hand, follows Freud in this regard: "This not-I, so essential to articulate for the essence of being, is what Freud brings us in the second step of his thinking called the 'second topography', as being the Id (*ca*)" (Session of 21 December 1966).

Lacan is relating the not-I to the essence of being while he is also struggling to articulate being on the side of consciousness and the defences of the ego. The operative term here is essence of being. The essence of being differs from being. The essence of being and the being of essence is emptiness.

The ego's repression of thought and the opposite undoing of the ego by thought or free association result in the emergence and production of a new subject. The id depersonalises the ego, and replaces identity with non-identity. Out of this non-identity emerges a new subject of the unconscious. The new evanescent I, or adverted subject, takes responsibility for desire and love and can make use of the Name of the Father.

Now it is unclear to me whether Lacan speaks of this "not-I" or "I am not thinking" in the sense of the ego not doing the thinking, as a negation of unconscious thinking, or as the absence of thinking in general. When the ego was not thinking, the ego erred, and the unconscious appeared to disturb the ego's defences. At other times of direct inspiration, thoughts emerge from a different place and are geared in an entirely different direction. In such cases, spontaneous thought turns out to be the first and best thought. At yet other times, non-thinking has nothing to do with a suppression of thought by the ego. Non-thinking arises from a different place than either the ego or unconscious thinking.

For Lacan, signifiers and the unconscious think automatically and spontaneously without any ego. The unconscious is a kind of knowing without a subject or without an ego. The subject of the unconscious represents an instantaneous manifestation of unconscious structure. This notion of unconscious thought without an ego is similar to what Bion called thoughts without a thinker, with one notable exception. For Bion, these thoughts are in search of a thinker who can think them into a symbolic form of organisation.

In this regard, Bion preserves, however disguised/modified, an ego notion that he links to the mother's alpha function. Bion's ideas about thinking are linked to Plato's ideas and to Jungian archetypes (that lead to an idealism of the Self), while Lacan is Aristotelian or Buddhist in the way that thoughts can be thought without a thinker or a subject. Organisation is given by an impersonal or transpersonal symbolic structure. For Lacan, the "not-I", or the "I am not", represents a negation of being and of the ego, and a substitution of the being of the ego. The being of the ego or the essence of being becomes non-being.

> Now, Descartes' *cogito* has a sense: *the fact is that for this relation of thinking to being, it substitutes purely and simply the instauration of the being of the I.*
>
> Because, for us, there is not only this *not to be*, since moreover the fate of *being* which is important for us as regards the subject, is linked to thinking. So then what is meant by *not thinking*?

> (Session of 6 December 1966)

Lacan does not answer this question, but provides a hint of an answer by posing a different yet related question.

> Let us take it up: *I do not desire.* It is clear that this *I do not desire*, just by itself is designed to make us ask what the negation is brought to bear on ... . But, in fact, the negation could mean that it is not I (*moi*) who desires, implying that I take no responsibility for desiring, which may also indeed be what carries me while at the same time not being *me*. But again it remains that this negation may mean that *it is not true*, that I desire, that desire, whether it is from *me* or from *not-me*, has nothing to do with the question.

> (Session of 11 January 1967)

Using the above as a model, I can now consider what Lacan may mean by not-thinking. In contrast to Descartes' "I think, therefore I am", Lacan links thinking to non-being and the unconscious and being to not thinking, and (ego-) consciousness.

The Cartesian "I" (*moi*) here represents the ego rather than the subject (*Je*) of the unconscious. The latter is equivalent to unconscious thinking whether in the sense of the dynamic or descriptive unconscious. In this formulation, the unconscious is equivalent to non-being or the lack of being.

Just as Descartes links thinking to the "I" and to being, Lacan creates a forced choice between "I am not" (the unconscious) and "I am not thinking" (being and the ego). "I am not thinking" could mean that I am not thinking because the unconscious is thinking, or because no thinking is taking place, whether conscious or unconscious. In addition,

"I am not" could be linked to Being as emerging from the unconscious (non-being is being) or "I am not" could be linked to the cessation of thinking (being is associated with thinking). Lacan does not appear to explicitly consider the possibility that non-being could be being or that the unconscious could be related to Being. All of these questions and permutations involve the question regarding the being or the nature of Being: is it non-being, is it desire, the ego, wishing and fantasy, thinking, not-thinking, or non-thinking?

Colloquial language has a variety of expressions for thinking. The subject may say "I was not thinking", or "What was I thinking?", or "First thought is best thought", or "Think twice before you act", or "On second thought …", or "I am having second thoughts". It is difficult to reconcile and make sense of these apparently contradictory statements. Only a topological or topographical perspective can begin to render intelligible the internal relations among these sentences.

In spoken idiomatic language, "I was not thinking" refers to a compromised or eclipsed capacity to prepare and organise intelligible action. Here, thinking goes together with second thoughts or thinking twice as a secondary process linked to the reality principle. The phrase "What was I thinking?" points to a wishful primary process thinking that is in conflict with reality or the capacity for realistic symbolic functioning. In turn, "First thought is best thought" refers to a primary form of spontaneous thinking that is not in conflict with reality and is in accord with Lacan's notion of the symbolic subject (*Je*) and the unconscious structured as a language. This first principle of thought is akin to an authentic intuition or apperception and insight into the internal workings of phenomena. Intuition here becomes identical to counter-intuition, if by intuition we simply mean common sense. Having second thoughts instead refers to a degraded egoic form of secondary-process thinking for which sceptical or obsessive doubt and rumination would be the prime example.

I speak of an authentic intuition in order to differentiate it from both magical or wishful thinking and common sense. In science and physics, theory is considered counter-intuitive because it violates our usual way of understanding reality. For science, intuition coincides with common sense at best, and at worst intuition represents pre-scientific, if not mythical or mystical, forms of thought. In Zen and Buddhism, intuition is the human function needed to understand or operate in the world according to the way things go or are beyond rational comprehension.

The so-called higher psychical functions are not secondary but rather primary functions equivalent to intuitive forms of unconscious knowing that are consistent with Bion's understanding of the dream-work as an alpha function. The same difference exists between intuition and projection, or between authentic intuition or even rational intuition and superstitious projection/intuition, than that which exists between primary beta thinking and secondary alpha thinking, or between a first that is second and a second that is first. This phenomenon is covered under what Bion called reversible perspectives and what Lacan viewed as the functioning of the psyche within a Möbius strip. There is a difference between primary and primitive or between the archaic and the ancient.

In Heidegger, Being is not determined by the ego or by representation, or by thinking for that matter. Being is used as an alternative to having to speak of a human capacity in terms of an ego or self. Strictly speaking, Being is non-self, it is neither the imaginary ego, nor the symbolic subject: Being is the subject of the Real. The essence of being or the non-being of Being or the Real of being is emptiness, although Being can also appear as the Lacanian symbolic lack of being and as the Freudian wishing or fantasy that closes the gap and emptiness of being.

Finally, beings are speaking beings and, therefore, being also appears within the house of language and within the signifiers and ciphers that articulate/organise the experience (mind/body) of a subject. In other words, non-being is being, and thinking is non-thinking (the unconscious is doing the thinking). Corresponding to these three levels of being, Heidegger (1949) noted that the philosophical tradition has generally presupposed that being is at once the most universal concept (Symbolic), the concept indefinable in terms of other concepts (Real), and the self-evident concept (Imaginary).

However, the fantasised object that occupies the place of the other, or that fills the lack in the Other, cannot give Being its being. In this sense, Lacan's dichotomy between unconscious thinking, in the sense of wishing, and Being is preserved. In addition, the signifier, or the subject for that matter, cannot represent itself. The subject in the Real as a form of *jouissance* remains unrepresentable and unsignified (in language). It is here where Freud, Lacan, Heidegger, and Zen meet. Freud is included in this meeting because the core of being has something to do with *jouissance*, although not exactly wishing as Freud conceived it. Juxtaposing the ideas of the three thinkers leads to a more complex conception of desire and of how *jouissance* transforms in the direction of how Being was understood by Heidegger. In *Existence and Being*, Heidegger (1949) wrote:

> That Being itself and how Being itself concerns our thinking does not depend upon our thinking alone. That Being itself, and the manner in which Being itself, strikes a man's thinking, that rouses his thinking and stirs it to rise from Being itself to respond and correspond to Being as such.

There is a different meditative form of thinking that responds and corresponds to Being and that Heidegger says is directed to the point of origin of Being. Being is like the self-notion that we assume to be the same with our self and yet can also be "extimate" to the ego, as Lacan puts it. Self can be no-self or no-ego. It is in this sense that the answer to the question of being comes in three voices: self-evident fantasy, symbolic interdependent existence, and the mysterious Real or emptiness as a form of *jouissance*. I advance the notion that thinking at the point of origin of Being or at the point of non-knowing corresponds to Lacan's concept of a new signifier/subject emerging as a result of the analytic process.

> To the early Greeks, Being, unlimited in its dis-closure, appears as an abyss, the source of thought and wonder. Being calls everything into question, casts the human being out of any habitual ground, and opens before him the mystery of existence.
>
> (Heidegger, 1949)

Lacan asks the question regarding the properly Heideggerian formulation of Being in the following way.

> Does this not mean placing oneself, as *ego*, outside the grasp in which being may embrace thinking?
> To posit oneself: *ego, I think* as pure thinking being (*pense-être*), as subsisting by being the *I* (the *Je*) of a local *I am not*; which means: *I only am on condition that the question of being is eluded,* I give up being, *I* ... am not (non-being is being), except there where—necessarily -I am, by being able to *say* it. Or to say it

better: where I am, by being able to say it to *you*, or more exactly: by making it be said to the Other, because this is indeed the process, when you follow it closely in Descartes' text.

(11 January 1967—English brackets are mine)

In this quote, Lacan's text evokes the possibility that being may embrace thinking outside the ego and that Being comes back to the subject via the Other. This is a different and new I. No longer the I of the ego, there is a new I that emerges when the ego is negated (I am not), or when the I of the ego and the *objet a* (i[a]) have been separated or fallen off from each other (i ∥ a). In its imaginary autonomy, the ego lives in denial of the Other, but by speaking to the Other, the subject may recover a true form of autonomous Being (not an ego any more). When the imaginary being of wishing has been spoken and dissolved in speech, the I of Being itself, or the subject of the Real becomes a meeting place between *jouissance* and the instantaneous manifestation of the signifier (Other) in the present moment of being and non-being.

When the ego is either thinking or wishing, Being is lost or covered over (Imaginary). In this formulation, the ego is on the same side as wishing and the Freudian unconscious wish in the sense of a primitive primary process. The ideal ego and the ego-ideal are contained within the closed narcissistic libidinal box of the unconscious object. Instead, the subject of the unconscious or the unconscious structured as a language is equivalent to a second that is a first or to the Freudian unconscious in a descriptive sense. Being and desire are revealed by the instantaneous manifestation of the thoughtful signifier (S_1). In addition, there is a non-thinking that is not egoic and that is in fact linked to the larger Being. I will distinguish this non-thinking of unknown knowing from the not-thinking that Lacan links to the ego, the *cogito*, and the "I am" or "I know" of ignorance. In truth, I (*Je*) am where I don't know or where the subject (of the Real) and *jouissance* are non-thinking.

In addition, the notion of unconscious thinking or not-thinking or non-being which Lacan opposes to being is also in contradiction to the Lacanian notion of human beings as speaking beings (*parle-être*). In the latter, language is on the side of being, and one would be hard-pressed to argue that in Lacan language is linked to the ego, and not to thinking. We already know that Lacan stated that the unconscious is structured like a language. The Lacanian notion of speaking beings is also in agreement with Heidegger's notion of language as the house of being or as what allows for Being to be shown/said.

On the other hand, according to Lacan, language or the Symbolic (symbolic castration) also generates desire as a lack or absence of being, and this in turn leads to how the ego seeks being within fantasies and the Imaginary. The lack of being has a particular and developmental/ structural signification with respect to the loss of "being with the mother" and the loss of the mother's imaginary phallus as the signifier of the (m)Other's desire.

In this case, unconscious thinking and the lack of being are on the same side as language. As mentioned earlier, non-being or the lack of being and the unconscious can be on the same side of Being and language as the house of Being.

Within the Symbolic, the ego is always under the threat of disappearing and of feeling like nothing with respect to the totally different experience of being that imaginary fantasies seem to offer. Thus, language precipitates the disappearance of being within the subject, and at the same time human beings access being through language. Being is now found through metaphoric substitution, naming, and the function of the father or the paternal metaphor. Lacanian theory advances two contradictory propositions: being disappears with language and yet being only appears within language. In my opinion, this dialectical contradiction can be overcome by considering the lack of being as non-being in a negative dialectical relationship with being.

I mention negative dialectics because the negation of being, or non-being, do not produce a more substantial being than being the mother's imaginary phallus or merging or being with the mother. Non-being leads to being yourself without self-representation other than that provided by a signifier that cannot represent itself outside relationships (to other subjects/signifiers). Emptiness or the Real permeates language as the house of Being. Being yourself means a "you" in relationship to everything and everyone else.

What Bobrow (2010) calls "presence of mind" or "coming forth" represents the embodied flow of *jouissance* and signification as brought forth by the speech acts and actions of a subject with an empty heart/ mind. The presence of the subject in the here and now requires the manifestation of being and the manifestation of being requires the absence of ego-consciousness. We let go of the ego in order to find the self as the presence of serenity without representation. It is the Real subject that can be cool under pressure, judicious in action, tolerant of complexity, uncertainty / contradiction, and thoughtful in action without self-consciousness. At the same time, the subject of the Other *jouissance* can also remain connected to others while not engaged in speech or communicative action. This is what Winnicott (1960) called the incommunicado core of self / non-self that can remain silent and at ease in the presence of others. In zazen, a group shares the agreement to not speak and to practise zazen together in silence.

Emptiness precisely refers to a dialectical interdependence between non-being and being, self and other. Emptiness differs from non-being because emptiness is the relationship by which being and non-being, self and other, co-arise together. Between the Symbolic and the Real, being and non-being are different and yet contain one another, while between the Symbolic and the Imaginary, and between ego–object relations, non-being is completely devoid of being and vice versa. Rather than think of the lack of being as an absence of being or a nothingness, which is the opposite of being, if the lack of being is conceived of as the emptiness at the core of being, then emptiness, more than non-being, is wondrous being itself.

Finally, I will differentiate the "I am not thinking" of the ego, as a lack of critical thinking, or as a lack of unconscious knowing or a knowledge of the unconscious, from what, following Zen, I will call the non-thinking of the Real. And although the non-thinking of Zen does point to the Real, sometimes in Zen non-thinking is confused with not-thinking, and the ego and a false sense of self and being enters back into Zen via the back door of a rejection of language, critical thought, and unconscious dharmas (phenomena). Silence or not speaking is used as a defence against unconscious thinking.

In contrast to not thinking, non-thinking overincludes unconscious thinking as well as Being and a consciousness beyond ego-consciousness. This is one way of understanding Buddha as a bodhisattva or an enlightening being, in contrast to the *arahats* (ascetics) of Hinayana Buddhism who represent not-thinking and the rejection of words and the world.

For Lacan, there is also an anterior lack or loss with respect to sexual reproduction and the loss of infinite Life that goes with the birth–death life cycle. What Lacan calls the *lamella* represents the placenta, as a mythical *objet a*, and represents not only the loss of the body of the mother, but also the loss of immortal life. Developmentally, the loss of the *objet a* is anterior to the loss of the imaginary phallus, although structurally the two are interdependent.

Non-thinking and unconscious knowing which take place between analyst and analysand, and that are included in the experience of zazen, point to the origin of Being and to the mystery of infinite Life that overincludes birth and death. Infinite Life is there when there is no-thing, "It" moves when the mind is still, and when the mind is moving "It" stands still. It is silent when the mind speaks, and speaks when the mind is silent.

> Once, when the Great Master Hongdao of Yueshan was sitting [in meditation], a monk asked him, "What are you thinking of, [sitting there] so fixedly? "The master answered, "I'm thinking of not thinking." The monk asked, "How do you think of not thinking?" The Master answered, "Nonthinking."
>
> (Shobogenzo, Book 12, Lancet of Zazen (*Zazen shin*))

Once, when I was about ten years old, I walked into the living room of my parental home and found my stepfather sitting in a chair in silence. Impressed by the situation and the figure before me, I asked him, "What are you doing?" Jorge Bosch, my stepfather, answered: "I am thinking my boy, I am thinking".

In the quote above, the monk could have asked: "What are you doing?" instead of assuming the teacher was thinking. In fact, this is the theme of another famous Zen koan:

> When the Chan master Daji of Jiangxi was studying with the Chan master Dahui of Nanyue, after intimately receiving the mind seal, he always practiced seated meditation. Once Nanyue went to Dajii and said, "Worthy one, what are you doing sitting there in meditation?"
>
> (Shobogenzo, Book 12, Lancet of Zazen (*Zazen shin*))

Dajii answered that he was trying to become a Buddha, and in the ensuing dialogue Nanyue tries to show Dajii the fruitlessness of "becoming" in Zen Buddhism. I will take this up in the next chapter, but for now, let us examine the relationship among thinking, not thinking, and non-thinking in Zen Buddhism and their relationship to unconscious knowing and what I am calling infinite Life.

In the first story, the monk assumes that if the teacher is sitting, he must be thinking, and thus begins the dialogue by asking the teacher what he is thinking about in meditation. The teacher replies that he is thinking not-thinking. It is interesting to consider this story in the light of Lacanian thought. The teacher is both thinking in the usual ego way and at the same time trying not to think which is also an aspect of the ego's defences. Trying to attain a non-ego mode of thinking is still an ego mode within the logic of attainment (attaining non-attainment). Trying to attain a non-ego or selflessness is still making a self out of non-self.

Now if thinking not-thinking means "I am thinking that I am not thinking" or that "the ego is not the one that is doing the thinking" or that "there is no subject in thinking", then the "I" here would be the new "I" mentioned above rather than the ego. The teacher is engaged in unconscious thinking instead of conscious ego thoughts.

Finally, thinking without an ego is not that different from non-thinking. Non-thinking in Dogen's Zen refers to the non-duality of thinking and not thinking in zazen. Non-thinking points to thinking with the body: breathing in and breathing out with the belly, or what the Japanese call the *hara*. Non-thinking is keeping the back upright, letting go of the tension in the jaw and in the shoulders, letting go of stressful thoughts of me and mine, enjoying the serenity of the body/mind, and so on. In his visit to MIT, the linguist Noam Chomsky asked Lacan a question about thought that provoked a scandal and Chomsky's dismissal of Lacan as a madman. Lacan told him that we think that we think with the brain, but that he thought with his feet because it is the only place where he found something hard and solid (Roudinesco, 1993, p. 551).

It is unclear, however, how thinking or non-thinking with the body would point to the origin or to the mystery of Being. Non-thinking does not only point to thinking with the body, but also points to the emptiness of the forms of the body/mind. Unknown knowing is like the unthought known or thinking with the body. The body is an aspect of the Real or of knowing within the Real. The Real is associated with the organism independently from human construction and fabrication. The body of the Real differs from the Imaginary or Symbolic body. The Imaginary body is the libidinal body and the body of narcissism and of the ideal ego or bodily image. The symbolic body is the social body of language and perception; in other words, the subject as a signifier.

Distension in tension and intention represents the stillness that emerges and is invoked in the zazen posture. Bodily zazen and sitting still sets in motion the flight of the bird of the unconscious. In other words, with awareness of the body comes awareness of the incessant and impermanent stream of thoughts, feelings, and sensations. In unconscious thinking, the ego is also included as a narcissistic rather than as a reality object. Since in zazen there are thoughts that are not revealed in speech or free association, making the primary process of thoughts conscious involves transforming their energy not through speech but through the serene quality of the mind realised in zazen.

The flying birds and the rushing streams of emotion, as currents of unconscious life or of consciousness, are perceived against a background of luminosity and spaciousness that gradually transforms the quality of the mind. The bird is moving but it is also standing still, the sky or space is standing still yet is also moving with the bird. The standing still of the bird of thought or of the psyche, and the movement of the sky of mind, represents the emptiness or non-duality of infinite Life or of the birth—death cycle (birdeath).

Of course, this seems to be quite different from the analysis of how thoughts and feelings are derived from primary relationships, from love and hate, attachment and detachment from mother and father, and from the conflicts between law and desire that are the basic themes and staples of speech in psychoanalysis. However, upon closer examination, many of the themes electrifying or occupying the mind of Zen practitioners have to do with the relationship with the teacher and other members of the Sangha. The Sangha is a family composed of parents/leaders, mothers and fathers, children and siblings. If this is not immediately obvious in Zen teaching, or how meditation is described, it has become abundantly evident in the many sexual scandals and conflicts that have rocked North American Zen communities.

In fact, it is psychoanalysts or psychoanalytically informed practitioners who have been called upon to help these organisations with interpersonal/intersubjective difficulties. Despite years and decades of practice, the birds of the unconscious are still flying, and thoughts have been split between wishing/fantasising and the "ought" or regrets of thoughts. I believe that these problems have something to do with the dearth of speech in Zen practice and the confusion between not thinking and unconscious thinking and between unconscious thinking and non-thinking or emptiness. It is the difference between the unknown repressed unconscious and the unconscious of the unknown or the Real that is beyond known and unknown, conscious and unconscious.

Concluding poem

Infinite Life is like the vast sky that flies with the bird and the deep ocean that swims with the fish. The bird and the fish are contained within human thinking and feeling and the treasure chest of the signifier reveals and manifests the mystery of *jouissance*. With respect to the bird or the fish, the sky and the ocean are infinite in time and extension. Although the birth–death cycle of the bird and the fish are surrounded by the larger birth–death cycle of the ocean and the sky, the four are contained within the Infinite life of emptiness. Emptiness is truly empty without measure.

CHAPTER THREE

Meditation as thinking and non-thinking in Lacan and Zen

Purposes, meanings, and the Other

The notions of meaning, purpose, or intentionality are mostly associated with a psychology of consciousness, and with personal and/or spiritual development rather than psychoanalysis. People want to find meaning and purpose in their lives and for this they appeal to religion, spirituality, Jungian analysis, or to humanistic, existential, or self-help psychologies/philosophies. Victor Frankl (1975) invented an entire new school of psychology and psychotherapy on the basis of this idea alone (logotherapy). In addition, the search for meaning is also linked to teleological forms of thought. Jung borrowed the teleological principle from Von Hartmann's philosophy of the unconscious. According to the latter, the teleological principle is unconscious and yet drives all of life forces in the direction of its aims. The desire or the striving towards the goal of attaining happiness, virtue, knowledge, or serenity is an example of a teleological form of thinking or psychic functioning.

The same could be said of the pleasure principle: purposive action consists in attaining the desirable and avoiding undesirable pain or suffering. However, pleasure is not identical to serenity or happiness. For the Greeks, the latter comes from virtue and character rather than from pleasure. Freud faced this problem when defining the relations between the pleasure principle and the reality principle. Is hedonism the craving for destructive lust or the search for a reasonable, legitimate, harmless and socially permitted pleasure?

In addition, the fulfilment of ego purposes can bring a sense of satisfaction or happiness, or a temporary feeling of success, yet this feeling may change or turn when circumstances are no longer favorable to the ego. In this way ego purposes differ from intentions to live within a plane of being beyond ego purposes and intentions, or worldly failure and success. Beginners' mind, for example, remains neutral or serene with respect to the successes and failures that determine feelings linked to the ego and ego-representations. The happiness of the ego is dual while the joy associated with beginners' mind is non-dual or unconditioned.

From a spiritual and a psychoanalytic perspective the striving for virtue, as self-denial or the capacity to postpone gratification, can also be fraught with defensive purposes and an avoidance of passion and desire that can also lead to suffering as Freud has amply demonstrated. Striving after both pleasure and virtue can carry obstacles and impediments linked to very idea of striving, ambition, attainment, and purposeful activity.

Striving after virtue or happiness ends up inevitably wound up or entangled with what Freud called the ego-ideal. The ego-ideal in turn is fraught in two directions. First with the sense of duty, obligation, shame, and guilt linked to the superego. Second, with the ambitions, self-pride, and narcissism of the ego no matter how spiritual these may be.

Within Zen, this phenomenon is known as the Zen illness or sickness wherein practitioners are practising meditation with what is called a gaining idea aimed at advancing self-centred purposes or a personal enlightenment. The Heart sutra provides the antidote to this poison with the teaching of no path, no enlightenment, and no attainment. On the other hand, there is no pure Zen uncontaminated by the dust of the world. In the first century of the Common Era, Nagarjuna, the great Mahayana sage, already taught that Nirvana is Samsara and Samsara is Nirvana. Most practitioners bring their ego into the practice of meditation as the manure and fertiliser that will facilitate a transformation within their own being. Meditation represents Nirvana, and the ego represents Samsara. People want to feel good and happy but eventually begin scheming after and holding on to position, rank, financial resources, living conditions, security, and so on.

Nirvana within Samsara also means that there is something altruistic or even spiritual about egoism that is distinct from the contamination of spirituality by egoism or self-centred ideas. What could this be? In Lacan, the ideal ego comes from an Other-centred source. The ideal ego is seeking after the love and approval of the mother and to identify with the object of the mother's desire. This is the source of the ego and of the mother–child, *Madonna col Bambino*, union. The mother is perceived as the source of all that is good in the experience of the child.

However, there is no return or looking back at what already took place and has been inevitably lost. Looking back to the mother–child dual union produces the frozen effect of Lot's wife who turned into a pillar of salt when she turned back to look at the burning biblical town of Sodom (Genesis 19:26). The ego as a mental formation is formed as a scar or a bubble in the place where a satisfaction with the mother was experienced and then lost. From then on, repetition takes place in relationship to the ideal ego rather than the desire of the mother. The ideal ego is the dust in the mirror of the mind, or what in the Mahayana Lankavatara sutra is called the uninvited guest. In Lacanian theory, the *jouissance* of and with the mother of early childhood can only be recovered, if at all, via the Other *jouissance* that requires the prior intervention of the father.

The symbolic father/mother is the teacher or Buddha. In Soto Zen, Dogen (1200–1253), the founder of Soto Zen in Japan, occupies the place of the symbolic father. In the fascicle Zazenshin (Bielefeldt, 1988), he writes: "If you think that meditation is about sitting at peace/ease in a quiet place you don't realise that sitting is simply like a stone pressing on grass." Within Zen, intention is the intention to practice or of making effort or striving without a gaining idea (of dual union at the mother's breast or of being a warrior/hero for the father), but also without sloughing off, or laziness. Intention is an effortless effort or an intention without a specific object. We never loose sight of the thought of enlightenment although this thought remains undefined. We intend to practice and awaken together with other speaking beings, although this heartfelt or compassionate aspiration may also remain free or empty of rules or specific content. Intuitively or unconsciously, we know what this means and this unknown knowing remains fresh and distinct from common sense.

Sitting in zazen is the practice of immobile sitting without thinking anything in particular or thinking that we are doing anything special but also without trying to suppress thinking or thinking that by not thinking or by sitting without thoughts or without a gaining idea that we achieve a state of pure or uncontaminated Zen. Sometimes thoughts or intentions are gaining ideas (defences against loss), sometimes they are about not having gaining ideas or about not thinking, but at other times thinking is simply thinking without an ego or thinker. There is also non-thinking that does not have the purpose of suppressing thinking. There is both thinking and not thinking with and without the ego. Not thinking without the ego is non-thinking and non-thinking is the source of true thinking without an ego or thinking that is simply like a stone pressing on grass or a bird flying in the sky.

Non-thinking that does not think of itself as not-thinking, does not differ from the thinking that does not think of itself as thinking. Non-thinking is not the opposite of thinking and therefore is not without thinking and true thinking is not without non-thinking. The practice Buddha does not seek to become Buddha nor hinder actualising Buddha. Buddha is already Buddha because of practising without thinking of becoming Buddha and by not thinking that he/she is becoming Buddha by practising without thinking of becoming Buddha. Both thinking and not thinking are without ulterior motive, both thinking and not thinking are non-thinking.

The question of meaning and purposes is not only linked to intentionality (without an object), and to consciousness of something or of an object (as in phenomenology), but intention is also extended towards the desire and recognition of the Other. In other words, other than awareness without a content or object, thinking with purpose in the sense of a consciousness of an object, can represent meditating or thinking with the aim of obtaining something material or spiritual. The ulterior motive can also be obtaining the love, approval, and recognition of the Other. A Zen student is trying to become or make a Buddha, to get meaning or "the" meaning (enlightenment), in order to get the approval and love of a teacher.

But when thinking and not thinking are realised as non-thinking and Buddha is actualised beyond striving and not striving, approval or disapproval, Buddha and no-Buddha, isn't this precisely the realisation of Buddha's unknown love that loves and knows without knowing? Realising or actualising Buddha's love (Real) is beyond self-love

(Imaginary) and the Other's love (Symbolic). Buddha's love is the love of Big self which includes self and other and the Other's love that already includes the subject. The One manifests Buddha's love without the approval or disapproval of the teacher or Other.

At first, a student may approach Zen practice as a subject and receive the practice with beginner's mind. This in turn may lead to an awakening of the subject of the Real or of subjectivity without a subject. Zen tradition describes this experience as one of suddenly running into your father at a crossroads. But pretty soon an ego-ideal and a sense of meritocracy will begin to seep in. The student wants to be seen by the teacher as a good student or even as a better student than other students. The intention or desire to practice becomes a desire of the other's desire and approval and a false self or ego-ideal is constructed in the process.

Once a student begins speaking in a Buddhist language, and following the rules of the practice, he/she secretly begins to desire the love and recognition of the Other, and desiring to be desired by the Other. Depending on the sexual orientation and gender of teacher and student this may also have a sexual dimension. Or if the Sangha (community) represents the precepts of the practice, which include sexual prohibitions of one form or another, then a sexual desire for someone of the opposite or same sex may ensue.

At this point meanings, purposes, and intentions are no longer synonymous with consciousness or realistic ego-functioning. Now we are caught in the web constructed by our own wishes and actions. In *The Interpretation of Dreams* (1900), Freud used these categories to describe psychical processes that were ostensibly unconscious. Freud used the term "symbol/representation" to represent something standing in the place of something else that remains unconscious. According to Freud and Lacan, it is the Symbolic order rather than conscious intentions that holds the keys for the knowledge of the subject.

This is obviously a different starting point, than the way most subjects experience their thinking about themselves or the world, whether in daily life or in meditation experience. In daily life or meditation, people experience their mind and its contents, from the point of view of their ego or personality. It is them that are doing the thinking, and most commonly people identify with their thoughts. What is non-self or unwelcomed is often ignored if not actively rejected.

According to Buddhism, the self and non-self elements of thoughts, that are either liked or rejected, are mental formations of the storehouse consciousness. For psychoanalysis, they are formations of the unconscious. However, both the storehouse consciousness and the unconscious have a social dimension. The storehouse consciousness is the repository/storehouse of species knowledge, memory, and dynamic activity since times immemorial. In addition, the unconscious for Lacan is the discourse of the Other and language includes not only grammar rules but also the language of desire.

According to Mahayana Buddhism (in the Surangama sutra), the storehouse consciousness, as a collective effort over time, has the social karmic effect of leading us to believe in the existence of an outside world independent from consciousness. In actuality, the real images and words associated with the objective world are constantly being projected out of the *Alaya vijnana* or storehouse consciousness. Individual karma is what causes human beings to be born into the human form of species-being within this particular universe. Once born, through volitional action or doing human beings continue to build the storehouse consciousness for future generations. The storehouse consciousness is conditioned and conditioning, determined and determining at the same time.

The Other or the Other-dependent consciousness, or what Lacan calls the symbolic order, is what constructs the experience of empirical reality, the words and images that bring together sense organ, object, and perception. Representations according to Freud are made up of thing and word representations. Things are not things in themselves but the real-images and signifiers that define them. Memories are based on the seeds that were laid down by mnemic traces or representations.

For Buddhism, perception is in fact non-perception for we do not perceive real objects only representations (real images and signifiers). The Real is what things are in themselves as representations taking place within the empty infinite mirror, otherwise known as ultimate reality. In the Real, there is no subject or object, and therefore the Real can be equally described as mind or matter, mind within matter, and matter within mind. The subject and the object both arise together as the other-dependent nature.

The infinite mirror that contains the seeds laid down by doing and experience is equivalent to the Real unconscious. In addition, using concepts derived from quantum physics (Deutsch, 1997), seeds can be understood as entangled forms of information that are superposed or condensed (to use a Freudian concept). These seeds are both S_1 or a representation and S_0 or an entangled form of knowing that is beyond the space/time parameters of experience. S_0 refers to unknown forms or Q'bits, or unary traces (traceless traces) of knowing that cannot be perceived. In this formulation, the unconscious refers to unknown knowing held within entangled particles. To emerge from S_0 unknown knowing has to become S_1 and eventually S_2 thereby loosing its original place of superposition.

Perception stems from what Freud called the preconscious-conscious system. We seem to be conscious when perceiving but in fact perception is preconscious. For Freud, the preconscious was the sense of the unconscious in a descriptive sense. The preconscious, otherwise known as the descriptive unconscious, is not repressed. Rather it reflects the fact that the process of perception as a construction or mental formation is unconscious. We are not aware of how language and the Other-dependent nature is determining or conditioning our perceptions of reality.

Thoughts and thinking are built on representations that are thinking us rather than the other way around. Individuals build a sense of ego out of appropriating the store consciousness and thinking that there is a thinker doing the thinking. In this sense, thought differs from thinking. A single thought in the present moment may be the place where a new subject/signifier arises unconditioned by the established serial process of thinking. This would be one way of understanding what the Buddha called the thought of enlightenment.

For Buddhism, consciousness is something more than what is commonly understood to be conscious experience. In fact, the Lankavatara sutra (D. T. Suzuki, 1931), and the teaching of Vasubhandu (Indian Zen ancestor from the second century) emerging from it, already anticipated the Lacanian theory of the Borromean knot. The symbolic Other is similar if not identical to the Other-dependent consciousness (*Paratantra*), the Imagined (*Parikalpita*) is similar to the Imaginary, and the Real (*Parinishpanna*) is similar if not identical to the Real of the later Lacan. Subjective structure is the structure of the Lacanian Borromean knot (Real, Symbolic, Imaginary), but the individual misapprehends the structure of the knot for the structure of their ego or personality.

It is language, for example, that holds together the subject/object structure of a sentence, and the metaphoric structure of the subject, but the ego mistakes this structure as one of or his/her own making. Language is the language of the Other because the relative truth of a proposition depends on the emptiness of the author as the foundation of the statement. When we realise that language is without an ego, and that it is inter-dependent or Other-dependent (on all other signifiers within language), then according to Vasubhandu this is the consummate nature (Real or *Parinishpanna*), and according to Lacan it is the subject of the Real.

In learning how to speak and verbalise, within a cultural context, a subject acquires not only the laws of the culture but also a practice of self-regulation of their desires and impulses. Ego-functioning is the functioning of the symbolic function, and the sooner the subject depersonalises and symbolises the function, the smoother and efficient the functioning of the subject becomes. The unity of experience is derived from the interdependency of the structure, not from the ego imposing his/her "master" will on its objects. Therefore, egolessness or non-self does not lead to disintegration, as people usually fear and believe.

However, the interdependence of the repressed and the repressive differs from the interdependence of subject and object, self and other. In Buddhism, the teaching of interdependency, or "independency" as Suzuki Roshi called it, is the same as the teaching of emptiness. The latter is the condition of the former. Things are related because they don't exist in a vacuum and also because they are empty. Relativity means that if you pick up one corner of a napkin you have the other three at the same time. If you say napkin you have four corners and you have the words table, food, utensils, etc. But this is not yet emptiness. Emptiness means that all these things exist in our mind and at the same time they don't. When they are not there where did they go?

What makes them be there and not be there, is not only the need or the context but also their use within language. With language we can talk about them when they are not there but also when they are there we know them through their names. What is a napkin without the associative context? What is it? The fact that a napkin is not actually a napkin, that it's absolute difference points to the void or emptiness, is precisely what sustains its relative value beyond the sum of associated words and functions.

In the case of repression, the emptiness of a repressed word or signifier is missing. Repression reifies a signifier like the frozen picture of a trauma or fantasy. S_1 becomes S_2 or vice versa. The tracelessness of a trace is missing. Repression and the repressed represent a false hole. It looks like something is missing but there is something there lurking behind the veil or wall of censorship and repression. A gaping gaze, for example, returns from repression and appears in the hole left by the disappearance and absence of the repressed.

This is consistent with the teaching of the two voids promulgated by Manjushri, the legendary bodhisattva of wisdom. Lacan also spoke of a true and false hole. There is a void of absence and the true void of emptiness. Repression is a false hole of absence rather than emptiness.

Letters represent things that are no longer there but are not repressed. The void or the paper/parchment represents the thing, and the void or the paper are then replaced by the letter. In turn, other letters represent letters, and things become represented by the relationship among signifiers/words that themselves represent subjects. A table is and is not a table because it is only a table for a subject who is another signifier and who is and is not a signifier because the signifier cancels the subject who nonetheless can only be represented by a signifier. Subject, object, and void all arise together.

This differs from the interdependence of the repressed and the repressive in the repressed unconscious. In repression, zero or the void is represented by a repressed signifier. The hole of repression is a false hole because in the hole there is a repressed signifier. What is missing in repression is emptiness because the subject becomes reified as an object/signifier, or as the object of a repressed fantasy (i.e., the imaginary phallus). The relationship to the other then becomes mediated by an imaginary fantasy object.

The imaginary fantasy object differs from the imagined externality of the world of objects although only to a certain point. I say only to a certain point because as a projection of the storehouse consciousness, that I have already said is the product of species being and effort over the generations, the external world can be perceived as the gaze of the Other. The eyes of our ancestors are watching us in trees, on the road, the windows of buildings, and the stars in the sky. This is another example of how the alleged primitive mentality of animism, known as a precursor of religious thought, would contain a truth about the nature of consciousness.

When we realise that the external world arises within the interdependent nature of the mind, then the world can also be perceived in all its transient beauty. A human being then becomes a pillar between heaven and earth as a figure/category of the creative imagination. Rather than things or objects, real-images become creative epiphanies or flowers in the sky, as Dogen calls them.

In the *Genjo koan* fascicle, Dogen (*Shobogenzo*) writes: "Nevertheless, flowers fall with our attachment, and weeds spring up with our aversion." This statement combines both types of causality, natural and human or volitional. Dogen is combining nature's cycle of bloom and decay with the human pleasure principle by means of which we attach to pleasant things or states and avoid unpleasant things and states. Flowers are going to fall anyway despite our attachment or non-attachment, but when we become attached to things then transience or impermanence becomes a source of suffering. In addition, the enjoyment of a flower or a pleasant state may be disturbed by attachment. To really enjoy things we have to enjoy them from the perspective of impermanence. In addition, in order to enjoy things we also have to let go of detachment or not be attached to non-attachment.

Letting go of attachment also applies to development. For a child to enjoy the attachment to the mother, the child also has to accept the separation from the mother and the intervention of the father. Consequently, to enjoy the father, the child also has to accept the law that comes with the father, and accepting the law does not mean the loss of desire but rather the access to desire, and so on and so forth.

Symbolisation, in fact, begins as an attempt to represent the loss of the object. The object/cause/other is represented by a signifier/effect/subject or S_1. Then S_1 becomes the cause of a new effect or S_2. Although both the law of karma and the law of symbolic organisation produce effects in conscious or preconscious experience, a theory is required for their correct understanding/apprehension. At the same time, an experiential/clinical method is also necessary in order to work with mental formations that are beyond the grasp of the conscious ego. In Buddhism, this method is called the practice of mindfulness of mental formations (within the practice of zazen, not separate from it), also known as thinking non-thinking, while in psychoanalysis the method is called free association. The first requires the help of a teacher, the second of a psychoanalyst.

For Freud, symbols and thoughts were substitute representations for repressed sexual and aggressive fantasies/desires. But desire, as a repressed meaning that remains unconscious, also functions according to signifiers and symbolic representations. A symptom, for example, is a symbol of a repressed idea/signifier, a dream image is a symbol of a dream-thought, and the manifest content of speech or of any symbolic expression both conceals and reveals a latent content or meaning. The Freudian notion of symbol is closely tied to the function of defence and repression. The symbolic order is a double structure of meaning that encompasses both desires and more normative unconscious structures.

A symbol points to something other, and desire itself is a vestige of the desire of the Other and for the other. Both desires and their prohibitions, or wishes and their disappointments, function according to purposive aims and representations. At the same time, the later Lacan came to speak of a symptom and the letter or S_1 as a form of *jouissance*. The repressed unconscious has to be taken once step further beyond the construct/duality of the repressive and the repressed that mutually condition each other. S_1 has to be freed from the chain of rational or semantic interpretation.

Going from the unknown of the repressed to the unknown of the unknown requires a different function of language based on the Real within the Symbolic. This is the meaning of "turning words" as small units or Q'bits, or as the brevity associated with wit, and the letter as a unary trace. Now instead of being linked with other words or letters, S_1 as the *objet a* is linked to a form of *jouissance* in the here and now that is beyond meaning and no meaning.

There is a *jouissance* within desire that has nothing to do with either desire or the Law and the same is true for the Law (something within the Law that is not Law-bound). Emptiness is found at the end (and at the beginning) of the teleological process and puts an end to the search for meaning and signification. Meaning becomes the same as no-meaning or senselessness.

Awakening in psychoanalysis and Zen

Let us begin with the desire to sleep versus the desire to be awake. Both sleep and awakening will acquire different meanings in relationship to the Other. In childhood, children want to stay awake at night to play and be a part of the adult world, while parents want the children to go to sleep at a bedtime set by the parents and cultural norms. Most commonly, parents want children to go to sleep, not only for their own good, but because parents want to rest and be able to have sex.

Therefore, going to sleep can have the meaning of the law and of Oedipal exclusion. Conversely, staying awake can have the meaning of desire and Oedipal inclusion. Once the bedtime battles are over and children have accepted going to sleep at a prescribed time, the cultural imperative changes. Now they have to learn to wake up not to play or enjoy forbidden things, but to go to school or work.

Therefore, both sleep and awakening can mean either something desired or mandated. Moreover, parents want their children not only to *have* to go to sleep or to awaken but to desire both to sleep and to awaken. By telling their children to go to sleep, parents are compelling them to desire what they desire (have sex), and by the same token they are conditioning them to desire what they desire in a different sense (that the children desire to go to sleep so that the parents can have sex). This is an example of how both desires are simultaneously being set up or established: the desire to transgress the law and the desire for the law. Therefore, that desire is the desire of the Other, means both the desire for the phallic signifier of sexual desire that comes from the Other, and the desire for the law that has the same source.

People, and particularly women, could object on the grounds that sex is not the only thing that parents have in mind once their children go to sleep. Rest or other adult activities may be more important than sex. Moreover, mother and father often fall on different sides of this issue. Stereotypically, the father wants sex whereas the mother is concerned about the children and the possibility that the children could hear them. Mother's could feel that they are hurting their children by having sex with their husbands. Despite appearances and common sense, altruistic concerns for the children are not the only thing that is at stake in this example. Just like the children would like to jump in bed with their parents, the mother may put the children in the place of the father or in lieu of sex with the father. This is how the child can function as the mother's imaginary phallus. On the other hand, and non-stereotypically, it could be the mother that desires to have sex with the father and the father does not. However, the father's not wanting would be for reasons other than a concern for the children. The psychical differences between the sexes are not symmetrical in this regard.

I have an analysand, who could not sleep alone and always wanted to sleep between his parents. The mother did not mind and could not say no and the father hated it but could not say no to mother or child. However, client's "insecure attachment" to his mother was not based on lack of good enough mothering. The problem was the reverse: that parents and the father could not say no to the analysand. Eventually, in my opinion, this resulted in an addiction to heroin that lasted many years. The analysand could not say no to heroin and let go of a certain impossible *jouissance* with the mother. Attachment theorists often assume that insecure attachments are always the product of lack of consistent or good-enough mothering. The problem here was the opposite to one of attachment. What was missing was the cutting function of the father that leads to non-attachment to a deadly *jouissance* with the mother. This function of the father is consistent with Buddha's (symbolic father) teaching of non-attachment. But far from extinguishing desire, putting a stop to the *jouissance* of the Other is what makes a lack and therefore desire possible.

Finally, being asleep or being awake can have a similar symbolic or spiritual meaning to being blind or being able to see or have insight. Insight in Buddhism includes reflection, mindfulness, and attention, and as such is distinguished from thinking, wishing, or analysis. Nevertheless, awareness also presupposes, whether consciously or unconsciously, knowing the factors at play in any situation on a moment to moment basis as well as the capacity to make judgements and decisions (yes/no) on the go and at a moment's notice. In a practical everyday sense, being awake represents the intention to get up in the morning to practice meditation or to initiate the activities of the day. Fundamentally being awake means being aware of the present moment as something new and fresh and unconditioned by the dreams, individual or collective, that we all live in.

At the same time, whatever we say about the present moment or about awakening is another dream we call Buddhism. Thus Dogen speaks of awakening from a dream within a dream. In psychoanalysis, awakening represents knowing oneself and being awake to the nature of the Other and unconscious desire. In both cases, being awake is privileged over being asleep although they both include one another.

Now is the spiritual intention to awaken closer to the desire to stay awake in childhood or adulthood? Actually, a case could be made for either one of the two. To the extent that "sleepers awake" represents a spiritual form of commandment, the desire to awaken seems similar to a desire for work or creative productivity. It would be easy to tag along the desire for spiritual enlightenment to some kind of developmental line and place it as a later acquisition to the establishment of the reality principle in childhood (as in Erikson's work). However, the sense of immediacy, timelessness and innocence of childhood would be lost. The childhood desire to be awake refers to a very primal desire to directly know something about the origin of things.

In childhood, this desire is represented by a desire for a forbidden knowledge of the flesh. In a classic paper, Laplanche and Leclaire (1968) observed that Freud's proto-fantasies had something to do with the question of the origins: the origins of life (primal scene), the origins of sex (seduction fantasy), and the origins of sexual difference (castration). To this I would add the Lacanian question regarding the origin of desire: what do I want, what do I really want, and what does the Other want, and more importantly, what does the Other want from me? Despite differences between secular and sacred phenomena, this is not unlike the question of wisdom and compassion in Buddhism. In some way, the three proto-fantasies refer to the mental origins and knowledge of the body, the Zen body/mind, or the origin of Being as Heidegger would call it. In addition, such mental knowing of the body is very much embedded within a bodily experience or a *jouissance*.

In Zen, the desire to awaken is associated with a wisdom-seeking mind. In seeking a practice of meditation, it is wisdom that is seeking for wisdom. This kind of wisdom is devoid of content or is the wisdom of emptiness or what Lacanians would call a desire for knowing or for an enigmatic knowledge without meaning. A human being wants to know itself as a human being, just as a tree wants to know itself as a tree, with its roots, trunk, branches, leaves, and flowers. According to Buddhism, we want to know two things: what we are made off and that fundamentally we are empty in our own being.

These two forms of knowledge are related given that we are made of non-self elements and therefore our independent small self is empty of content. It is only as Other that we realise our true self or Big mind. In addition, there is also an Other *in* the Other (the Real). A principal bodhisattva (enlightening being) vow is the intention or desire not only to awaken but also to awaken with and to hasten the awakening of all beings.

Other beings here represent other subjects and yet at the same time how things are linked up or held together. Since the subject is nothing but this relationship between subjects, between signifiers, between subjects and objects, and between things, awakening actually represents the effective functioning or the articulation/realisation of a structural relationship. We come from the Other and from the comings and goings of the Other. It is understandable that children would want to know this.

At the same time, we can't all be in bed at the same time or all the time—it is not workable, not to say abusive. We have to make do with knowing that we are an impermanent aggregate or assemblage despite the appearance of autonomy, unity, or singularity. Ultimately, we also have to realise that the Other is our own mental construction and, therefore, have to find things out for ourselves. The Other is only "This I am, just This, or This". Every singularity is a One that contains the Other, or the part or unary trace that contains the whole or the hole within the whole, the emptiness of the whole. The subject has to realise that the self as aggregate and phenomena in general, are empty in their own being, and actualise this perceptual realisation in specific implicit actions, beyond knowledge, in accordance with the symbolic principle of cause and effect at work in any given situation. Emptiness, the unconditioned, or the Real lies right at the heart of the symbolic cause and effect relationship.

Knowledge, knowing, and compassion

According to Ricoeur's and Derrida's hermeneutics, there is no self-understanding that is not mediated by signs, symbols, and texts, whereas in Zen there is a transmission of ultimate psychical reality outside all scripture or beyond the bounds of words and the symbolic order. Zen teaching recommends a direct plunge into the Real through the experience and practice of meditation. The Zen Buddhist concept of truth, as emptiness, implies an impotence of language to represent the Real. Lacan also incorporated this notion of the Real into his theory of the three registers or the Borromean knot. Within psychoanalysis, a repressed and often traumatic signifier of desire (of the Other) occupies the place of truth. However, from a Buddhist perspective, the signifier of desire is the signifier not only of a lack of an object but also of a lack of a signifier or a fundamental emptiness at the core of the Symbolic. This is what Lacan called a true hole.

From this perspective, truth is a psychical or subjective position which calls for the presence of the unknown rather than the known and for the need to let go of ego-knowledge in order to access an unknown form of knowing (*L'insu qui sait*, according to Lacan) not only about desire but about reality itself. This perspective also overlaps with the emphasis given to subjective truth and experience within the school of existential analysis. It is well known that Lacan sought to incorporate the existential thinking of Heidegger into psychoanalytic theory and practice. According to existential analysis, "truth is a subjective relationship produced in the course of action and in our own consciousness" (May, 1957b, p. 29). Both Zen Buddhism and the school of existential analysis emphasise experience as opposed to the abstractions of reason.

On the other hand, neither Buddhism nor existentialism gave us the view of the family as an aspect of the symbolic and mythical structure of the mind. The latter has been an important contribution of psychoanalysis not found within Buddhism or existentialism. Freudian psychoanalysis brought the structure of the Oedipus myth out of the unknown and into the known structure of mind/consciousness. The symbolic structure occupies a fundamental function in the human experience of reality. In this respect, Rubin (1996) has noted an absence of a psycho-historical-symbolic principle within Buddhism and an unnecessary rejection of psychoanalytic insights, which he calls Oriento-centrism. In my opinion, Lacan's triad of the Imaginary, Real, and Symbolic registers of *experience* (Borromean knot) constitutes an improved framework by which to understand the complex and multifaceted relation between experience and representation.

On the one hand, it is true that there is an aspect of experience that is different than or not reducible to symbolic or linguistic representation (the Real in Buddhism and Lacan) and yet, on the other hand, the Symbolic and Imaginary also condition the experience of reality. Vasubhandu (Kochumuttom, 1982), the second-century ancestor and theoretician of the Yogachara school of Buddhism, anticipated Lacanian theory. He spoke of the three aspects of the self-nature: the Imagined, the Other-dependent, and the Real. Finally, the later Lacan added a fourth dimension/ring to the Borromean knot. He considered the Name of the Father as the fourth dimension that ties the other three together. This would be equivalent to the names of the Buddha, Vasubhandu, or Lacan who have presented or revealed the teaching of the aspects or rings of experience.

The Buddhist Therevada tradition (Silva, 1979) distinguishes the means to knowledge into the two categories of reason and experience. Experience can be subdivided again into sense experience and authentic intuitive experience. The average educated human being or even a scholar can make use of reason and sense experience. But the authentic intuitive function becomes manifest through a spiritual practice such as meditation and the practice of analysis broadly and deeply understood. Spiritual insight includes a perceptual realisation, a seeing into the nature of Reality that is not dependent upon perceiving or naming the objects of the senses. For Buddhism, wisdom is not the product of the accumulation of information acquired from without and over the life span. The source of wisdom is intrinsic to the nature of the mind defined writ large. The Buddhist tradition uses the example of a jade stone or a diamond to illustrate this state of affairs. The formless jewel is in the ordinary stone but needs to be chiseled out and brought forth. The *practice* of chiselling, of concentrated effort, of listening, meditating, observing, and experimenting, is what reveals the intrinsic jewels of wisdom.

Psychoanalysis also differs from a tradition of transmitting knowledge or technical know-how through the exclusive mediums of teaching and learning various kinds of information whether rational or factual. Psychoanalysis is founded on a different kind of knowing of the unconscious that is actualised through the opening and clearing of subjective experience. This form of knowing, although not exactly the same as the intuitive function in Buddhism, also occupies the place of a third form of knowledge beyond those of reason and practical sense experience. For example, every analyst must undergo a personal analysis in order to engage in the clinical practice of psychoanalysis. This kind of subjective and personal knowing of the unconscious cannot be measured or evaluated according to oral exams or objective tests of various kinds. It can only be authenticated, in the intimacy of the analytic situation (personal and supervised practice of analysis), and transmitted by the recognition of a symbolic lineage consisting of a group of peers and more experienced analysts.

Etchegoyen (1991) has pointed out that throughout his work Freud affirmed that what is fundamental to psychoanalysis is knowledge. Analysis aims to offer the analysand a better knowledge of himself. At one time it will be focused on memories, at another on drives, but the aim is always knowledge, in the sense of the search for subjective truth. In the metapsychology, knowledge consists in making conscious the unconscious. In the structural theory, self-knowledge is described by the formula "where id was ego shall be". In my opinion, Lacan permutated and improved this formula by stating "Where it was I shall become". The latter proverb or aphorism could also be rendered as "I am This I am", "I am This", or simply the Zen "This". The emphasis here is on "this" rather than "the I". In fact, philologically speaking, first names were coined to replace and represent "this".

In psychoanalysis, personal self-knowledge seems to be produced in an opposite direction to scientific knowledge. Psychoanalysis includes subjectivity and vital interests and desires while scientific empiricism appears to produce a severance of knowledge from subjectivity and the natural interests of life, as Habermas has pointed out. However, the contradiction may be only apparent, given that psychoanalysis achieves objectivity by an inclusion of subjectivity and by bringing forth the realisation of "It", or "This". Technology, in turn, shows to what extent scientific empiricism can also be used to provide all kinds of vital satisfactions.

However, in contrast to the empirical sciences, psychoanalysis shares with Buddhism a keen interest in a systematic work with and permutation/transformation of subjective experience. The source of knowledge regarding the mind comes from within rather than without. In addition, the function of knowledge or self-knowledge within the practice of psychoanalysis differs from cognitive intellectual ego-knowledge or information. Lacan makes a distinction between knowledge and knowing and identifies knowing, or *savoir*, with unconscious enigmatic knowing or knowledge of the unconscious both within meaning and beyond meaning and no meaning. The knowing that psychoanalysis offers the client is not the cognitive knowledge of the analyst but the experiential knowing of the unconscious contained within the client's own mind. Thus, I have translated the Lacanian term *savoir* as "unknown-knowing".

But in psychoanalysis unknown-knowing has to do with the structure of the Symbolic and the signifier and not with what the ego or the individual could gather of his own experience via a method of solitary introspection. In different ways, both psychoanalysis and Buddhism issue strong cautions and concerns regarding introspection as a method for the study of subjectivity. Buddhism encourages mindfulness of mental formations but warns against over interpreting mental contents. Buddhism focuses on perceiving the ultimate emptiness and impermanence of all mental formations.

In my opinion, however, the Buddhist concern with over interpretation refers to the danger of interpreting meditation or psychoanalysis as a kind of ego-analysis. To guard against the illusions of introspection or self-analysis, psychoanalysis requires the intervention of the Other. In the analytical situation, the analyst interprets from the place of the third or of the symbolic function of the Other. Psychoanalysis, and particularly Lacan, stresses the importance of the function of the third or the big Other as representing both the importance of the unconscious for subjectivity as well as the need of an Other (analyst) and a symbolic perspective for its correct apprehension. Left to its own devices, the ego will arrive at an imaginary interpretation of subjective and inter-subjective experience. Ultimately Lacan also goes beyond symbolic perspectives and arrives at quasi-Buddhist positions when he stresses the ultimate emptiness or vacuity of the Other and the symbolic in relationship to the Real.

For Zen Buddhism, insight also refers to a direct perceptual realisation of the self-nature or the ultimate nature of the subject. Beyond the recognition of various mental objects and their relations, the study of subjectivity includes the study of the perceiving subject or self itself as well as the interdependency of subject and object. If one asks who resides at the seat of awareness, "Who" is knowing or aware, the answer is not given by any particular self-representation verbal, or otherwise. Buddha is not who we usually think we are, it is not the conscious ego.

Moreover, a classical Zen koan also asks "Who is this Other?", meaning that the Other is none other than our true selves. In Lacanian psychoanalysis, the question of the subject is not unlike the question regarding the Other of the unconscious. Buddha is a consciousness beyond ego-consciousness. The unconscious is the unknown within the subject but it is also the unknown subject, both as subject and object of knowledge. Thus, it is possible to argue that Buddha consciousness and the psychical position of the analyst both constitute variations of the seat of unknown-knowing. Making conscious the unconscious refers to a paradoxical consciousness beyond consciousness rooted in the intrin-sic nature of the subject.

Fromm already pointed out that self-realisation occurs via an affec-tive rather than intellectual knowledge. He and Lacan agree on the fact that self-knowledge is experiential as well as sudden and spontaneous, but disagree on the question of its affective dimension. In general, Lacan has been criticised for disregarding affective experience. However, even though the Buddhist sutras regard compassion as a self-evident truth and as a fruit of the dharma, compassion is a function of wisdom and must be described and qualified by wisdom. For example, compassion is described in the sutras with the simile of the love of a mother for her only child, but this could be misleading because the sutra also says that a bodhisattva does not prefer her children to those that are not hers. A bodhisattva is not attached to her children as privileged or special objects of her own narcissism.

In addition, Bion, for example, establishes equivalence between reaching the unconscious in a session and arriving at the emotional truth of a session. However, when by a combination of catharsis and insight, a subject works through the experience and meaning of certain affective states, the emotions of love or hate, depression or anxiety, are transformed in the direction of a certain serenity that Freud recognised as the hallmark of the secondary process. It is important to remember that the calmness of mind that comes with this subjective position, the sense of serenity and equanimity and even compassion are not necessarily feelings or emotions *per se*, or perhaps they are affects but not feelings or emotions. In this regard, the Heart sutra says that in emptiness, feelings are empty in their own being. The Heart sutra is the heart of emptiness or the empty ventricle of the heart.

According to object relations and Kohutian psychoanalysis, emotional knowing or understanding, also known as empathy and the emotional correlate of insight, has a root in the undifferentiated state of infancy known as symbiosis or what Lacanians would call *jouissance*. However, I argue for the need to distinguish a symbolic from an imaginary empathy, a symbolic interdependence between self and other from a primitive imaginary fusion between subject and object. This distinction is important not only to distinguish object relations from a Lacanian perspective but also to distinguish a primitive fusion between mother and child, from the non-duality of authentic spiritual experience. The latter requires the intervention of Buddha consciousness or the symbolic father and mother.

Both Winnicott (1960) and Kohut (1966) use the mirror metaphor to describe the mother–child relationship. Mirroring is defined as what the mother does in response to the child's behaviour (Baker & Baker, 1987; Post, 1980). The mother sees herself reflected in her child and vice versa. "Who's little finger is this?", "Isn't this expression cute?", "Listen to this cooing sound!" The mother supports the child's functioning and self-regard or healthy narcissism by choosing the child, or perhaps more accurately by the child's causing the mother's desire by virtue of their shared reflective similarities.

However, what the Winnicottian and Kohutian analyses miss, and what Lacan emphasises, is that maternal desire for the child is mediated by the mother's own desire for a fantasised object capable of producing an illusory narcissistic completion of the ego. In other words, any mother loves the child because she sees her own virtual mirror-image projected and incarnated in her infant.

But how can the subject know that what he/she understands really constitutes the other and is not merely a projection of subjective experience in the narrow or limited sense of the term? The object relations school proposes that "objectivity" distinguishes empathy from identification and projection (idem). In maternal empathy, for example, in the attunement to the experiential state of the child, also described as mirroring, the mother not only identifies with her child but also views her infant objectively. The child may be sad or angry, and the mother understands on the basis of her own experience but her own sadness and anger, for example, do not interfere with the experience of the child.

Within object relations, higher order empathy includes boundaries, separateness and differentiation. Thus, in the language of object relations one can distinguish between lower-order empathy that cannot be distinguished from projection and identification, and higher-order empathy that includes boundaries and differentiation. However, the problem with this notion is that the use of the term "objectivity" gives the impression that subjectivity is not involved in higher order empathy. Rather, I would argue, so-called higher-order empathy is a different subjective position or structural element within subjectivity.

I propose to distinguish between two forms of empathy: Imaginary and Symbolic. The first consists of an empathy with the other as an object of the subject (a subject–object relationship), while symbolic empathy involves a relationship with the other as a subject/signifier with his or her own desire. For Lacan, both love and the subject constitute a relationship between signifiers: the lover and the beloved. The subject is already an Other and both are empty in their own being. The Other is empty because it only consists of a series of relationships and the subject is empty because the subject is a metaphor within language. I realise that this is counter-intuitive, but what we love in the Other is our own emptiness or the emptiness that we recognise as our own.

Moreover, symbolic maternal empathy also implies the participation and involvement of the symbolic father, as a function already established within the mother/woman from where in she also relates to her child, while imaginary empathy does not. Symbolic empathy also includes the capacity not to be empathic with the ego but ultimately empathic with the subject. So-called "good-enough mothering" is a complex function composed of both Imaginary and Symbolic empathy.

Buddha's compassion is based on wisdom and the realisation of the mind as an empty mirroring function that reflects everything without having a fixed image of its own. The round mirror of wisdom reflects things as they are and whatever appears in front of the mirror is the self. Thus, whatever the empty mirror subject does to what is in front of the mirror, it does to itself writ large. Since self-love or self-interest is assumed and generally accepted as a motivation, when self is expanded to include the Other, then narcissism is also modified accordingly. The Other is also included under self-interest in the large sense. Having included the Other of the unconscious, the analyst is in a better position not to project their own unconscious unto the intersubjective other. The analyst sees the other for who they are as a function of Big self (Other) and responds from the basis of knowing and compassion rather than from an imaginary form of love and hate. On the other hand, given that the other does project their Other unto the analyst, the analyst uses the symbolic mirror to reflect back the images and signifiers of the unconscious of the subject.

CHAPTER FOUR

True subject is no-ego

The self as a contemporary concern

In his well-received book, *Thoughts Without a Thinker*, Mark Epstein (1995) points out that nowadays:

> As the emphasis in therapy has moved from conflicts over sexual and aggressive strivings to a focus on how patients are uncomfodrtable with themselves because, in some fundamental way, they do not know who they are, the question of the self has emerged as the common focus of Buddhism and psychoanalysis.

(p. 6)

Contemporary forms of Anglo-Saxon psychoanalysis no longer interpret the Socratic dictum of "Know Thyself" as did Freud, who took it to mean knowledge of unconscious thoughts, impulses, and representations. Rather, ego-psychology, self-psychology, and the object relations school focus much more on identity problems as a function of a relationship between the self and its environment. Presumably, people in advanced technological societies no longer suffer from traditional conflicts with sexuality and aggressiveness but are rather afflicted by identity confusion and problems with "self-esteem" or narcissism.

However, although both contemporary psychoanalysis and Buddhism share an interest in the self, there is also a fundamental contradiction between them. Self-psychology, ego-psychology, and object relations focus on the importance of having and building an ego/self, while Buddhism focuses on the importance and reality of no-self. As I will discuss in detail in a section further on, this fact has been identified by prior authors such as Engler (1981), Suler (1993), Rubin (1996), and Epstein (1995) as the most salient point of difference or contradiction between contemporary psychoanalysis and Buddhism.

Engler advanced the well-known formula that you have to be somebody before you can be nobody. In other words, it is necessary to have a self before you can let go of it. This is usually understood in terms that if you don't have a healthy sense of self then this leads to a fixation to a pathological form of narcissism. If you have a self then you don't have to think about whether you have one or not or be concerned about the self at all. This can easily lead to the belief in an enduring or substantial self that forms the ground and basis of our sense of reality: the "reality ego" as Freud called it. In addition, the self of psychoanalysis and psychology is something that is built in the family and family relationships in childhood.

In early Buddhism, no-self is also related to the question of leaving the world and family relationships behind. If we make having a family and having a self equivalent or correlative to one another, then it is easier to understand how one has to have a family before leaving one behind. Not having parents would be the equivalent of not having been born (which at an entirely different metalevel, Buddhism says it is exactly the case anyway: the unborn aspect of us was not born with birth and will not die with death).

The question that follows from this, then, is what kind of self does the teaching of no self realise (when leaving home or family life), and what kind of no-self was already there throughout development despite the imaginary ego and the family? This question is important for two reasons: first, because it points to the Mahayana teaching of later Buddhism; and second, because in North American Buddhism, teachers are also getting married and having families.

From a Lacanian psychoanalytic perspective, the ideal ego and the ego-ideal are necessary constructions or mental formations but which are nonetheless imaginary rather than substantial. They are an inevitable form of alienation that nonetheless needs to be overcome. We don't know "Who" we are because of not knowing what we are made of or if who we are has to do with us or with how the Other has shaped us. The self hurts, is not our own, or appears to acquire an eerie quality of its own. The ego is an unconscious mental formation that has the distinctive task of covering over or defending against the lack or absence of self. It is this emptiness of self, or what following Lacan I call the subject of the Real, that constitutes our true self. Thus the real self is the same as no-self. The ego instead is a defence against the real self/no-self. According to Buddhism, the ego is a swollenness to cover the voidness of self.

Nevertheless, although not healthy or pretty, ego defences are necessary defences. The ideal ego defends against the absence of the mother or of the *objet a* by erecting a specular body image in the place of the Other. The specular image is also a gift from the Other, to facilitate the child's own independence from the Other. The ego-ideal defends against symbolic castration, the loss/lack of the Other, or what is missing in the body/self, via identification with ideals of perfection, with dominant or ruling ideas. One can see how Buddhism and religion, and even psychoanalysis, could be implicated in this defensive process.

Both Kohut and Winnicott, and even Bowlby's attachment theory, start out from the premise that problems with self-esteem or low self-esteem are the result of lack of adequate mirroring, good-enough mothering, or secure attachment in early childhood. The presence of all of these three in a child's life lead to a healthy sense of self or ego, whereas the absence of the mother's desire and attention/concern leads to ego deficits and the absence of a cohesive self. Although it is true that the mother's desire and preoccupation is fundamental, what is often overlooked is that the mother's desire is never free of narcissism and therefore is also in need of a paternal intervention under what Lacan called the Name of the Father.

In other words, the attachment of the mother and child leads not only to a healthy and secure sense of self but also to an ideal ego shot through with narcissistic investment. To the mother, the child not only represents a subject, self, or human being, but also an unconscious object that complements her own sense of self-worth or ego. This is what Lacan, following Freud, called the imaginary phallus. The latter represents a self or S that needs to be barred ($). Within Lacanian psychoanalysis, $ is a symbol that represents the divided self, but it can also be used as a symbol to represent the Buddhist teaching of no-self. This no-self is essential to the development of the self, just like cell division is essential for the reproduction of life. Both self and no-self, attachment and detachment, binding and unbinding, are fundamental for healthy development.

From this perspective, there is no conflict between the perspective of the self within contemporary psychoanalysis and the no-self perspective of Buddhism. Both are potentially contained within a Lacanian–Freudian perspective. Thus, it is also possible to argue that the modern malaise of identity confusion or narcissism is not only due to the absence of self but also due to an excess of self. If there is a necessary maternal investment and love of the child then this will lead to the ideal ego as well as to ego-inflation. Self is both necessary and a problem. If the ideal ego is not developed, then this is a problem, although the ideal ego will also have to be frustrated and found lacking for further self-development. Both are aspects of the parental or paternal function, as Lacan called it. For different reasons, maternal and paternal attachment and detachment are both necessary and problematic.

Although the intervention of the Name of the Father is necessary to bar the self that functions as an imaginary phallus of the mother, the father as the holder of the imaginary phallus generates the next major challenge for psychical development associated with symbolic castration. At this point the danger is no longer psychoses or borderline character pathology but neurosis. In addition, before briefly examining the problem of neurosis from the self/no-self perspective, a few words are necessary regarding the early failure of the function of the father.

I have mentioned the *no* of the father that bars the self as an imaginary phallus. However, this *no* can be compromised early on, not only by the mother but also by the father himself. If the intervention of the father is too severe or too brutal, as in the example of Schreber's father in Freud's (1911) famous case of psychosis, then this can also affect the no or the letting go of self. Instead of the ideal ego being replaced by the ego-ideal (in the direction of no-self and eventually the Lacanian subject), the ideal ego is replaced by a primitive and tormenting superego that prevents and perverts a necessary detachment or no-self function linked to the beneficence of the Name of the Father. This primitive superego is built on top of the bad or depriving breast of the bad mother.

Now does this then mean that too little or too much here function in the same way that with the desire of the mother? If this is true, then both would lead to an attachment to an imaginary sense of self. The no of the father represents a qualitative symbolic shift of registers: from the Imaginary to the Symbolic. Within Lacanian theory, the Imaginary represents first the realm of wishes and fantasies and a relationship of alterity (dual unity) with the mother prior to a differentiation between self and other. The differentiation between self and other evolves out of a relationship to the Other who represents symbolic rules (of grammar, prohibition of incest, kinship rules, sexual difference, murder prohibition).

However, under certain conditions, such as those already mentioned, the Symbolic can be subsumed under the Imaginary rather than the other way around. In such cases, "no-self" does not lead to a true self or to a true negative; instead, it produces a false negative. Too little or too much of the no of the father produces an imaginary rather than a symbolic sense of self and no-self. In other words, a false negative fails to transform a false positive into a true negative, leading therefore to a failure in the shift of registers from the Imaginary to the Symbolic. The Name of the Father is foreclosed in the Symbolic and remains stuck in an imaginary and perverted version of it. The Symbolic is subsumed by the Imaginary both under the desire of the mother and a brutal version of the negative.

Conversely, when the Imaginary is subsumed under the Symbolic, then the Imaginary can produce generative effects within the Symbolic. Here, we have the example of the imaginary father and the arrival at neurotic capability and Oedipal structure proper. The values are now inverted, the father represents self and the mother and child represent no-self. The father is perceived as having the imaginary ego/phallus that was denied to the mother and the children ($).

But this imaginary function of the symbolic father is only temporary and is not to be confused with the brutal father discussed above (although it often is). It is this imaginary function of the father that will give rise to the castration complex or the rock that will cause the shipwreck of neurosis for human beings. In turn, the castration complex is the motor for the development of the ego-ideal. Identification with ideals or norms covers over the loss that takes place under the castration complex. At this point, the loss represents not only being a special self-object for the mother but also a loss associated with sexual difference. The girl will not have what the father has, and the boy will have it but fear the inevitable loss that comes from entering the symbolic order.

Nonetheless, the relationship to the Symbolic needs to evolve beyond this point. Otherwise, in the Imaginary, the boy and the girl will think that the boy has something that the girl does not. By accessing culture, a girl will gain something she thought she was deprived of, and the boy will lose something that he thought he had. Only within the Symbolic can one have by not having and not have by having. The sexes differ by whether the Symbolic loss happens at the entry (girl) or exit point (boy) of Oedipal structure and not by whether one has it and the other does not. Within sexuation or zenxuation, as I could call it for the purposes of this book, sexed self and no-self have a different meaning.

For North American women, Buddhist teaching seemed particularly difficult where the teaching of no-self mirrors their experiences within patriarchal culture. Women felt powerless *vis-à-vis* men who appeared to have a self to speak of and who used women for sex. The teaching of no-self did not seem to deprive men from acquiring status and going on to become important selves within their respective Buddhist communities. This is the place where becoming nothing or realising no-self can degenerate into an ego-ideal or superego formation. Instead of realising emptiness, emptiness is covered over with religious or Zen forms: rank, status, position, and so on. In true practice, the forms of practice have to stand for themselves and not be a means for the power of emptiness or no-self. The power of no-self is the power of renunciation, not the power of domination.

For traditional Japanese Zen teachers, North Americans seemed very self-centred, always placing their interests and desires first. This has something to do with the value of the individual that emerged from the Renaissance and that led away from the traditional character of the Middle Ages. For the same reasons, Japanese youth have turned away from Buddhism in droves and embraced Western culture instead. But in addition to this, and as already mentioned, narcissistic individualism arises not only from bad parenting but from misrecognising the narcissistic dimension of selfhood itself. The Other of traditional culture is still necessary with the One notable exception produced by the advent of modernity.

As Lacan pointed out, the subject needs to appropriate desire from the desire of the Other. This is in contrast to the repression of desire and self-denial characteristic of Other-centred traditional societies. However, the appropriation of desire also differs from what in Buddhism is called the appropriated dimension of the storehouse consciousness. The latter represents how the ego appropriates elements or factors of the unconscious and preconscious Big mind and uses them to construct a self via an identification meant to bolster the ego and gain a desired social recognition from the Other (which would be equivalent to modern individualism). In contrast to this, the Lacanian recognition of desire involves recognising the desire for recognition, and making desire independent from this recognition and from using the Other or an object as a means to bolster or give the ego its Being.

Suffering: its causes and possible solutions

In some respects, the Buddhist tradition has a lot in common with psychoanalysis and its emphasis on sexuality and aggressiveness (the two "troublemakers" of the psyche). *Anusaya* or *Vasana* are the Sanskrit terms for unconscious drives or instinctual predilection. It refers in Buddhist psychology to the unconscious habit-patterns that underlie emotional responses such as desire and hatred. Sexual desire, aggressiveness, and ignorance are the traits or poisons that condition suffering according to Buddhist doctrine.

Of the three poisons, ignorance or illusion is what prevents human beings from realising the cause of suffering. Therefore, understanding and realisation are key factors of enlightenment for both Buddhism and psychoanalysis. They both cherish realisation as a solution to the problem of ignorance, but disagree on account of the Hinayana version of Buddhism that advocates the extinction of desire and hatred. The Mahayana teaching is different in this regard.

In addition, psychoanalysis and Buddhism conceive of the function of realisation in different ways. Freud considered insight a rational ego-function. Self-psychology and object relations privilege the function of emotional empathy over rational interpretation. In this respect, they come closer to the function of compassion in Buddhism. However, compassion in Buddhism has to be guided by the more fundamental function of wisdom.

Wisdom goes beyond the intellectual ego-function of reason. Lacan goes further than Freud in establishing the function of interpretation on the basis of an unconscious form of knowing beyond ego knowledge.

With Lacan, the psychoanalytic function of realisation comes very close to a Buddhist definition of wisdom. It is wisdom and the Mahayana *prajna paramita* sutra that brings out the deeper meaning of Buddhism beyond earlier views. Emptiness as the root of desire and of compassion is not unlike what Lacan calls the desire of the analyst. It is the desire of the analyst and the unconscious knowing of the subject that regulate the direction of an analytic treatment.

Nevertheless, Buddhism and traditional psychoanalysis make the same diagnosis of the cause of suffering yet differ with respect to the recommended treatments. Although Buddhism, in contrast to Western religion, focuses much more on meditation and mindfulness than on morality, in contrast to Freud, the Buddha never recommended the undoing of sexual repression or the exploration of unconscious fantasy life. Therefore, in psychoanalysis, the analysand does not cross to the other shore of a solution to the problem of suffering on the raft of meditation practice but through what Lacan called the crossing of the phantasm (unconscious fantasy). Both practices also differ in that what is specific to the analytic path is the use of the Symbolic and language to reach the Real but via the intermediary of the Imaginary. In contrast to this, although Buddhism shares with psychoanalysis a critique of illusions and the imaginary, Buddhism does not explore, track, or interpret the Oedipal fantasy material that lead to the construction of a false sense of self.

Buddhists often misinterpret the analytical function of interpretation. Interpretation has to be given by the analyst from the place of the Other or Big mind and not by the imaginary ego. Interpretation is not introspection. Lacan said that interpretation goes not from the known to the known, or even from the unknown to the known, but from the unknown to the unknown. Finally, there are limits to the practice of interpretation just as there are limits to the practice of meditation.

For Freud, traditional morality had become part of the problem rather than an aspect of the solution to the problem of desire. On the other hand, Freud was not a libertine, since he also conceived of desire as something that could only be completely realised in dreams and the Imaginary. Freud was not of the opinion that the sole unbridled pursuit of sexual satisfaction was the solution for the discontents of civilisation. Along the same lines, Lacan declared that the sexual relation as such does not exist. This, of course, does not mean that people do not have sex, which obviously they do, but that the other of a relationship can never have or be the actual object of desire for the simple reason that the object of desire is a narcissistic part-object of the subject. From this perspective, genital satisfaction is thrown into question as a model of happiness and stability for a long-term relationship.

A couple's remaining option is to play with the illusions of having the object for one another, but only as a dance of masks and semblances not as an actual reality. The difference between this kind of sexual play and perversion is the symbolic knowledge that masks and semblances are not reified fetishes but only playful illusions that are empty in their own being. Far from extinguishing all illusions, the wisdom of emptiness and the emptiness of wisdom conveys the ability to play with the illusory nature of reality.

Historical changes of character structure

Overall, the general cultural critique of the traditional repressive character (also known as the sexual revolution), which in many ways expanded and extrapolated Freud's consideration of the role of repression in the production of psychopathology, itself led not to a complete cure and profilaxis of neurosis, but rather to a change or reversal in its dual structure: from a traditional over-control of sexual and aggressive impulses to a generational problem with impulse control (for example, as seen in borderline character disorders). The lessening of traditional social repression, and the changes in traditional sex roles and mores regarding sexuality, have changed the face of neurotic complaints from one of traditional inhibitions to one of a sense emptiness, inauthenticity, identity confusion, and alienation.

Now if the problem for the self or subject is much more identity confusion rather than traditional repression, this is because the character of the subject has shifted in the West as a result of the Enlightenment, the sexual revolution, the feminist movement, and psychoanalysis itself. The West has gone from a traditional and modern (secularised) cultural paradigm that modified and scrutinised the subject in deference to the collective will, the paternal metaphor, and the function of the father, to a postmodern culture that modifies and scrutinises the paternal metaphor and the collective will in deference to the mother, the ego, and the child defined without the drives.

One of the key differences between object relations theory and Lacanian psychoanalysis revolves around definitions of maternal and paternal function and the relative importance and definitions given to both as organisers of the development and structure of the psyche. In addition, this difference in theory and focus arises in the context of a larger debate within Western culture regarding the nature of sexual difference, the nature of matriarchal and patriarchal social orders, and a feminist critique of the function of the father as an organiser of male supremacy and the subordination of women.

As Freud tended to explain development and psychical structure around the function of the father in the Oedipus myth, the object relations and self-psychology schools gravitate around theoretical explanations that focus primarily on the mother as a key organiser of subjective experience. As Freud developed his theory of the unconscious and of the function of the father around his analysis and treatment of hysteria and neurosis in general, object relations theory and Kohut develop their views of the self and of the maternal function around the analysis and treatment of character or self disorders as the most current prototypical psychical malaise of Western civilisation.

As Freud and Lacan could be criticised for being phallocentric and father-centric, contemporary Anglo-Saxon psychoanalysis can be critiqued for being mother-centric and container-centric. The presence or absence of the receptive maternal container as an explanatory concept is privileged over the presence or absence of the paternal phallus and the paternal function. The opposite is true in the phallocentric account, as amply discussed in the post-Freudian literature. In addition, the notion of a maternal container in contemporary psychoanalysis refers to pre-sexual, pre-genital, or asexual forms of love and attachment rather than to symbolic sexual differences. Finally, although on the one hand, this work does raise a critique of a mother-centric paradigm that ignores the symbolic function of the father, it also acknowledges, incorporates, and resituates the critique of phallocentrism and father-centrism.

In addition, the rejection of the function of the father associated with a feminist critique of patriarchal culture has also left the subject at a loss for an anchor in the symbolic order. I argue that this has been primarily due to confusing or collapsing the symbolic function of the father and the discourse of the analyst with the desire for supremacy and domination associated with what Lacan calls the imaginary father and the master's discourse.

In the heart of every man and woman lives the phantasm of an imaginary form of masculinity and of a primal imaginary father (Freud's father of *Totem and Taboo*) who would own all women and relegate all men to a position of subservience. This is part of the mythical structure of the unconscious. And from this impossible fantasy follows the notion that the symbolic order or the paternal function implies a submission to a form of second-class citizenship, and that the paternal function is exclusively a question of power and desire for domination and supremacy on the part of men. The more that men or women aspire towards an imaginary form of masculinity, the more this compromises the actual function of the symbolic father.

The general movement of Western society away from traditional values that emphasised self-denial and subordination to traditional authority is the background for a movement towards autonomy, emancipation, and the importance of the individual. The rights of the private individual have been privileged over the interests of the society and the community. The importance given to self-esteem is only a symptom of this more general social-historical context. North America represents the cultural apotheosis of the importance and value of individual ego-drives. The success and freedom of the individual ego becomes of paramount importance. Thus, the contemporary interest in narcissism can be seen as determined by the two sides of the following dilemma. On the one hand, the ego, desire, and children have been freed from traditional restraints and obligations; and on the other, parents were also freed from their traditional responsibility of putting their children's interests first. Parents are more tolerant or accepting, but also more neglectful and focused on their own needs and rights.

In this regard, Epstein points out that:

> When a child, seeking contact with another person rather than just instinctual gratification, comes up against a narcissistic parent, too preoccupied with her own search to attend to the child's, the child is left with a feeling of absence that becomes the seed of her own fear and insecurity. Such a child is forced to construct what Winnicott called a "False Self" to manage the demands of the alternatively intrusive and ignoring parent.

> (Epstein, 1995, p. 37)

There are several difficulties associated with the ideas presented above. First, there is an assumption of childhood innocence, that a child only wants a wholesome humanistic connection that is somehow unfettered by drives or impulses. Epstein's child does not rage, is not demanding, is not clinging or behaving aggressively towards the parents. Within that model, such behaviour would only manifest as a reaction to an abusive environment. The problem is that since most good parents experience that behaviour from their children, somehow now, according to this model, they are left with the uneasy feeling that they are presumed guilty of abusive child-rearing behaviour.

When the mother is turned toward the Other, whether towards her profession or towards the father, this may be experienced by the child as abandonment or rejection. The object relations and self-psychology models, embedded within Epstein's quote, collapse the distinction between the imaginary and the symbolic mother. The symbolic mother is the mother who recognises her own lack and desire for the child and at the same time desires something beyond the child (as she should), and also recognises/loves the child as a subject of the Other (the father and the society). The imaginary mother is the mother who gratifies the child too much, as a narcissistic extension, or does not fulfil her maternal responsibilities, and does not love the child beyond what the child can do for her.

Both the symbolic and imaginary mother will trigger defences, but of a different kind. The symbolic mother will generate a symbolic absence that will compel the subject to develop a negative capability and come to terms with the positive forms of the negative: privation, frustration, and castration. The symbolic mother is the most that can be expected from a mother, and yet she won't fail to have a part in the production of a normal neurosis, or an existential form of suffering.

Now the imaginary mother, whether in the form of too much gratification or not enough desire for the child (two sides of the same coin), will lead to the phenomena described by Epstein. The false self produced in relation to a responsible and conventional, yet distant and undesiring, mother will be more characteristic of the schizoid personality than the borderline or the new character disorders.

Otherwise all human beings could be said to have a false self in the form of the imaginary ego. The persona, or the ego, is the mask that we all wear in public in order to cover over the losses associated with subjectivity, and more fundamentally the absence of a substantial self. However, in neurosis, the persona is the ego-ideal, or the medals, banners, and identities associated with the Law and social ideals; while in the borderline condition, the persona or mask is the ideal ego as a narcissistic formation. The child is identified with being the imaginary mother's narcissistic object and social rules don't apply to them.

It is also true that men or fathers cannot be said to be entirely free of blame in this regard. Like in Freud's *Totem and Taboo* myth, because of the excesses of the imaginary primal father, the sons were forced to band against him. The excesses of the neurotic imaginary father lead to traditional neurosis and inhibitions that we all know in the form of the obsessive or hysterical character structure. But what appeared to be a riddance of the brutal father often turns out to be one of his innumerable new beginnings. Although women and children appear to become free of the excesses of authoritarian patriarchy, the omnipotent mother and child became the new incarnations of the tyrannical imaginary father.

The predominant view within Anglo-Saxon psychoanalysis that considers reported experiences of rejection or parental abandonment as a carbon copy or an isomorphic reflection of environmental parental failures co-exists with an opposite tendency within the culture according to which women have been abandoning the traditional maternal function in large numbers. Beyond rejecting the desire to have children, some feminists have gone as far as arguing that the biological reproductive function constitutes an oppression of nature against women.

In my opinion, this logical contradiction reflects an identity between opposites. The point of view that privileges the so called pre-Oedipal dyadic relationship to the mother as a response and correction to Freud's patriarchal tendencies ends up setting up an impossible expectation for women that runs contrary to the general tendency within the culture. If the presence of the mother is so important, then women should return to the traditional maternal role as soon as possible. What is more important than the omnipresence of the mother is the alternation of the presence and absence of the mother and father in the child's life. With the presence of the symbolic father, the absence of the mother plays a positive and necessary constructive function. Just like within the Lacanian framework, sexual difference is given by the relationship to the father, the presence of the father in the family, either as father or husband of the mother, frees the mother to have her own desire and life independently from the maternal function.

Nevertheless, the presence and absence of the symbolic mother and father will not come without a price for the subject. Symbolic castration and separation from the imaginary mother and the fantasy of the imaginary phallus is the price paid for civilisation. In this sense, the problems associated with injuries to narcissism and the imaginary ego may be unavoidable within culture. As Epstein has also observed:

> Buddha did not lay the blame for the compelling allure of grandios-
> ity or emptiness on inadequate child rearing; there is no Buddhist
> prescription for raising an enlightened child free from narcissism.
> According to Buddhist psychology, narcissism is endemic to the
> human condition; it is an inevitable, if illusory, outgrowth of the
> maturational process.

(p. 69)

What the so-called new wave of object relations and self-psychology misses is that despite the apparent aforementioned changes on the his-torical surface, the traditional character has not been completely super-seded. First, because large parts of the world, and minorities within the developed world, still live under its influence; and second, because, psychoanalytically speaking, the lessening of secondary social repres-sion still leaves intact the structural repression associated with the incest prohibition and the Oedipus myth. It is this structural repression that in Lacan's view produces a divided or dual subjectivity or self that accounts for the validity and relevance of psychoanalysis. No matter how good-enough a mother or father may be, the division between the law and desire lying at the root of character formation within cul-ture and family, however defined, will continue to plague the psyche of the subject.

As Epstein states with regard to Buddhism in contrast to an object relations perspective, for Lacanians a divided subjectivity is endemic to the human condition and a natural outgrowth not of a natural matura-tional process (as in the object relations school) but of a culture-bound and rule-bound structure of human subjectivity. This is not to say that given the deep structure of the incest prohibition, how a parent behaves, good-enough or bad-enough, is irrelevant or does not have an impact on a child's sense of wellbeing. The question becomes more one of needing to simultaneously hold both a structural and ahistorical or traditional perspective and an historical and developmental diachronic perspective.

More than constituting successive stages in the history of psychological thought, both of these perspectives within psychoa-nalysis, Freudian and contemporary object relational, follow from two independent streams of the Enlightenment and the modern scientific paradigm (modernity). The Enlightenment, as a social philosophical movement, contained, among others, two important themes.

First, an emancipatory cognitive interest or ideal consisting of a critique of traditional religious assumptions and dogmas which was part and parcel of the general movement towards a scientific analysis of natural phenomena (including human nature). As in the example of Freudian psychoanalysis, traditional knowledge was subjected to processes of secularisation, rationalisation, and demystification. Second, a humanistic vision of the world which runs through the social philosophy of Rousseau, the young Marx, and the psychoanalytic revisions of Fromm, Horney, the object relations theory of Winnicott, Mahler, Kohut, and the interpersonal school of psychoanalysis. These two strands of the Enlightenment result in different assumptions and views of human nature and the nurture/nature relationship. I postulate a distinction between dialectical and dualistic ways of formulating the nurture/nature question.

Both the traditional/secularist and the humanistic perspective can be critiqued for falling into dualistic rather than dialectical views of human nature. In a dualistic view, opposite terms are considered absolutely external to one another, while the opposite is true of a dialectical perspective. The traditional religious as well as classical philosophical view of human nature in the West was that the divine soul or rational principle was the better side which needed to preside over the lower tendencies of natural drives and passions. In terms of familial and political structure, the authority relationship between nurture and nature was embodied and distributed across parent–child, husband–wife, ruler–ruled, and priest–laity relationships. The source of problems in any of these relationships was usually attributed to the natural end of the relationship.

To a great extent, psychoanalysis maintains a secularised version of this traditional perspective, but with a few notable exceptions. Namely, that consistent also with a humanistic and dialectical perspective, some relativity is introduced into the model whereby the traditional authority can be questioned (that is, Freud's concept of the superego), and the controlled libidinal tendency is perceived as having a modicum of emancipatory and curative potential.

The humanistic perspective instead reverses the traditional values into their opposites but maintaining the dualistic structure of the relationship. The child, woman, and ruled are presumed to be innocent and good (not seekers of sexual or aggressive gratification) if provided with adequate parenting and a facilitating and supportive environment. In this model, the blame rests entirely in the nurture and power side of the relationship (parent, father, ruler, priest). This explains the tendency of relational theorists to attribute personal difficulties and character disorders on faulty or inadequate parenting.

Buddhist and Lacanian notions of self and subject

In general, the object relations (Fairbain, Winnicott, Mahler), ego-psychology, and self-psychology schools all privilege the importance of developing a coherent or integrated ego or self-identity. This fact has been identified by prior authors (transpersonalists, Engler, 1981) and within the psychoanalytic tradition, Suler (1993), Rubin (1996), and Epstein (1995) as the most salient point of difference or contradiction between contemporary psychoanalysis and the Buddhist doctrine of no-self.

These authors have forwarded several possible solutions to the self/no-self dilemma. Engler formulated a by now widely circulated idea that you have to be somebody before you can be nobody. In other words, Engler proposed that first the ego has to exist before a no-ego phase can begin. However, this linear developmental argument runs the danger of ego-reification illustrated by the following Jewish joke. Once a rabbi came into the synagogue and found the keeper praying out loud, saying, "Oh God! I am nothing, nothing ...", to which the rabbi responded "and who are you to say you are nothing?". In this model, being nobody is still under the influence of a false ego construct presupposed as a prerequisite. Not having an ego becomes a positive ego-identification, but an ego nonetheless. In the example provided by the joke, you have to be somebody (a rabbi) in order to say you are nobody (or be nobody).

In addition, the teaching of no-self does not represent a form of self-denial. "No-self" does not mean low self-esteem, low status, or lack of self-confidence because from a Buddhist perspective a negative ego is still an imaginary ego, nonetheless. Low self-esteem, or lack of self-confidence, is not caused by the denial of an ego but by the presence of an imaginary one.

No-self from a Buddhist or Lacanian perspective includes human faculties and functions not attributable to an ego. A problem in exercising human functions or with self-confidence does not exactly represent an ego lack. To the contrary, it could be argued that it is precisely the attachment to an imaginary ego that needs to be worked through and let go. The imaginary ego interferes with the symbolic functioning of the subject/signifier.

But although Buddhism shares with psychoanalysis a critique of ego illusions and the Imaginary, Buddhism does not explore and track the Oedipal fantasy material that lead to the construction of a false sense of self (as presented above). The imaginary ego represents what Engler (2003) calls "somebody". In psychoanalysis, this imaginary ego is analysed and worked through not simply dismissed or repressed. However, in working through the imaginary ego, either in Zen or psychoanalysis, the so-called ego-functions are not destroyed. For this reason, Buddhism considers these functions as functions of the true self, while for Lacan they are symbolic functions of the subject. To transcend the ego-functions means to strip them bare of their imaginary thought-coverings. To transcend the ego-functions means to have the realisation that memory, judgement, and insight or knowing are a function of the interdependence of the larger, unconscious, symbolic structure. I use the term "unconscious" in a descriptive sense to indicate "Big mind" and not the repressed unconscious. In truth, neither conscious nor unconscious applies to describe what Buddhism calls consciousness beyond consciousness and Lacan called a "knowing that does not know that it knows".

Rubin argues that the "different stories that psychoanalysis and Buddhism tell about selfhood … are alternative tools that are useful for different purposes rather than irreconcilable claims" (1996, p. 75). He criticises the negation of self in Buddhism as a defensive operation leading to denial and repression of desires and impulses that then return in destructive forms of acting-out behaviour. He rightfully points out, in my opinion, an absence of a psycho-historical dimension within Buddhism. He concludes that both a sense of self and no-self are needed for optimal psychological health. Epstein does not necessarily view a conflict between the Buddhist doctrine of no-self and the classical ego-functions that potentially can be used for spiritual purposes. On the other hand, he finds rudiments of a psychoanalytic theory of no-self in a few highlighted passages from Bion quoted further on.

Suler, in my opinion, in a few places comes very close in content to the interpretation of Lacanian ideas proposed in this book. Initially, he advances a linear developmental model of how the subject progresses from a pre-self phase to a self and object phase and finally to a no-self phase (1993, p. 58). However, further on he mentions the more interesting idea that subjective structures are processes at a slow rate of change in such a way that self can be thought of as a conventional name for a non-substantial moment of structural construction and no-self one of structural deconstruction or de-automatisation of subjective structure. He follows Bion and Eigen in describing how the condition of non-being and "catastrophe are the zero point that infuses and grounds the self" (p. 71). Zero, no-self, or emptiness can be regarded as "the primary binding force that holds the self together, a primordial source from which structure and function spring" (idem).

The Buddhist notion of no-self does not conflict with the Lacanian paradigm given that this is precisely a point where both traditions coincide to a significant degree. Both could be said to converge on the formula that "true self is no-self", or on the realisation that the true subject requires the symbolic death or deconstruction of imaginary ego-identifications and -representations. In reference to this convergence between Buddhism and psychoanalysis, Epstein mentions that:

> This emphasis on the lack of a particular, substantive agent is the most distinctive aspect of traditional Buddhist psychological thought; it is the realization that transforms the experience of the wheel of Life. But such a conception is not completely outside the realm of psychoanalysis. True thoughts "require no thinker," the psychoanalyst W. R. Bion echoed.
>
> (p. 41)
>
> Insight arises best, he said, when the "thinker's" existence is no longer necessary.
>
> (p. 222)

However, in contrast to Epstein's brief mention of Bion, within Lacanian theory one can find a well developed psychoanalytic body of knowledge to account for the non-substantiality of the subject in terms of Lacan's three registers of experience: the Imaginary, Symbolic, and Real. I argue that the Lacanian notion of the subject provides a viable alternative to either the psychoanalytic thesis of a substantial ego or self (which Buddhism rejects) or the Buddhist pitfall of ignoring the significance of both language and a historical symbolic subject.

Lacan's concept of the Real provides an answer to the valid critique that psychoanalysis lacks a positive psychology of meditation states. Finally, the practice of ego-deconstruction, or what Lacan calls benevolent depersonalisation, applied to both analyst and analysand, constitute the near equivalent of the experience of meditation in Zen and Buddhism in general.

For Buddhism, the ego is a false belief in a non-existing imaginary self. A false concept of ego "produces harmful thoughts of 'me' and 'mine,' selfish desire, hatred, ill-will, conceit, pride and egoism" (Rahula, 1974, p. 51). Instead, "What we call I is only a combination of physical and mental aggregates" (idem, p. 66). A true self or personality, or what Lacanians would call a subject, consists of the five "skandhas", defined as an "aggregate" of personality factors, a series of clusters or groups of self-functions and processes which conform the empirical, functional self. The five skandhas are body (five senses), perceptions, feelings, impulses as mental formations/representations (desire and its objects), and consciousness.

In Mahayana Buddhist psychology, consciousness is itself subdivided into nine levels of consciousness consisting of the five senses, analytical reason and language that organise perceptions (sixth consciousness), a self-consciousness which gives rise to a false sense of ego and a self-critical faculty (mental formations of the seventh cs.), a repository/storehouse consciousness which includes conscious and unconscious memory (eighth cs., or *Alaja vijnana*), and finally an awareness devoid of content (ninth cs.), also known as Buddha consciousness or consciousness beyond consciousness (D. T. Suzuki, 1968). It goes without saying that if consciousness is an independent self-function, then it follows that the other factors can occur with or without consciousness. In addition, it is worth noting that Buddhism distinguishes between self-consciousness and a consciousness beyond consciousness. Buddha consciousness comes right after the eighth consciousness that is as close as Buddhist psychology comes to a Western concept of the unconscious.

In Buddhism, the word "person" is used in a conventional sense to distinguish one serial process from another and in order to have some sense of a "continuing person" as an agent of responsibility. In a psychological sense, the word "personality" has merely conventional usage, referring to a certain unity of functions. The functional unity of the self is what is called a personality. However, for Buddhism, the ego is not the agent that organises the unity of the personality. The unity of the personality is conceived as a function of Buddha-consciousness beyond consciousness. Within Buddha-consciousness, all the interdependent factors and functions of the mind are realised as inherently empty. In Buddhism, emptiness means interdependence. Each mental factor or subject does not have a separate existence or an inherent being, because being is given by the relationship to all the other factors that determine or "co-arise" with it.

So on the one hand unity or unification is given by the interdependence of a structure that is linked together by a principle of numerical or symbolic unity. On the other hand, interdependence depends on the emptiness of each element that causes it to only have a relative meaning within the structure. From the point of view of form, 1 is different from 2 but only has meaning in relationship to 2. From the point of view of emptiness, 1 can function as a 1 in relationship to 2 because, 1 has no inherent meaning other than in a 1–2 relationship. However, when One functions as 0 or as having no inherent meaning, then 1 is completely independent from 2, and the same can be said of the number 2. Imaginary unity is produced when the ego appropriates this independent function of zero or of the Real.

The imaginary ego

Much like Buddhism, Lacan believed the ego to be an imaginary, although inevitable, construction. For Lacan, the emphasis given to the ego, to autonomy, mastery, and individualism, reinforces an imaginary register of human subjectivity. Lacan defines the imaginary register of experience as intrinsically tied to an inevitable function of illusion or misrecognition. As a dimension of experience, the Lacanian concept of the Imaginary is based on the premise of an imaginary ego as a false construct or fabrication. In addition, as explained below, the fabrication of a substantial ego is also linked to fantasy life and particularly unconscious fantasy life. Finally, the concept has an ambiguity built into it given that Lacan also links the Imaginary with visual perception and a general theory of optics. The imaginary ego is a correctable yet inevitable construction.

According to Lacan's theory of the mirror phase, when the child captures his/her reflected image in the mirror, he/she acquires an unsubstantial bodily ego-representation. Lacan links the ego to the imaginary because in his view the ego is tied up to the self-image, to how the self sees itself reflected in the mirror-like surface of the other. Lacan postulates that the evanescent immaterial reflection of a bodily ego in the mirror represents a concretisation of the mother's object of desire: "Oh! so it is this who my mother desires or does not desire."

Thus, the specular image, the image in the mirror, occupies the same structural position as the fantasised *objet a* that constitutes the cause of the mother's desire. According to Lacan, the individual derives his/her own self-image and body image, his/her narcissism, from an early identification with the mother and her desire. The first total ego-image is framed according to the desire of the other. The ego is a case where the subject constitutes a fantasy object for the mother. It is the identification with this imaginary object that lies behind the identification of an imagenic bodily ego-representation.

From then on, the specular image remains as a double of the subject that equivocally can represent either the self or the other. This is the place of projection and imaginary intersubjectivity where the other is narcissistically misrecognised in terms of the ego and where the ego is narcissistically misrecognised as not derived from identification with the other. From the perspective of the Imaginary, instead of actually seeing the other as a subject, what the self sees in the other is its own reflection. The ego-illusion and misrecognition is given by the fact that it is precisely at the place where the ego is most determined by and dependent on the other that the thought of a special and independent individuality arises. Lacan associated the ego with sibling rivalry and competition, where the other recognised as a brother and a like-minded member of the same species is perceived as capable of displacing and occupying the very place that the ego holds *vis-à-vis* the mother.

For Lacan, truth and reality have a fictional, illusory or fantasmatic structure. Not only the ego but also objective reality has an illusory quality. Reality is a construction and perhaps even a fiction. Not only subjectivity but also objectivity has an Imaginary dimension. Here, Lacan differs from Freud who, in classical Western fashion, clearly distinguished between fantasy and reality. In this respect, Lacan also inadvertently comes close to Mahayana Buddhist thought.

In the Zen tradition, Rinzai, for example, distinguished among four types of relations between subject and object. In the first type of relationship, the subject, knowingly or unknowingly, is completely in the shadow of the object. Western culture would be a prime example of this form of relationship between subject and object (a point made by Jung long before). Within fantasy life, the ego is defined by a relationship to the objects of desire. The ordinary human being has to develop a conventional notion of object as distinguished from subjective desires. Here the objects are regulated by law rather than by wishing. The relationship to the mother would be the prime example of a relationship to the objects of desire, while the father represents the relationship to the objects of external reality.

However, beyond conventional morality or rationality, Buddhism, psychoanalysis and postmodernism remind us that objectivity is inextricably mixed with subjectivity. Objective things are a product of the mind or of the subject. Being a product of the subject, objectivity is empty or has no objective or inherent existence. Just like in the first form of relationship the object cancelled or took out the subject, now the object is taken out or cancelled by the subject. Psychoanalysis and Buddhism require a focus on the self or subject.

However, Buddhism takes the relationship between subject and object one further notch or a quarter-turn of the knot. In the next phase or type, both object and subject are taken away. Since the objective subject or mind does not have an inherent existence, what remains is emptiness and emptiness only. But this is not the end of the story either. In a final twist or permutation between subject and object, emptiness itself has to be denied. Being empty or devoid of substance, emptiness can only exist within the forms provided by subjectivity and objectivity. Both subject and object are now functions of emptiness as a non-dual reality beyond mental/spiritual and material reality.

Subjectivity has an equivocal status within psychoanalysis. On the one hand, it represents desire and the pleasure principle, on the other hand, the ego is supposed to be the subjective correlate of the reality principle and the personal/cognitive foundation of objective knowledge. The child's body image represents the emergence of the objective world and of the ego out of the mother's subjectivity. But the object cause of the other's desire and the notion of an objective object world cannot be separated. Objectivity exists against a backdrop of subjectivity. Even if the ego and desire are differentiated, the ego still functions as a subjective support or function for the apparently independent existence of an objective world. Thus, Lacan deconstructs the notion of an objective reality and of a reality ego by braking down the ego into its constitutive Imaginary and Symbolic elements. The Imaginary ego is an object of subjective desire, while the reality ego is a symbolic subjective structure linked to what Lacan calls the subject.

Without analysis or meditation practice, the conventional ego always remains prone to function according to identifications. The social other as object is perceived through the screen of fixed and fantasised self-representations. Along the way, the other and the imaginary ego become easily confused. Thus, Lacanian theory offers a historical/structural explanation of the arising of the problem of me and mine, pride and rivalry with the other. The Lacanian critique of the ego and the Imaginary coincides with the Buddhist critique of egocentrism and of the ego as an illusory and artificial entity.

On the other hand, although Buddhism and Lacanian psychoanalysis regard the ego as an imaginary construction, Buddhism, unlike psychoanalysis, is not interested in deconstructing and tracing back the sources of ego-identifications or of desires to the familiar and symbolic history of a subject. Here, I agree with Rubin when he observes an absence of a psycho-historical dimension within Buddhism. But from a Lacanian perspective, the presence of a psycho-historical dimension does not necessarily provide evidence and support for the actual existence of a substantial self or ego. Beyond the Imaginary, and within the Symbolic, the subject is a metaphor and a name for a series of functions and processes that occur within language and discourse.

The subject and the symbolic

The participation of the individual in a symbolic register of human experience is what begins to brake up the apparent solidity of the Imaginary. According to Lacan, it is the symbolic order (a set of laws, values, myths, etc.) and the order of language, which establishes many of the structures and functions of the subject that in the ego-psychology school are attributed to non-defensive and "realistic" ego-functioning. For Lacan, reality is a social construct entirely given by the culture-bound and rule-bound order of language. The rules of language and the rules of kinship are conceived as two fundamental and integral elements of culture.

But in contradistinction to the ego-psychology school, Lacan does not formulate the existence of an ego entity in order to explain linguistic functioning. The same can be said with regard to the concept of reason as a faculty of the subject. Reason and language as functions of the subject, do not require the belief in an ego as an organising agent of the personality. Language and the symbolic unconscious constitute an Other to the subject because they mediate the relationship between the subject and the object, self and other. The Other is capitalised because the unconscious and language are the larger structures which condition the experience of reality of the subject.

In addition, the Other also refers to parental figures and figures of authority from whom the subject receives both social rules and the rules and content of language. Just as the ideal ego and narcissism are derivative objects of the desire of the mother, it is the relationship with the symbolic father that frees the subject from narcissism and from being an imaginary object of the mother's desire. The identification with the symbolic father, in the sense of identification with symbolic rules and social laws that the father represents, establishes the subject as a pivot of the Symbolic and the Symbolic as a pivot of subjectivity. The Symbolic is what organises human subjectivity, and in so far as symbolic rules and social laws are embodied in concrete singular "citizens", the subject functions as an agent/pivot of the Symbolic. Herewith, an individual can hardly be distinguished from the grammatical subject of the statement and the attribution and location given by the circulation of a proper name within language and culture. The subject is identical to a name which represents "so and so" within a particular society.

The point of biggest difference or distance between Buddhism and Lacanian psychoanalysis lies on the importance attributed to language and the Symbolic. Buddhism does not have a concept of a symbolic subject or of the function played by language as an organiser of perception, thinking, and subjective experience. Buddhism, and particularly Zen Buddhism, consider words to be a hindrance to understanding because words are dual logical elements, inherently discriminative and inadequate to express the non-dual nature of reality.

It is interesting to discover, however, that there are, in fact, many commonalities between how Lacan and Buddhism conceive of language. For Lacan, whatever we say and perceive of reality is always mediated by the signifying system of language. Naming things differentially through the pre-existing structure of language creates the sense of an objective reality. However, whatever is captured of reality within the net of linguistic phenomena misses the immediacy of the noumena that water-like escapes through the holes of the symbolic. This limitation of language is also related to a limitation of objective reason itself.

No matter how much one tries to reflect on and dissect and analyse perceptions and achieve relative degrees of objectivity and critical thinking, the immediacy of the Real will continue to evade us for it lies beyond the *a priori* categories of reason and language, although it does not exist independently from them. Thus, Zen contends that emancipation and illumination cannot be realised at the level of language because as soon as things are named we are caught and limited by a net of symbolic designations.

This problem is also related to a dialectical contradiction in Lacan's thought. On the one hand, lower-case social reality is entirely given by language both in terms of what is allowed and what is forbidden; and on the other, Lacan postulates a dimension of experience existing outside or beyond language and symbolisation (Real). Thus, although Lacan and psychoanalysis privilege the function and use of words and language as vehicles of understanding, and Buddhism considers them a hindrance or obstacle to understanding, Lacan also postulate a third register of subjective experience (the Real) which comes very close to describing the reality of meditation experience.

Some of the confusion regarding the interpretation of Lacan's ideas about language and the unconscious stem from his initial non-differentiation between a preconscious, rational, and social language (unconscious in a descriptive sense) and the language of the unconscious which he later came to term *lalangue*. This difference is also related to another distinction that Lacan makes between an ego-based imaginary use of language and the function of language in psychoanalysis as a function of the subject of the unconscious. It is in this latter sense that language can articulate an emancipatory rather than limiting function for the subject. Both in Zen and psychoanalysis, a different function of language articulates something of a Real beyond symbolisation.

The function of language in Dogen Zenji

Zen teaching is commonly understood as a direct pointing to the mind (the finger pointing at the moon), as grounded in direct experience, and/or as a mind-to-mind transmission outside the scriptures. The latter statement is usually attributed to Bodhidharma, who brought the Zen teaching and the practice of meditation from India to China. Before Bodhidharma, Buddhism in China consisted primarily of a scholastic study of text or sutras.

The contrast between Bodhidharma and the prior transmission of Buddhism in China, via the translation and study of the sutras, corresponds to a division or duality between meditation and intellectual study, practitioner versus scholar that runs through many of the schools of Buddhism both in China and Japan.

Bodhidharma, and Zen in particular, is often associated with the Mahayana Lankavatara sutra. It is said that it is the only sutra that Bodhidharma brought into China. The Lankavatara sutra is related to the Yogachara school and to Zen because it stresses inner realisation as the fundamental source of religious understanding and virtue.

The sutra teaches that ultimate reality is unconditioned and therefore beyond categorical or rational description in terms of causes and conditions or words and letters. This distinction between the unconditioned and causes and conditions continues a duality between the two that the Mahayana is supposed to overcome. Inner realisation is a pure perception that cannot be made the object of discursive understanding. Like the Diamond Sutra, the Lanka teaches the non-dependence upon any formulated teaching. From this point of view, there is no absolute within the relative or non-duality within duality.

Buddhist scholars often contrast the Yogachara and the Middle Way or Madyamika schools of Buddhism. Madyamika is the middle way between absolute and relative truths. For the Madyamika, the absolute is also manifest within the relative, but the relative applies not only to ordinary activities (cleaning, cooking, and physical labour) but also to the life of the intellect. The Zen school, as commonly understood, would be a direct descendant of the Yogachara or mind-only school of Buddhism, while the schools that do not reject intellectual study of the sutras can claim a line of descent from Nagarjuna or the Madyamika school of Buddhism. An example of this would be Tibetan Buddhism.

It is common for the Zen school to think of Mahayana Indian Buddhism as purely intellectual, discursive, or speculative/ philosophical. However, these distinctions are artificial since Nagarjuna was also steeped in meditation practice, and Vasubhandu, the founder of Yogachara, was also quite intellectually complex.

Nagarjuna emphasised that when Buddhism denies the importance of words, it uses words to deny words. If words are meaningless, or "just words", then how can one deny the meaning of words with words? The denial of words would itself be meaningless. The Lankavatara sutra is very meaningful despite the fact that it is using words to point to the limits of discursive understanding and to point to the importance of zazen or meditation as the supreme vehicle or first principle of inner realisation. Tozan, the founder of the Soto school in China, in a famous poem wrote that the meaning is not in the words but that it is also not beyond words either. One has to use the suchness within words (just words) to reach the suchness beyond words (words are just or such). For the purpose of recovering suchness without words from within the suchness of words, Nagarjuna formulated the teaching of the twofold truths: absolute and relative.

The teachings of Dogen, the main figure in Japanese Soto Zen teaching, differ from the Zen tradition founded on a dualism between intuition and intellect, meditation and wisdom. As Kim (2007) has pointed out, Dogen restored language, thinking, and reason—the familiar tools of duality—to their fully deserved legitimacy in Zen. Non-duality does not signify the transcendence of duality so much as the realisation of non-duality within duality. Dogen's manner of approaching duality and non-duality was not hierarchical.

Dogen's teaching is rooted in the context of the Rinzai and Soto schools in China and these schools themselves are rooted in the context of the Yogachara and Madyamika schools of Buddhism. Within contemporary Japanese Soto teaching, there are also two schools of Dogen studies, those that privilege Dogen the meditator and those who privilege his wisdom or critical thinking. Dogen actually represents a non-duality between these two schools of Buddhism, sometimes revealed as zazen-only and sometimes as right thinking.

The consequence of the duality between intuition and intellect, meditation and wisdom, is not only the creation of a duality between insight/discernment and intellectual discrimination but also between enlightenment and delusion. Non-duality is construed as the neutralisation of discrimination/delusion and thus has little to nurture duality or reason as such.

Neither enlightenment nor delusion can exist without the other and one always attains enlightenment through delusion. The intellect also has a role to play in enlightenment. Right thought or thinking, or right analysis includes and realises the ineffable or the Real within thought itself.

Dogen differs from the forms of Zen that deny or attack the function that the intellect plays in the manifestation of wisdom. Words can reveal or conceal experience beyond words. For Dogen, the sutras are the entire universe. Words reveal what is concealed about the universe, and words have to be revealed through the universe.

According to Kim, Dogen's work distinguishes the instrumental from the "realisational" view of language. The beyond the signifier is itself a signifier (of the Real and *jouissance*, however) not a reality that exists outside or is unrelated to language. In addition, Dogen uses many hermeneutic devices similar to those found in Jewish Kabbalah (see the upcoming chapter). Both writings (Dogen's and that of Spanish/French Kabbalists) are products of the twelfth century, although from very different parts of the world at a time that transportation was difficult. Dogen transposes Chinese lexical components to produce a similar effect to that of Temurah that consists of permutating and rearranging sentences to arrive at new meanings and forms of *jouissance* contained with the text.

Just like Lacan, Dogen used homophony (similitude in sound between words: e.g., meditation and medication) and other language resources to arrive at previously unknown significations. Lacan considered homophony as a main form of association or combination characteristic of unconscious signification. For example, according to Kim, the statement that Dogen used to designate the awakened state, or his experience of awakening was generated by homophony. In the Chinese spoken at the time, dropping body and mind sounded similar or the same to dropping the dust of the mind. His teacher may have said the latter, and Dogen heard or understood the former.

The permutations of cogito ergo sum

Following Lacan, the permutations of the Cartesian *cogito ergo sum* will be used to illustrate the three dimensions of the subject. "I think (I speak), therefore I am" represents the imaginary ego and the self-image as aforementioned. When utilising social language, the *moi*, the ego, says, I think, I speak. As Fink (1997) has pointed out, when the ego says I speak "What he means thus refers to a level of intentionality that he views as his own; it refers to an intentionality that fits in with his self-image" (p. 24). This is why Lacan distinguished between the enunciating ego and the subject of the enunciation and between meaning and signification. Meaning is imaginary because "it is tied up with our self-image, with the image we have of who and what we are" (idem).

Instead, Lacan conceives the subject of the unconscious, of signification, of the enunciation as an effect of the operation of the signifier.

The classical Freudian slips, the parapraxis, the double meanings, the polyvocal significations, in short, all of the formations of the unconscious, are seen by Lacan as effects of the language-like symbolic structure of the unconscious. These psychic formations have the effect of breaking the imaginary homogeneity of what the conscious ego intended or meant to say. The unconscious and the signifier speak through the subject. The thing speaks for itself or "It" speaks in me. In this respect, Lacan (1972) modified and permutated the Cartesian cogito ergo sum by stating "I think where I am not" instead of the classical "I think, therefore I am". It is not the ego but the subject who speaks the reality and truth of the unconscious.

"I think where I am not" represents what Epstein (1995), following Bion, calls thoughts without a thinker where, from a Lacanian perspective, thoughts are signifiers that speak for themselves and articulate the symbolic existence of a subject. The autonomy of the signifier or of symbolic thought is experienced as a negation of the ego: I am not. My thoughts work autonomously and not always in alignment with my intentions and desires. But the "I think" aspect of "I think where I am not" refers to the fact that the Symbolic also represents an aspect of my subjectivity although not of the ego. It is a larger me doing the thinking activity although in a way which appears to be ego-dystonic. Although unconscious thinking negates or eclipses the ego, in analysis a new I emerges that can take responsibility for unconscious thinking and thought.

Numerous "I think" are within the track of goal-oriented thinking, of goals and objectives and anxieties about what will I become at the level of an ego-representation. Where the ego says and thinks "I am", in the *moi*, the I is an imaginary object of desire of the social other, of the dreams and frustrations of parental figures. This is the illusion of ego-autonomy. "I think where I am not" signifies that it is desire as the desire of the other that is doing the thinking activity. The I is being lived by the dreams and desires of many generations before.

Lacan's aphorism that the unconscious is the discourse of the Other highlights such involuntary and unconscious functioning of language and identity: how the laws of language, the rules of syntax, of metaphor and metonomy, of how words/signifiers are connected/disconnected with one another, condition what and how something can and cannot be said, and how the self-imputed sayings of the ego unconsciously represent quotes and identifications with the discourse of significant others (the discourse of the other in lower case). In this latter sense, the ego consists of identifications with signifiers coming from the Other (both from the symbolic order and significant/signifying others). The ego represents an imaginary use of the Symbolic to stitch and cover over the ultimate non-existence of both the Other and the subject. When signifiers representative of ideals become invested with the narcissism of an ideal ego, then identifications become idealisations of an ideal father or fatherland and the signifier functions as a false identification.

No-self and symbolic emancipation

The critique of ego—or self-psychology constructs is usually countered with the objection that:

> Decisions and planning cannot occur without a human agent who envisions possibilities, examines alternatives, and chooses specific courses of action. To deny this mode of being is to create chaos and undermine the basis for choice and action … If there is no subject, then there is no agent to evaluate phenomena and no previous experience from which to learn.
>
> (Rubin, 1996, p. 76)

For both ego-psychology and self-psychology, the self "appears as a fundamental organizer, and unity of initiative that is more than simply a content, structure, or experience" (Suler, 1993, p. 41). Both Buddhism and Lacanian psychoanalysis have to answer to the commonsense appearance that, of course, there has to be someone there who responds to a name, culture, and language, provides a continuity and orientation across time and space, and decides on courses of action and knowledge. But isn't this line of reasoning also the most obvious way of succumbing to illusory appearances? Can there only be organisation on the basis of an ego-principle? Can there be a non-imaginary unity principle? For Lacan, it is the signifier (the fact of being named by the other) that organises the experience of the subject and, according to Buddhism, only in the Buddha mind can the subject realise the actual unity of reality. In the Genjo Koan, Zen teacher Dogen (1231–1253) wrote: "To advance the self and realize the ten thousand dharmas (phenomena) is delusion; that the ten thousand dharmas advance and realize the self, is enlightenment."

The problem with the formulation of language and the symbolic order of law (rules of language, culture and kinship) as a principle of organisation is that it only provides a traditional concept of identity and determination by the Other. Lacan ambiguously uses the concept of the Other to represent both the law and the superego as well as the concept of desire and the desire of the Other (unconscious desire). On the other hand, he also formulates a psychoanalytic ethic of never giving up on one's (unconscious) desire. In this latter sense, Lacan also articulates a classical and modern psychoanalytic interest in emancipation from the tyranny of the Other as traditional judge and superego. But is he, like Reich and Marcuse, advancing a libidinal id interest as an alternative to a classical ego-autonomy? Is there any possible emancipation from the Other which does not consist of an illusory id hedonism or romanticism or a modernistic/rationalistic ego-autonomy?

If the ego as an organising agency is only an illusion, and a traditional patriarchal symbolic order precludes the possibility of change and emancipation, then what is it that gives not only organisation and efficacy but also originality and flexibility to the activities of the subject? Following Buddhism, it can be argued that, beyond the registers of the Imaginary and the Symbolic, there is, as Suler put it, a primordial binding source which holds the self together, a synchronic first principle that unifies the subject as a symbolic and real subject.

Within the symbolic register, the noumena, or what is beyond the categories of logic and language, manifests as the simultaneous interdependence of elements within a structure. In Lévi-Strauss's (1958) work, symbolic effectiveness represents the manner in which symbolic elements in synchronic combination articulate something of a Real beyond rational comprehension. Only in the arrogance of reason and the reifications of the master's discourse can such functions be attributed to an ego agency. The formless or invisible principle at work within the synchronic efficacy of interdependent elements can never be stated completely by language. Since the One of the Real can never be said completely in words one easily hypostatises and theorises the existence of an ego agency.

A first level of psychoanalytic emancipation (autonomy) is reached through finding the heteronomous "not-I" within the symbolic pathways of desire. "I think where I am not" signifies that it is not the "I" that is doing the thinking. The ego is merely a toy of desire within the signifying chain. This sense of the ego, or I, needs to be transformed into a new I or "me" that Lacan calls the subject of the unconscious and that can be appropriated and permutated in the practice of analysis.

However, a further, larger "me" still needs to be reached beyond the pathways of symbolic desire on the level of emancipation and autonomy corresponding to an authentic spiritual function. "I think where I am not" needs to be permutated into "I am where I do not think". This permutation has two aspects: an ego aspect, and a non-ego or non-self aspect.

The ego aspect refers to the ego's thinking and "not-thinking". For Lacan, the "I am where I do not think" points to the ego's refusal of unconscious thinking. "Not-thinking" is equivalent to the repression of thought. The being of the ego and of consciousness also includes ego-syntonic thinking according to the ego's character traits. "This is the way I am, and what I think, and nobody knows better about this or about me than me." Here, "I am where I do not think" refers to the ego not being able to "not-be" or think in a non-ego-centred way. Thinking in this case refers to thinking outside of the box of the ego. The symbolic subject requires the acknowledgement that the ego is not the one doing the thinking. At the same time, "I am where I do not think" also refers to the subject of the Real and to non-thinking in the sense of a mind beyond thinking.

Non-thinking points to the realm of being beyond signification and representation: our Real self, the Big me which is beyond thought and which is capable of saying: "I am Who I am" (Exodus 3:14). "I am who I am" does not mean the ego's "Well, this is who I am, a guy from the South, or from the North of England, or the United States, and this is how I am, and what I do, take it or leave it." "I am Who I am" in Exodus refers to the mystery of Being and of the Name, which is the true foundation, the groundless ground of subjectivity, rather than the ego.

Thus, through psychoanalytic practice, the subject can find and appropriate his or her own symbolic identity within the laws of desire and language, but the subject is also capable of doing the same with respect to an ultimate identity (which is no identity) within the Real. I submit that this is similar to what Lacan calls the not-All. The Real represents neither the All of the Imaginary (the false appearance of wholeness), nor the All of the Symbolic (the law, the phallic function, the serial chains of letters and numbers, the sum of the parts, the skandhas in Buddhism, etc.)

According to Lacan, something of the order of the Real and of truth is always left half-said and in the silent obscurity of the unknown. Reason is impotent to describe the mystery of Being. No one can really or in truth say "I" because what the "I" is at the level of the Real is ignored. In other words, the real self is not the sum of self and object representations as formulated by Jones (1991) and Masterson (1985). Such is only true in the dimensions of the Imaginary and the Symbolic. The Real subject of experience and awareness is not a self-representation.

The unity of an image is imaginary and the signifier is multiple and polyvocal. In addition, a battery of signifiers never exhausts the meaning of the unrepresented subject; the ignored me, remains shrouded in a mystery beyond signification. Real unity lies within a post-representational realm. In this sense, sophisticated mythological thinking, which always leaves things half-said is in a better position to present the real meaning of the subject. The discourse of social science, of the University, of rationality, is always falling into one form or another of "egocracy".

Jung referred to the "autonomy" of unconscious contents in the same way that Lacan refers to the "heteronomy" of the signifier. To the ego, the unconscious appears to have a mind of its own. The autonomy of the Real and the Symbolic is experienced as heteronomy and as compromising the autonomy of the ego. Nevertheless, once the heteronomy of the Real and Symbolic registers is appropriated and chosen by the subject (of the unconscious), then the so-called autonomy of these worlds becomes the autonomy of a new centred subjectivity without a subject.

Thus, the heteronomy of the Symbolic and the Real (that which decentres conventional ego-identity) is not transformed into an imaginary ego-based autonomy, but rather, dialectically speaking, the "heteronomous autonomy" of these registers is transformed into an "autonomical heteronomy" of the subject. Heteronomy because no-self signifies that multiple structural processes, elements and conditions provide the context for a subject, but autonomy because when no-self is actualised then things advance the self or things, structures and processes become the activity of Big self.

To quote Dogen (1985) again:

> To study the Buddha way is to study the self. To study the self is to forget the self. To forget the self is to be actualized by myriad things. When actualized by myriad things, your body and mind as well as the bodies and minds of others drop away. No trace of realization remains, and this no trace continues endlessly.

(p. 70)

To forget the self is to be confirmed or enlightened by all phenomena (dharmas). According to Zen, a special concept or entity to describe the self is unnecessary. To study the self is to forget the self, and to "know thyself" is to know thyself as no-self. The self is what we are or what we do as an effect of knowing what to do with the mystery of *jouissance*. To know what to do with the mystery of *jouissance* means to know nothing of it and from there to go on and enjoy our ordinary life activities. The Other third *jouissance* of the mystic is like streams that flow in the dark without self-consciousness.

The drive in Lacan is related to *das Ding* as the no-thing. The drive is a push/intention towards realising the emptiness of being. In sublimation, the drive becomes the basis or the groundless ground for the Symbolic order. As Grotstein (2003) has observed, following Bion:

> The infant who is able to tolerate frustration is able to tolerate the absence of the breast as a "nothing," while the infant who cannot tolerate frustration attacks his image of the breast, and this attacked image deteriorates into the no-thing as a concrete phantom-object that represents what he has done to the breast and its transformation into a conscience. The faeces represent the mode of attack. The concrete "no-thing" becomes a phantasmally real object that falsely fills the space for thought, thereby preventing any possibility of real thoughts emerging.

> (p. 21)

In Bion's work, the meaning of "nothing" and "no-thing" is reversed. In my view, nothing refers to an absence while the "no-thing" signifies a presence that is not a thing, rather than a thing that is marked by negativity as an absence. According to Grotstein, the concrete "no-thing" fills the space of emptiness, making sublimation impossible. This would be the equivalent of the imaginary face of the *objet a* in the Lacanian framework. The Real face of the *objet a*, however, is the *a* as the presence of an absence that is benevolent rather than persecuting. The good object is internalised, not as a thing but as the space that makes subjective life and sublimation possible.

Instead of pursuing concrete things or objects, the drive circulates around an aimless aim. The real source of enjoyment is simply to go on being, and beyond on-going being, and to walk in a circular path around the object once more. The object here is the *objet a* in the form of an absence or emptiness. For the later Lacan, the drive is not biological but is not simply a symbolic or imaginary construct either. It interacts with them but remains something Other within the Other rather than an Other of the Other. Seeing is seeing, for example, as the *jouissance* of the One, sometimes as the gaze of the Other, sometimes as the look of the subject.

A functioning human being represents in Suzuki's (1970) words "the true activity of Big existence". Wherever we go or whatever we do we meet our self in the process of being confirmed by the activities of daily life. In Big Mind, or consciousness beyond consciousness, the universe works in a surprising, sudden, spontaneous way, automatically, unconsciously without self-consciousness. When the self is not defined by anything in particular or any special form, then in emptiness (of a fixed self-definition), forms and functions confirm us in our selfhood and thusness.

From this perspective, the process of self-transformation in psychoanalysis and meditation experience can be understood, following Zen and Lacan (1960), not as an ego-function, but rather as a process of discarding imaginary ego-representations and revealing benevolent depersonalisations and creative subjective destitutions. Structural permutations of subjectivity within the practice of psychoanalysis, I argue, evoke an order or state of mind, an experience of subjective destitution and realisation that is the near equivalent or friend of the meditation mind or Buddha-mind in Buddhism.

> Conventional notions of ego as that which modulates sexual and aggressive strivings have led many Americans to mistakenly equate selflessness with a kind of "primal scream" in which people are liberated from all constraints of thought, logic, or rationality and can indulge, or act out, their emotions thoroughly.

> (Epstein, 1995, p. 93)

As Epstein notes, selflessness does not mean an absence of ego strength in the sense of what from a Lacanian point of view I would consider the effective action of a symbolic subject. Selflessness or no-self is not symbiotic union but rather the effective functioning of a symbolic subject who in renouncing and working through imaginary and fixed ego-identifications (including imaginary uses of language and despotic representations of the Other) acquires a greater flexibility to flow with, deconstruct and permutate structural symbolic elements at work in a given situation or circumstance.

The subject of the Real

This brings me to the third permutation of the Cartesian cogito leading to a third dimension of experience and of the subject: the register of the Real and of Being beyond thinking.

Lacan differentiated between social reality and the psychical Real or what in Zen would be called ultimate reality. As aforementioned, in Lacanian theory, social reality falls under the category of the Symbolic. The Real refers to the Freudian unconscious in the wider sense of the unknown and not just the repressed. Lacan gave varying definitions of the Real among which the following should be noted.

The Real and the subject within the Real is a breach or an empty locus or space that allows for a nexus of relations to exist, for the movement of the signifier within a signifying chain. As Fink (1995) has pointed out:

> In his seminar on the purloined letter, Lacan states that a signifier marks the cancellation of what it signifies. ... Once the subject has said his or her piece, what she has said usurps his or her place; the signifier replaces him/her; he or she vanishes. ... The signifier takes the subject's place, standing in for the subject who has now vanished. ... This subject has no other being than as a breach in discourse.
>
> (p. 41)

Thus, on the one hand a signifier for another signifier represents the subject. The subject is a metaphor located within the Symbolic register. On the other hand, the subject within the Real is a breach or a hole within discourse. Moreover this breach, gap or hole has been described by Lacan as the point of non-knowledge. As Nasio (1992) has stated, "As subject, I realize myself where I do not know." In addition, on the one hand, this point of non-knowing refers to the *lacunae* in the act of forgetting as an effect of the repression of signifiers within the Symbolic.

On the other hand, the point of non-knowing also refers to the unknown in the sense of what lies within the Real and beyond language and the existing battery of signifiers. In this latter sense, the subject within the Real and the point of non-knowledge also function as a source of new significations. The engendering of a new signification implies that, up until the moment at which this was engendered, a hole existed in the field of the signified or of signification. Since signification is given by the relationship of one signifier to another signifier, when signification is not known, meaning there is no signifier for it, then one can say that there is a hole in the field of the signified. And it is indeed in this same hole (and not in the act of knowledge or symbolic representation) that the subject is located according to Lacan.

The Real is also the Other *jouissance* which women and mystics are said to experience but know nothing about (the experience which knowledge or language cannot describe). The Real is that which the signifying chain encircles and yet remains inaccessible to language and signification. Therefore, Lacan speaks of a lack or impotence of language to pinpoint the Real. It is this impossibility to symbolise and understand by means of reason and language which lends the Real its essentially traumatic and anxiety-producing quality. Finally, for Lacan, the Real is a plenum without fissures, divisions, oppositions, or differentiations, and this is to be distinguished from the illusory wholeness ascribed to the Imaginary. When the ego thinks of itself as being whole, in New Age or humanistic fashion, this is a self-image hyper-cathected with narcissistic energy.

For Buddhism, true self is no-self because phenomena in their own being are empty and only exist as a function of the relationship with everything else. What we call our self is a convention, a fabrication or confection. What are actually there are the five streams of existence: namely, forms, feelings, perceptions, mental formations, and consciousness. But there is no permanent or inherent self within these five streams. These five streams are empty in the sense that nothing stands by itself separate from everything else. As Lacan would put it, the self is the other or the other in the self. Thus, emptiness in Buddhism means interdependence.

For example, the body is within the stream of form, and each part of the body is interdependent with every other part. The nose is only a nose in relationship to the face, and the nose is inherently empty because without the face the nose does not exist. Thus, to express the emptiness of form (nose), a Zen teacher may say something senseless like the nose or the mouth is hanging from the wall. Another aspect of emptiness is that things are empty because they are constantly changing: the five streams are in a state of constant flux and transformation. Sometimes Buddhism uses the sky or space as a metaphor for emptiness. Space is like that in which everything can move and the groundless ground in which things exist. The clear blue sky is a metaphor for essence of mind and the thoughts of an enlightened person are like birds flying in the sky without leaving any traces. Thoughts without a thinker don't give rise to a false sense of self beyond the true self-experience of birds flying in the sky.

It is thus possible to find areas of intersection between the Buddhist notion and experience of emptiness or ultimate Reality and the Lacanian register of the Real. Although Lacan stresses the importance of language as an organiser of experience (of thoughts, feelings, and consciousness) in a way that Buddhism does not, he not only describes language in the language of interdependence but also includes a register of experience beyond language. The finger is the signifier pointing at the moon, but the finger/symbol is not the moon itself within the experiential register of the Real. The signifier is the signifier and the moon is the moon. The Real is that which the signifying chain encircles and yet remains free of a fixed signification within language.

The signification of a word or letter depends on its relationship to all the other words and letters within language. Each word or letter in-itself is empty of its own meaning and it is this emptiness which causes the constant dynamic movement of meaning within a signifying chain. On the one hand, the meaning of words is entirely dependent on other words, and at the same time this relationship and movement or circulation of meaning is generated and dynamically activated by the fact that in themselves or by themselves words are inherently devoid of meaning. Words are pointing to the moon but are not the moon because words are always pointing to other words and thereby remain within a symbolic register that circumscribes the Real as a realm outside meaning.

On the other hand, because words by themselves are empty, the signifier, the pointer, or the finger is already the moon. The signifier or the finger pointing at the moon is already the moon and at the same time is not the moon. Is this a formal contradiction? How could both statements be possibly true at the same time? Well, in this example although they are true at the same time they are not both true in the same respect given that one refers to the Real within the Symbolic (the letter) and the other to the Symbolic within the Real (the signifier as semblance).

Emptiness as the clear space which allows for the movement and translucency of meaning is the larger "me" that can be reached on the level of the Real. "I think where I am not" needs to be permutated into "I am where I do not think" which signifies the realm of being or non-being beyond signification and representation aforementioned. In the "I am Who I am", "Who" is Being at a point beyond ego-knowledge and even beyond unconscious knowing (the unknowable or unconscious non-knowledge). The Other (I think where I am not, or "I am where I am not thinking" in the sense that it is not I who is doing the thinking) cannot give the subject its own being yet the Other represents a necessary moment in the disclosure of Being.

The Being of the subject emerges out of the Other *within* the Other (Real). The Real is the Other within the Other not the Other of the Other (God, for example). By addressing the Other and being addressed by the Other, the imaginary enclosure/bubble of being (I think, therefore I am) is cracked/popped and opened/disclosed.

Within the subject of the Real, being is dis-closed as a One *jouissance*. Dis-closure is a non-dual word that contains a closing and an opening at the same time. It is like the homophony between the word reveal and the neologism re-veil that would mean the opposite (to re-cover or cover/conceal once again). In this sense, revealing contains the opposite effect of concealing. This is how for Lacan *lalangue*, as a letter, a Real within the Other, constitutes a presentation of *jouissance*, a *reveil* or awakening, rather than a symbolic or imaginary substitution. Freud had already anticipated the meaning of non-duality with his notion of the antithetical meaning of primal words. One could paraphrase the concept by referring to the primary antithetical signification of language. The word primary here refers to a first principle, to something original or ancient but not aboriginal, primitive or archaic.

Moreover, as noted above, the hole in the field of the signified or, put differently, the hole which appears within the Symbolic when the signified is within the Real, the empty a-territoriality or groundlessness of the Real, begets a non-conventional and evolutionary leap beyond the established uses of language and ideology. Thus, no one can really or in truth say "I am" or "I know who I am" because what the "I" is at the level of the Real is unknown. Lacan (1968–1969) argues that the subject is actually lacking/absent in the Other or that there is no subject that represents the Other (\$[Ø]). The subject then demands (\$◊D) that the Other or language tell him/her Who s/he is. However, no answer is forthcoming. This lack of an answer in the Symbolic returns as a no answer in the form of a question (Who am I?) or in the form of the negative (I don't know).

Not-knowing the meaning of identity within the Real and the fact that no-self or no-ego is more me or myself than the ego is precisely the source of both new meaning and what articulates the elements of subjective structure. This view is compatible with Suler (1993), who following Bion and Eigen describes how non-being and "catastrophe are the zero point that infuses and grounds the self" (p. 71). Rather than the ego, it is non-being or no-self which functions as a primordial binding source which holds the self together. The answer to the question of self comes from the Real in the form of an emptiness of self that binds the self together.

Thus, I have argued in favour of a marriage of the Lacanian concept of the Real with the Buddhist notion of the Real in terms of emptiness. Lacan often described the Real in terms of an absence or a lack within the Symbolic to pinpoint the Real. Such lack alludes to a limitation of language to represent a Real beyond symbolisation. Lacan defines the emptiness of the Real as a lack in the Other. This relates to the experience of dread many Zen students report when first attempting to give talks and use words to speak about Zen experience. Zen teaching describes this predicament as a mosquito attempting to bite into an iron bull. Symbolic castration or psychical impotence would not be too far off in describing this experience.

For Lacan, the missing signifiers to represent the Real, the lack in the Other, or the symbolic phallus as a signifier of a lack, constitute the subject as barred, as divided, and as desiring something of the Real which the Symbolic or the Imaginary will never fully grasp. Neither language, nor the ego or drives will render the Real to the subject. The drives, commonly understood, do not render the Real to the subject, because the drive is a demand of the Other (\$◊D) and the Other cannot ultimately give the subject its Being.

As experienced in the practice of Zen meditation retreats, the encounter with the Real is impossible and yet also possible at the same time. Such paradox is also conveyed in the Lacanian aphorism, "be realistic, ask for the impossible". Conventionally, to be realistic signifies to only ask or engage in things that are possible. To ask for the impossible is to be unrealistic. In Zen fashion, Lacan turns the conventional under-standing on its head. To access the unconventional Real one must dare to engage in what appears to be impossible at least initially. For exam-ple, who as a Westerner would think of spending sixteen hours a day in meditation—certainly someone who must be a bit crazy!

In addition, the lack in the Other can also be linked up with two other properties of the symbolic order as well as likened to the well-known Zen line from the Heart sutra, "form is emptiness and emptiness is form". As aforementioned, given that every signifier is defined only by its differences from other signifiers, this emptiness of meaning of each singular signifier by itself is what sustains the interdependency of meaning within the structure. Nothing stands by itself separate from everything else. Second, the symbolic order is characterised by the fun-damental dialectic of presence and absence.

In the symbolic order, everything exists upon a background of absence. Language arose in human beings as a way to represent things in their absence. Lacan notes that the signifier is used in the absence of the thing and that signifiers only exist in relationship to other absent signifiers. Thus, in the first case the emptiness of the signifier, or the fact that the self-existence of each singular signifier by itself is devoid of its own meaning (form is emptiness), enriches and supports the meaning of the signifying structure (emptiness is form); while in the second, the emptiness or absence of the thing and of the structure (form is empti-ness) supports the symbolic form of the signifier (emptiness is form). The structure is absent because we are not aware of all words or gram-mar rules as we speak.

In either case, emptiness or dialectical absence (which is also a pres-ence) represent positive terms that do not annihilate either form or structure. Symbolic absence generates the production of new meaning, the shading and cascading of meaning within the function of metaphor and metonymy in language. Thus, within the Lacanian paradigm the lack in the Other represents not only the finitude of discourse and the impossibility of ever having the last word, but also a source of creativ-ity and inventiveness. For Lacan's barred subject under the Symbolic not only undergirds the positive function of social laws but also the possibility of desire. Symbolic castration under the law of language is the price paid for accessing both desire and the emptiness of the subject.

Thus, when Lacan refers to the subject as a metaphor or a signi-fier which cancels/produces the subject as a breach or hole within discourse (the self is made of not-self elements), such negative terms (breach/hole) also need to be considered and understood in terms of the positive creativeness of the Buddhist not/naught or of the true self/ subject as emptiness. Creative emptiness is more than just the absence of something. It is only within the Symbolic that emptiness appears as a negative lack or hole. Within the Real itself, emptiness is a plenum, as Lacan has pointed out. It is the Real as an empty plenum (*vacuum plenum*) that turns the hermeneutic wheel of enlightenment and begets the sparks of new poetic significations. Finally, in my view, the no-self or non-being under the Symbolic and the Real also has an affective and energetic dimension. Non-being represents a creative symbolic death that in conjunction with Eros and life provides the quiescent energy that illuminates and holds the self together writ large. The latter would be consistent with the entire concept of *jouissance* within Lacanian theory.

Lacan also poses the concept of an anterior lack prior to the lack within the Symbolic (Verhaeghe, 1998). The lack within language refers to the fact that once being appears within language it also disappears under language given that there is a dimension of the Real and of being, therefore, which cannot be said by language. But more fundamentally, there is an element of the Real that is lost in the process of birth itself. Being appears with birth but also disappears under birth. This process is repeated once again in language. What is lost with birth, life and under language is the Real, the unborn, the thing or no-thing without a name that Lacan says is eventually spit out of the Real in the form of the Name of the Father. In relationship to this Real, the subject occupies the place of the unborn and the unrealised. The question is whether following Buddhism, this subject is realisable?

With his notion of the alienation of the ego under language and the signifier (the divided subject or $), Lacan purports to argue (not unlike Buddhism) that the subject has no substance and that therefore there is no self-realisation. However, in Buddhism self-realisation precisely signifies the realisation of no-self or that the ego has no substance. It is also expressed paradoxically when within the Zen tradition enlightenment and no-enlightenment or Buddha and no-Buddha are identified as the same thing. This point can be clarified by replacing the Lacanian "no self-realisation" with "no ego-realisation". There can be self-realisation but only as a non-ego.

This point is sometimes missed in Lacan due to confusion between the ego and the subject (Moncayo, 1998). Moreover, as aforementioned, Nasio also articulates the point of self-realisation as a point of non-knowing when he says, "As a subject, I realize myself where I do not know." Thus, to understand the self-realisation of the subject within a Lacanian framework, one need only apply Lacan's concept of "unknown knowing" or of the "knowing that does not know that it knows" (*l'insu qui sait*) to the question of the subject. Unconscious knowing or not-knowing refers both to repressed knowing in the analysand and non-repressed unconscious (non-)knowing in the analyst as manifested in the act of interpretation. Unconscious knowing refers to a knowing subject that does not exist or know as an ego but only as an evanescent and momentary subject.

Unconscious or unknown knowing refers to an ego that is not and to an unborn subject that is the aspect of being lost in the process of becoming and gestation. But what is it? What is this subject? What is this unborn Real which is a no-thing. Here both Lacan and Zen Buddhism tell us that the answer comes from the Real and not from language or the Symbolic. Developmentally for Lacan the subject has to separate not only from the mother and the Imaginary via the father and the Symbolic but also from the symbolic Other and the ideal father by realising the non-existence of the Other and of the ego-ideal. This paves the way for the real being of the subject, *son être du sujet*. The act of *autopoeisis*, or *se parere*, as Lacan called it, of self-creation or self-realisation, is linked to the emergence of a new subject or the being of the subject within the Real as well as to the emergence of new signifiers and poetic significations.

Knowing and non-knowing

I stated above that no one can really or in truth say "I am or I know who I am" because what the "I" is at the level of the Real is unknown.

Lacan finds antecedents for the position of the analyst in the Stoics and the Socratic mayeutics. Socrates went around town engaging people in conversation about different subjects, appearing to know nothing and being willing to learn from everyone who professed to know. Socrates made profession of no knowledge except of that of his own non-knowing. He believed that people know both less and more than what they think they do. To those who appeared to know he showed them that they actually did not know; and to those who appeared not to know, he showed them that in fact they did know. The key point is that access to the larger unknown subject requires an ego-death. Although the ego claims to know, in reality it does not know, because it is the subject that in truth knows. Conversely, although the ego claims not to know, in reality it does know because the subject knows. In analysis, it is the unconscious subject of the analysand who knows, not the ego. The analyst also needs to maintain a similar subjective position.

The distinction between ego and self or subject also corresponds to a distinction between formal reason and dialectical reason, or between reason and intuition. East and West converge on a category of rational function that in the West achieves its maximum expression in the philosophy of Hegel and the post-Hegelian thought of Adorno (negative dialectics). Dialectical reason is consistent with a Buddhist principle of non-duality given that it conceives and perceives opposites as containing one another. However, dialectical reason also contains formal reason because things also need to be seen as independent and different from one another: this is this and that is that. Emptiness or negative dialectics is what links formal and dialectical reason to one another: because things by themselves are empty, they are interdependent and at the same time independent. From the perspective of the Imaginary, things are similar; within the Symbolic, they are different or function as difference; and in the Real, they are marked with a traceless trace, or Unary trace.

In Buddhism, intuition is the psychic function needed to arrive at and reveal an understanding or realisation of non-duality. Both Freud and Jung postulated that formal logical oppositions or dualities do not exist in the unconscious. For Freud, the pre-dual unity of the unconscious constituted a primitive mentality, irrationality without negation, whereas the dialectical unity of non-duality contains a negative moment as an element and step of the dialectical process. The non-dual unity of opposites is post-dual and post-rational while synchretic and idiosyncratic unity or symbiosis is pre-dual and pre-rational. This argument is consistent with Ken Wilbur's (1984) pre-trans fallacy. Freud only explicitly differentiated between irrational or pre-dual unity and the duality of formal reason. He did not have a category for dialectical non-duality, although the knowing of the unconscious by the analyst requires it to a significant degree.

Lacan makes explicit the connections between Hegel and Freud as does Jung with respect to this aspect of his own psychology and Eastern thought. Nonetheless, there is a still some distance between dialectical reason and the intuitive function in Buddhism in that the latter is rooted in a yogic bodily practice of meditation absent from the Western philosophical tradition. Intuition is a function used to reveal Reality in a descending moment once a post-rational perceptual realisation has been attained. In this sense, truth or the Real is utterly inconceivable by reason, whether formal or dialectical. The most one can say is *neti, neti,* not this, not that (a negative dialectic, therefore). In the koan tradition of Zen Buddhism, dialectical reason, as exemplified by the use of logical paradoxes, is used not to explain reality but to open the mind and transport the subject to a level of no-mind or beyond mind.

In passing, it should be noted that Jung (1953) had already realised the significance of paradox as a form of spiritual expression. He pointed out that most spiritual statements contain logical contradictions that are impossible in principle. Only paradox comes near to expressing the non-dual basis of life. Non-ambiguity and non-contradiction are one sided and therefore unsuited to express non-duality. True intuition is the psychic function needed to apprehend a subtle dimension of reality that exists (or not) beyond wishful thinking and discriminative consciousness.

Intuition and understanding in Lacanian psychoanalysis can be associated with a symbolic perspective rooted not on rational preconscious language but in the language of the unconscious. Lacan (1961) redefines the classical psychoanalytic concept of transference around the question of knowing (*savoir* in French). Knowing is not knowledge (*connaissance* in French) because Lacan makes a distinction between the referential knowledge of science and a textual knowing in the psychoanalytic situation regarding the text of the unconscious. This latter form of knowing would not be characterised by the formal dual logic of ego-processes.

Unconscious knowing needs to be contrasted with the usual psychoanalytic conception of both knowledge and insight. Although the word insight does not appear in Freud's work it has become a standard concept in psychoanalytic practice that closely follows Freud understanding of the function of knowledge in psychoanalysis. In Freud's metapsychology, knowledge consists in making conscious the unconscious. At one time, this will be focused on memories, at another on desires and fantasies, but in either case, as Etchegoyen (1991) has pointed out, from the dynamic point of view, something becomes conscious by working through resistances and the lifting of repression.

Moreover, following standard psychoanalytic understanding on the difference between scientific knowledge and the function of knowledge in the practice of analysis, Etchegoyen points out that, in contrast to scientific knowledge, analytic knowledge is personal self-knowledge acquired by working through resistance and undoing repression. From my perspective, unconscious knowing is subjective but is not based on the formal and dual rational knowledge associated with ego-consciousness.

In formulating his conception of the transference, Lacan redefines classical concepts derived from Freud's metapsychological papers. The unconscious has to do with an associative chain of signifiers or representations that convey a knowing apparently ignored by the ego. The analysand does not know that he/she knows. Following Freud, Lacan elucidates the understanding and usage of the symbolic function in psychoanalysis within the context of linguistics. From the field of linguistics Lacan borrowed the concept of the linguistic signifier as a similar (although not identical) concept to the Freudian concept of representation.

Nevertheless, Lacan's aphorism "the unconscious is structured like a language" should not be interpreted, in my opinion, as meaning that the structure of the unconscious is identical to the structure of social language. Rather, the unconscious has the structure of a different kind of language—the language of the unconscious or what Lacan called *linguisterie*. Social language is equivalent to the preconscious or to the unconscious in a descriptive sense. *Lalangue* as the text or language of the unconscious escapes the grammatical and formal organisation of discourse. The signifying chain is composed of key signifiers which are polyvocal and equivocal in nature. *Lalangue* thrives on the symbolic rather than the logical, grammatical or syntactic elements of language. I argue that this is similar although not identical to a non-dual use of language in Zen Buddhism.

Thus, Lacan can be understood when he says that analysis is about a searching for an experiential knowing that is not based on book knowledge. For example, the analysand often says: "I do not know what is wrong with me." The analysand knows that the symptom means something (has symbolic significance) although this something is unknown. In other words, in every session the analysand is looking for "unknown knowing" (*L'insu que sait*).

Lacan has coined the expression "subject supposed to know(ing)" (*sujet suppose savoir*, or the S.s.S. position) to account for the crucial place of knowing in the analytic situation. This is my translation of Lacan's concept. Alan Sheridan has translated it as the "subject supposed to know". However, such translation does not underscore the fact that the analyst is not the source of "knowing"; rather, the analyst is being attributed to knowing. The process of attribution of knowing is the reverse of the process of appropriation of the knowledge of the Other. Individuals usually appropriate knowledge, make it their own, and in the process construct a unique marketable ego. In the transference, the ego transfers the knowledge of the Other or their own unconscious knowing to the analyst. Instead of appropriating this knowledge, the analyst has to return this knowledge to both the dynamic and descriptive unconscious.

Sheridan's translation of the subject supposed to know concept emphasises the imaginary ego of the analyst who is expected to know something. By translating it as knowing, I emphasise the subject (of either analysand or analyst) who is secondary to knowing and a vehicle for the unconscious and the symbolic order. As in the case of the English word "understanding", the analyst is standing under the unknown-knowing within himself and within the analysand. I will distinguish between these two further on.

In analysis, the analyst should not respond to the analysand from the place of his own ego. If the analysand, in the transference, asks for a master of knowledge (subject supposed to know), the analyst should act from the place of not knowing, the equivalent of Socrates showing people that in fact they did know. But it is the unconscious subject of the analysand who knows, not the ego. Thus, in the concept of the subject supposed to know, the ego of the analysand supposes that the rational ego of the analyst has scientific knowledge, while in fact the analyst is being attributed the knowing of the subject that the ego of the analysand ignores.

The French expression for this concept has the advantage of containing the ambiguity of the double meaning under discussion (the knowledge of the ego and the knowing of the subject). If the ego of the analysand claims to know and that the analyst does not (desupposing the analyst of ego knowledge, "I know and you don't"), the analyst still responds without self-consciousness from the place of a knowing that does not know that it knows. The analyst needs to acknowledge that the individual knows but point in the direction of unconscious knowing by the subject and not the ego.

Thus, whether in the case of the analyst or the analysand, unknown-knowing appears from the unknown subject in the form of the innovative or surprising utterance which escapes the binary formal structure of conventional language. Thus, insight, thought of in this way, refers to cases in which a new, fresh meaning/signification emerges from a new combination/articulation of the relationship between the signifier and that which is signified.

Knowing, or "realisation" in Zen Buddhism (D. T. Suzuki, 1968), also refers to something that cannot be experienced by means of rational ego-discrimination. Strictly speaking, knowing is subtle and inconceivable, and therefore, there are no appropriate words to express it. Knowing comes from the depths of unconscious existence where there is no dual gap between subject and object. "What" is it that is known and "Who" is it that knows and "Where" is the knowing taking place? However, the existence of the Real as a plenum, as a higher order unity or as mindfulness, has to be distinguished from symbiosis or the illusory completion/unity provided by fetishes and imaginary phallic objects at the level of the ego. This distinction needs emphasis, because psychoanalysts often misunderstand Zen Buddhism or meditation because of a confusion of the different levels of analysis and experience. Moreover, Zen Buddhists often confuse merging with realisation. Just to say that all is one is not enough.

Insight in Zen refers to a direct perceptual realisation of the self-nature or the ultimate nature of the object. Zen meditation cultivates a themeless awareness or awareness without a specific content. If one asks who resides at the seat of this awareness, "Who" is knowing or aware, the answer is not given by any particular self-representation verbal, or otherwise. Buddha is not who we usually think we are, it is not the conscious ego. I have said that Buddha is a consciousness beyond ego-consciousness or self-consciousness. When Bodhidharma, the Indian Buddha who began the Zen school in China, was asked by Emperor Wu: "Who is standing before me?", Bodhidharma answered: "I don't know". This is a concrete example of how the knowing of the subject can only be affirmed in the negation (of the ego) of not knowing that one knows.

Buddha consciousness is a consciousness beyond ego-consciousness that does not know that it knows. Thus, it is possible to argue that

Buddha consciousness and the psychical position of the analyst both constitute variations of the seat of unknown-knowing. Making conscious the unconscious, on the basis of an awareness of Big mind rather than an ego-consciousness, refers to a paradoxical consciousness beyond consciousness rooted in the intrinsic nature of the subject.

In the act of interpretation on the basis of unknown-knowing, the analyst does not self-consciously mimic the unconscious but rather does what the unconscious does, not from a place of ego-knowledge or ego-ignorance (the dualistic "I know" and "I don't know" of ignorance), but instead from the psychical/topological space of a knowing subject that does not know that it knows (the non-dual "I don't know" of knowing or of a non-knowing which in not being the dual opposite of knowing, includes knowing in a dialectical moment).

Although the ego claims to know, in reality it does not know, because it is the subject that in truth knows. Conversely, although the ego claims not to know, in reality it does know because the subject knows. But the critical point is that the knowing of the subject can only be affirmed in the negation of even not knowing that one knows (I don't know that I don't know); of not being ego-conscious of our knowledge or of our no-knowledge which is another way of referring to unconscious knowing.

Winnicott defined the true self as an inherited potential that is experienced as a continuity of being (1960, p. 46). Following this definition, Bollas (1989) wrote that:

> That inherited set of dispositions that constitutes the true self is a form of knowledge which has obviously not been thought, even though it is "there" already at work in the life of the neonate who brings this knowledge with him as he perceives, organizes, remembers, and uses his object world. I have termed this form of knowledge the unthought known to specify, amongst other things, the dispositional knowledge of the true self.

(p. 10)

Bollas associates the unthought known with the instinctual knowledge, for example, which predisposes a bee to build a beehive without recurrence to well thought-out inductive or deductive logical reasoning. He adds that the actualisation of this instinctual unthought known or latent knowledge in human beings depends entirely on the maturational environment provided by the parents. In addition, Bollas points out that:

Infants also learn rules for being and relating that are conveyed through the mother's logic of care, much of which has not been mentally processed. Children often live in family moods or practices that are beyond comprehension, even if they are partners in the living of such knowledge.

(p. 213)

However, a problem with Bollas's definition is that he seems to confound natural and cultural processes. Rules of being and relating fall within the scope of a cultural symbolic order. In addition, as aforementioned, he presumes that an instinctual and natural true self or an environmentally produced false self is solely a function of the maturational environment provided by the parents. But what about the divided and dual subjectivity produced by structural cultural rules?

In separating human beings from the natural world, culture introduces rules of a different order than those of the regularity found in nature. Culture separates the subject from the immediacy of knowing and being found in nature and non-human species. This separation produces a division and a duality between nature and culture, desire and the law, good and bad. Moreover, ever since such separation, a longing remains to return to the immediacy and the participation in the natural order of things. Thus, Bollas's definition of instinctual knowing or Winnicott's concept of the true self as an inherited biological potential refer to a holistic view of the natural/biological world and of the unthought known acquired in the process of evolution. In many ways, such view coincides with an Eastern view of nature as an expression of the Tao or Buddha-nature.

However, in the animal world, animals eat each other and are subject to the rule of force, violence and domination. If anything, Buddha-nature is a non-dual dimension of existence where the duality of human nature and animal nature, law and desire, are reconciled or entangled after having gone through the alienation of symbolic forms and cultural mediations. Buddhism seeks an immediacy or directness of experience that is a higher order synthesis beyond the positive immediacy of desire and the negative mediation of the law. In animals, this immediacy is also there, but it quickly turns into the instinctual activity associated with eating and the fight/flight response. As a Zen saying goes: first, there are mountains and rivers, then there are no mountains and no rivers, and finally, there are mountains and rivers once again. From this perspective, as aforementioned, there is no prescription for raising children into a natural and effortless enlightened true self.

In human beings, as Freud and Lacan taught, the natural order of instinct is mediated by and known through symbolic pathways and the network of language. What is human is the order of law and prohibition that, as Lacan argued, is coextensive with the order of language, symbolisation, and kinship. Thus, there is no way of avoiding in culture the condition of a divided subjectivity, between an ego and a subject, a false self and a true self. Cultural forms determine what will be allowed and disallowed, desired and forbidden, for the subject.

It is easy to confuse imaginary unity with the One of the Real. The natural unity of spontaneous instinctual knowing in human beings is lost in the process whereby an instinct becomes a representational drive pitted against an opposing symbolic form. Imaginary instinctual knowing is split into a knowing of desire and a knowing contained within symbolic forms, language and the knowledge of reason. In addition, Bollas's concept of the unthought known does not include the phenomena of repressed or forgotten knowing or of unconscious thinking known to the subject but not the ego.

Following Lacan, the concept of unknown-knowing (*L'insu que sait*) conveys the paradoxical nature of knowing as well as the possibility of theorising repressed knowing, unconscious thinking as well as non-repressed knowing contained within symbolic forms and the more general activity of biological and physical life processes in the universe. The expression (unknown-knowing) sounds awkward or strange because we are used to using a subject and presuming an ego when we speak. Knowledge has to be known to a knower. But knowing can also be thought of as a process or an activity that is taking place without requiring the existence of an ego. Such knowing also includes thinking activity as exemplified in Bion's expression: "thoughts without a thinker." Bollas's concept of the unthought known appears to assume that once something is thought it is automatically known to the conscious ego.

I stated above that the analysand does not know about an associative chain of signifiers or representations that convey a knowing apparently ignored by the ego. The analysand knows that the symptom means something (has symbolic significance) although this something is unknown to the ego. This type of unknown-knowing on the side of the analysand refers to unconscious knowing in the sense of the repressed. Something is unknown in the sense of the repressed unconscious. In the transference, the analyst is unconsciously presumed to be the holder of a repressed subjective knowing of the analysand under the veils of the ego-to-ego alliance where the analyst is supposed to have professional and technical knowledge about psychical processes (i.e., repression).

The professional or technical ego-knowledge of the analyst is not what facilitates the process of the treatment. In analysis, the analyst is working with the core of his/her subjective being. Herein unknown-knowing on the side of the analyst, refers not only to the analyst having been an analysand, but to an unknown- knowing not in the sense of repressed unconscious knowing but in the sense of the consciousness beyond self-consciousness described above. In consciousness beyond consciousness, the heteronomous autonomy of the unconscious that produces symptoms and divides the ego is transformed into the autonomous heteronomy of the subject, the surprising, spontaneous, unconscious workings of Big mind.

When the analyst functions out of an attitude of not knowing, in the non-dual sense of a not-knowing which includes knowing by the subject and not the ego, he/she becomes a vehicle for the non-repressed unknown-knowing and understanding contained within the Symbolic, or what Lacan calls the treasure chest of the signifier. Unknown-knowing here includes both the repressed signifying chain of the analysand and the participation of the analyst in the larger unknown (unconscious in a descriptive sense) structure of language and the Symbolic. In addition, the "I don't know" of unknown- knowing also extends into the experiential mystery of an unknown Real emptiness beyond Symbolic forms and beyond the knowledge derived from the combined action of reason and the experience of the senses.

Aphanisis and epiphany in Zen and Lacanian psychoanalysis

I have stated that within Lacanian theory one can distinguish between a preconscious, rational and conventional language (unconscious in a descriptive sense) and the language of the unconscious and that this difference is also related to another distinction which Lacan makes between an ego-based imaginary use of language and the function of language in psychoanalysis as a function of the subject of the unconscious. I argue that it is in this latter sense that language can articulate an emancipatory function rather than the limiting or conventional function ascribed to language by Buddhism.

This line of analysis also provides an answer to the aforementioned contradiction in Lacan's thought of on the one hand defining reality in terms of language and postulating a Real beyond language on the other. Conventional language refers to social reality as constructed within (preconscious) language, as a function of the relationship between one signifier and another signifier (S_1-S_2), whereas the language of the unconscious refers to psychical reality in the sense of both repressed signifiers and to a meaning or signified beyond language (S_2-S_1 in the former and S_1-S_0 in the latter).

In addition, this distinction also addresses another contradiction within the Lacanian corpus. Lacan theorises the benevolent action of the signifier that separates the subject from the immediacy of a maternal imaginary or symbiosis. However, symbolic castration under the signifier, although normal and normalising, produces an irrevocable split, division, and alienation within the subject. This is Lacan's version of Freud's well-known pessimism: the symbolic subject always remains a lacking, dissatisfied, and unfulfilled subject.

Lacan's position oscillates between these two conceptions of language. His conceptual stance is consistent with the concept of nothingness found in secular existentialism and in contemporary depictions of character pathology. In self disorders, the sense of emptiness and of a lack of self-identity is not attributed to a basic existential condition but to a parenting fault or defect. If only the parents had provided good-enough mirroring and recognition, the self would have been naturally whole and integrated. In contradistinction to this perspective, Lacan and existentialism conceives of negative nothingness as an existential condition and as a function of the hole left within the subject by an inevitable absence of the object and the insatiability of human desire. The absence of the object of desire represents the presence of a negative nothingness that the signifier cannot fill because language is impotent to represent the Real.

A double negativity can be discerned within human subjectivity. There is the hole left by the absence of the object and the hole or missing place within the Symbolic to represent the Real. Lacan argues that the paternal metaphor (the Name of the Father) as a key organiser of language, or as a symbolic identification, is used as a stop-gap for this hole or missing place within the Symbolic. When the parental or paternal metaphor fails, which it inevitably does, then this existential predicament gives rise to all kinds of fanaticisms, ethnocentrisms, and dogmatic views whether secular or scientific. The only way out of a regression from the Symbolic to the Imaginary is to turn the identification towards the end of identification (from S_1 to S_0 rather than from S_1 to S_2) or to drive the identification towards the empty place where the Symbolic meets the Real.

Lacan explains the crisis of the family and of the social order in terms of the twilight or decline of the function of the father in Western civilisation. But even in well-established patriarchal orders, human beings are forever attempting to close the gap of negative emptiness with all kinds of objects, ideals, and ideologies. This is what Lacan considers the imaginary use of language and Buddhism envisions as the limitations and dualism of words and language. The imaginary function of language is also described by the concept of the imaginary phallus that invests the self and its objects with an illusory sense of narcissistic completion. In this case, and in Zen language, the finger is not the moon. The finger, words, and the signifier, conceal the moon or the direct experience of the Real.

Language can either lead to the Imaginary, to the signifier as semblance (of another signifier), or reveal the Real within the Symbolic where letters and words are semblances/vehicles for the mystery of being (being as wondrous emptiness). The latter is what I call the emancipatory, liberating, or evocative (Kim's realisational) function of language.

Buddhism and the negative theology tradition in the West both have a concept of a positive and creative emptiness. Such positive emptiness allows for a different definition of the Real, and hence for a different interaction between the Real and the Symbolic. I believe that this view can also be found implicit in Lacan's work although under-represented within his key well-known formulations. The positive Real refers to a bodily experience of wellbeing and meaning beyond words and language (the Other *jouissance* of sublimation).

Language as a medium lacks the words to represent this experience. I say this knowing full well that there are schools of Buddhism and other forms of spirituality that make plentiful use of language to describe the benefits and advantages of meditation or spiritual practice. However, these descriptions are still within the duality or imaginary use of language and within dual forms of unity experience. People can speak about being enlightened or compassionate when in reality, and when push comes to shove, they are still under the effect of delusion and hatred.

It is in this sense that Zen experience can be described as being empty of signification yet it has a meaning beyond language or beyond meaning and no meaning. Sawaki Roshi, a contemporary Japanese Zen teacher (1880–1965), described Zen as "good for nothing". Instead of describing Zen as the wonderful thing we would expect from the Imaginary use of language, Roshi appeals to the primary antithetical significance of language to point to non-duality. With the imaginary word, we speak but we don't actually say anything. The imaginary word is the empty or idle word, while the interaction between the signifier and the Real as a plenum, as mindfulness, produces the senseless full word. Turning words turn the medicine wheel of enlightenment and of the poetic function.

In Lacanian psychoanalysis, the experience of the body is approximated not with yogic postures and breathing but through what Lacan calls the materiality of the signifier as a representation of the drive. This can be understood as a total determination of the body by language, a perspective that is often associated with a critique of Lacanian theory and practice as overly intellectual and attributing too much importance to language. However, in this latter view language is seen as something separate from the body and from experience.

In my opinion, the problem is not of language but of self-consciousness or of the small mind that ignores the amplitude of both bodily experience and how the Real and the body are implicated in language (the Real within Symbolic). The body that is restrained or controlled by symbolic values and practices (that is, meditation in the lotus posture) can also be viewed as a symbolic body or a true non-substantial/spiritual body. The signifier and the name of the father (that is, Buddha) organise the materiality of the body. The signifier of the name of the father is an embodied form of signification, what Lacan calls a *jouis-sense*: an enjoyment or pathos of meaning. However, the signifier both inhibits and facilitates the *jouissance* of the body. It inhibits one kind of *jouissance* but facilitates another.

The analyst needs to use the language of the Other in the double sense of the words of the analysand and the place of his own symbolic function. The latter is unconscious or preconscious to the analyst at least in a descriptive sense. The analyst does not speak with her ego or her small self but with the words of the Other.

There are two aspects to the words or speech of the Other: how the ego of the analyst is cancelled by both the words of the analysand and his own symbolic unconscious. But the words of the analysand that the analyst uses in the practice of interpretation are not the analysand's ego-statements but the unconscious signifiers that appear within the dross of ordinary speech. In fact, such unconscious signifiers often appear to contradict and alienate the statements of the ego. Thanks to the personal analysis, and the resulting ego loss, the analyst can tolerate being cancelled or "duped" by the Other. Again, the Other here means both focusing on the words of the analysand rather than his/her own and if the analyst uses his/her own words they are enunciated from the place of no-self.

With this formulation I am establishing equivalence between the Other and the Buddhist concept of no-self. Just like small self means no other/Other; other/Other means no-self. But in either Buddhism or psychoanalysis, the subject does not disappear in its true sense. In Buddhism, no-self means true self or Big self; and in psychoanalysis, the act of interpretation cancels the ego but supports the insubstantial, evanescent subject. The effectiveness of the analyst is derived from the symbolic function as a pivot of the subject and subjectivity in general. A pivotal moment in the analytical situation brings forth the true meaning of the subject. When, on one side, the ego is cancelled either by words or by the silence within words, the subject appears as unary signifier/signification on the other.

> We can locate this Vorstellungreprasentanz in our schema of the original mechanisms of alienation, in that signifying coupling that enables us to conceive that the subject appears first in the Other, in so far as the first signifier, the unary signifier, emerges in the field of the Other and represents the subject for another signifier, which other signifier has as its effect the aphanisis of the subject. Hence the division of the subject—when the subject appears somewhere as meaning, he is manifested elsewhere as "fading," as disappearance. There is, then, one might say, a matter of life and death between the unary signifier and the subject, qua binary signifier, cause of his disappearance.
>
> (Lacan, 1964, p. 218)

For Lacan, the subject is helpless in the face of the Other and at the mercy of the pre-existing signifying structure of language. It is in reference to the symbolic Other, and to his formulation that the unconscious is the discourse of the Other, that Lacan (1966a) highlights what can be called the involuntary and unconscious functioning of language. He writes further: "The priority of the signifier over the subject is what Freud's experience teaches us ... . The signifier plays and wins before the subject can realize it ... . The illuminating sparkle of wit illustrates the division of the subject within himself" (p. 175).

However, the autonomous heteronomy of the signifier and the unconscious in relationship to the ego needs to be distinguished from the heteronomous autonomy of the subject under the operation that Lacan called separation. Otherwise, we remain subjected to the tyranny of the desire of the Other and unable to formulate any plausible notion of emancipation or change whatsoever.

Two levels of change could be distinguished at this point. The first level of change corresponds to the dynamism of the structure. A structure is in perpetual movement and transformation but the elements of the structure remain the same and are always found in a different place. For example, letters combine into different words leading to new names for similar things. For example, a same teaching can be packaged and repackaged under different names and persons who claim authorship for the same teaching under a different cover and title. This formulation can serve to describe much of what is published in spiritual literature, self-help texts, coaching, management, and so on. Sometimes a book itself can have the same structure: each chapter says the same thing albeit under a different title.

A tradition, a lineage, or a scholarly text differs from the above by virtue of reference, quotation, and citation. A name is placed in reference to other names that function as signifiers for the subject. Here we find the examples of writers writing within a tradition to disseminate the values, practices, and ideas of a particular school of thought. Finally, the second level of change is found when new ideas emerge within a particular tradition rather than at the expense of a tradition. In other words, by fulfilling/following the terms found within a tradition to their ultimate consequences, something new can emerge from within the tradition that revolutionises or evolves its own structure.

What is being advanced is not the individual although the permutations of the structure advance and realise the self (as Dogen put it). When the self is sufficiently and efficiently cancelled by the Other (traditional structure), then within the lack or emptiness of the subject, the lack or emptiness of the structure is realised (as well as vice versa), leading to the emergence of a new signifier/subject within the same. This is what I call the heteronomous autonomy of the subject, to distinguish it from both ego autonomy, and the heteronomy of the signifier. This concept is also consistent with Lacan's notions of separation (*se parere*: giving birth to oneself), a new ego in the Real, the unary trace, and the being or headlessness of the subject.

The cancellation of the self or the subject by the structure is an abstract way of speaking about something that often takes place in the imaginary dimension of group and family life. This is the beating that Stephen suffered under his peers in Joyce's (1916) *A Portrait of the Artist as a Young Man* (p. 82) and that Lacan theorised as the identification with the *sinthome* and the emergence of a new ego in the Real. A similar example is found in the biblical story of Joseph and his brothers. By telling his brothers that he had dreamt that the sun and the moon bowed to him or that his sheaf of corn was bigger than theirs, Joseph contributed to the emergence of envy and jealousy in his brothers. The latter reached a boiling point and resulted in Joseph being thrown into a pit and sold into slavery in Egypt. Joseph's pit or hole represents what the subject is within the Symbolic as a breach or hole in discourse. It is this nothing and the bubbles that arise from it that cause the movement of signification and the transformations within the master-servant dialectic. The mother's beloved child is the one that needs to be barred by the signifier and the process of signification.

A similar example is offered by the Oxfordian theory of Shakespeare authorship which Freud endorsed. The Oxfordian theory proposes that Edward de Vere (the Earl of Oxford) may have been the author of the plays and poems attributed to Shakespeare. In the film *Anonymous*, the Earl of Oxford is also depicted as both the son and lover of Queen Elizabeth. In the sixteenth century, appearing learned could discredit a nobleman or a court figure. An aristocrat, especially one in potential line of succession to the Crown, had to be a soldier/statesman/landlord, not a scholar or a writer. Scholarly writings could not appear to contradict or expose the shortcomings of authority and the monarchy. This was that century's version of "doctoral ignorance" or of the wish for wisdom to be concealed or suppressed in some fashion. Freud thought that the name Shakespeare referred to the name *Jacques Pierre* (to say that Shakespeare was French is not unlike saying that Moses was an Egyptian) but more importantly, for my purposes, the name Shakespeare can be rendered as "Shake Spear". Not only is the ambition (spear) of the true concealed author shaken by the pseudonym or metaphor (one name for another), but also the spear, as a metaphor for the military power of the Culture, suffers a similar fate. To comply with the demands of the Other, the author gives up the fame and power of the name (making a name for himself) but in turn the power of the written word ends up transforming the values of the institution or of the Other. Eventually the culture of true nobility triumphs over the culture of institutional power and domination. Finally, "shake the spear" is also a metaphor for the phallic function. Shake the spear can represent either a form of phallic *jouissance* or an antithetical metaphor for symbolic castration.

Additional examples of the heteronomous autonomy of the subject can be found in the lives of Moses and Jesus, Freud and Lacan. Moses had to escape the ire of the Egyptians, and later he barely escaped death under the very hand of G-d. In the biblical story, Zipporah, Moses's non-Jewish wife, quickly circumcised their son to avert the killing of her husband. In the Gospel, Jesus finally ended suffering the fate of the *Akedah* or the binding of Isaac. The father killed his son, and in the process his own Law was transformed for the generations.

Freud for his part suffered death threats under the Nazis, as well as rejection by the medical and social authorities of his time. Lacan suffered a similar predicament to Freud's under the very international organisation that Freud helped establish, as well as under the authorities that reigned over the academic institutions of his time. In the cases of Jesus, Freud, and Lacan, the hero's hubris played a role in their suffering in the hands of others. Jesus was the son of man or of G-d, Freud was his mother's golden "Sigi", he identified with Joseph, and saw himself as a conquistador of the new territory of the unconscious. Finally, Roudinesco (1993, p. 548) tells a story about how Lacan wanted to have a private visit to the Metropolitan in New York simply by announcing that he was in town. One of his hosts had to call saying that it was Sartre rather than Lacan who was visiting and Lacan never found out about the deception or the relative anonymity of his name.

In the case of Siddhartha, the harsh realities of life and the effects of signification on his own body provided the beating. He wanted to find an answer to life's suffering and this symbolic question led him to bind his own body in the practice of meditation in the lotus posture. Although after practising on his own for a long time, and once enlightened, Buddha was accepted and adored/honored by his peers, the path that he discovered, Buddhism, suffered a similar fate in India. Buddhism spread as a world religion owing to the fact that it was banned and nearly destroyed in its home country (by Islam and Hinduism). From India, it spread throughout the East and now to the West.

The symbolic order is a source of both alienation and enlightenment for the subject. Alienation because the subject becomes subordinated to the law of culture and the effects of the signifier but enlightenment because, with the renunciations and symbolic losses imposed by culture and language, the subject gains access to cultural symbolic forms which free the subject from the lower-order immediacy/unity of the ego and the Imaginary. Without the Real, however, the Symbolic within the Real also covers the Real with the lies and deceptions of words and speech. Words cannot convey the truth of truth.

Thus, I propose a use of the concept of aphanisis differing somewhat from that promulgated by Lacan. Lacan only considers aphanisis as a form of alienation and division of the subject. The symbolic frees the subject from the imaginary but also leaves him/her with the subjection/alienation/division produced by language and the subjection to the law and the Name of the Father. The concept of aphanisis needs to be considered as one of the terms of a binary pair for which the concept of epiphany constitutes the other. Life and death, the ego and the subject, appearance and disappearance, aphanisis and epiphany, need to be viewed as inextricably woven together in such a way that you cannot have one without the other.

I propose that the Real allows for a unity of experience, for the One of the unary trace that needs to be distinguished from both imaginary symbiotic unity and from the function of a symbolic unit/number within a series of signifying elements. As soon as we have one, we have two or duality because, as Lacan insisted, language and formal logic are organised as a binary order. The experience of meditative oneness rather needs to be located on the side of positive emptiness, of the zero that makes one and two possible. Zero in this case is the Real emptiness of the subject that lies outside and inside the Symbolic. The One as zero also produces separation by disqualifying the unity of the Imaginary, and by representing a dimension of truth beyond the legitimacy of words and formal logic.

The Real is within the Symbolic because the subject is nothing but the inter-connecting link and support of a symbolic structure. The Real is outside the Symbolic because neither a single element (a letter, word, or phrase) nor the totality of linguistic or representational elements or things constitutes the Real subject. The latter is the space in-between or the void which the signifying chain encircles and attempts to capture. Epiphany, then, is the experience of emptiness and release contained not only within "spiritual" symbolic forms but also within the material rims of the erogenous zones of the body (oral, anal, vaginal, phallic, etc.).

The aphanisis (disappearance) of the ego results in the epiphany (appearance) of the non-substantial subject (or of the no-self which is true self). When Lacan says that "when the subject appears somewhere as meaning, he is manifested elsewhere as 'fading,' as disappearance", this should be interpreted not only as a division resulting in a dual subject ($), but as a dialectic between the ego and the subject (8). When the subject appears as a signifier, the imaginary ego vanishes, and the Real subject is revealed as unborn.

The imaginary I (or rational ego) is not the agent of insight, rather it is the subject who bears witness to the lightening of wit and knowing contained within the treasure chest of the signifier. In the experience of psychoanalytic insight, it is the signifier that realises and illuminates the subject. The light and knowing contained within the signifier divide the subject, as Lacan points out. But this division exists only from the imaginary perspective of the ego who wishes to identify itself as the master of his/her own house.

The subject is both two and one and neither two and one. The subject is two because human subjectivity is divided between a symbolic subject and an imaginary ego. The subject is one because the ego lives under the illusory/imaginary unity of self-engenderment and autonomy and because the subject of the signifier is the "countable and namable one" within a group or battery of subjects or signifiers (that is, a number and a name in a class). But the subject is neither one nor two for the reasons aforementioned with regard to the Real subject or the One of the Real.

The determination and alienation produced in language and by language as an Other to the self or ego, needs to be understood as a function of the imaginary relationship which the ego has with language and the Symbolic. For the ego who wishes to be the master of his/her own house, language and the unconscious appear as a burdensome, ego-dystonic, symptom-producing determining structure. The ego wishes to stake a small claim on the Symbolic by saying "I speak, therefore I am", whereas from a broader perspective, the ego is only a drop, or a wave at most, in the large ocean of historical and symbolic experience (the Other).

Conversely, when the ego drops the imaginary presumption of being the source of speech ("I speak where I am not"), then the subject becomes a vehicle for the ocean of *lalangue* and the symbolic order ("I am where I don't speak with my ego"). The imaginary unit of the wave ego gives way to the primordial structure that unifies the subject as a Real and Symbolic subject. The symbolic subject becomes a link that supports the functioning and interdependence of a larger structure. This I have defined as the heteronomous autonomy of the true subject that actually constitutes a centred subjectivity without a subject. True subject is no-ego.

CHAPTER FIVE

Turning words and images of the unseen: symbolic uses of the Imaginary and the Real in Lacan, Zen, and Jewish Kabbalah

The Symbolic in Freud and Lacan

Lacan's aphorism that the unconscious is the discourse of the Other highlights the involuntary and unconscious function of language. Lacan (1966b) writes: "The priority of the signifier over the subject is what Freud's experience teaches us .... The signifier plays and wins before the subject can realize it .... The illuminating sparkle of wit illustrates the division of the subject within himself" (p. 175, the translation is mine). The linguistic signifier, like the intuitive function, has the quality of speaking through us.

Despite the fact that the reality principle governs thinking via words (words are logical elements) and that speech may be logically organised and controlled, sometimes enunciations appear to be inspired directly (without the mediation of inductive or deductive reason) by a latent symbolic meaning imposing itself in the creation of thought. Freud (1900) called such ideas as unconscious involuntary purposive ideas; by means of such ideas the unconscious governs the course of associations in abstract thinking, artistic creation and the production of jokes. For Lacan, unconscious or involuntary purposive ideas are an effect and function of the linguistic signifier.

Lacan conceives of the unconscious subject as an effect of the operation of signifiers. The unconscious and the signifier speak through the subject. The thing speaks for itself or "It" speaks in me. In this respect, Lacan modified and permutated the Cartesian *cogito ergo sum* by stating "I think where I am not" instead of the classical "I think, therefore I am". A creative pronouncement or enunciation is intransitive with regard to the subject of enunciation: who is speaking and about what? Who is the subject and "What" the object or "What" is the subject and "Who" the object. Consequently, the analyst aimlessly aims towards his or her own unknown knowing and responds to the analysand from the place of the free, automatic, intuitive association.

In free association, the signifier is attempting to apprehend a (No) Thing beyond signification. This No-thing that escapes signification is the Lacanian register or dimension of the Real. Psychoanalysis mostly operates over the Real from within the symbolic order (from the Real to the Symbolic), but in Zen and perhaps in Kabbalah as well, there is a leaping forth beyond symbolic thought resulting in a direct plunging into the ocean of the Real (from the Symbolic to the Real, from the land of the signifier into the ocean of the Real). The second part of the Lacanian proverb just mentioned, addresses this reality: "I think where I am not and I am where I do not think." Zen works with the Real beyond thought within the Real itself. Herein human experience acquires a further dimension beyond the play of the signifier within the symbolic order.

The relationship between experience and language, the Real and the Symbolic, can be understood by conceiving it as a form of experience/structure dialectic. Lefèvre (1975) has pointed out that experience can only be described by language even though language already filters experience thru something other than itself. Language does not exhaust experience itself. However, language does not exhaust experience not due to all experience being outside the Symbolic and the Imaginary. Rather language does not exhaust experience because experience includes an extra-social or extra-conventional realm that cannot be fully grasped in-itself by language. The range or spectrum of subjective experience includes a non-dual register which is transrational or beyond thought and speech (Real). This chapter propounds that the inclusion and articulation of such a register of experience is the meeting place between Lacan, Zen Buddhism, and Jewish Kabbalah.

On the other hand, experience also is the point of articulation of symbolic or linguistic structures. Conventional reality appears represented within language or is given by language and at the same time language appears incapable of representing further dimensions of reality beyond language. However, this extra-linguistic experiential domain can only be expressed thru a different and unconventional or extra-social use of speech and language usually not expressed in ordinary and conventional conversation. In this respect, the extra-linguistic realm within experience and the extra-social and unconventional use of speech and language seem to meet at this level. The ordinary meaning of words has to be transgressed in order to say something of reality beyond words.

This is what Ricoeur (1991) calls semantic innovation, peculiar predication and deviant naming. Thus, although Ricoeur and the school of hermeneutics do not recognise a Real outside the Symbolic, in contrast to Lacan the former theorises a difference between a conventional and unconventional use of language. At least initially, Lacan did not sufficiently differentiate between the unconscious and preconscious, unconventional and conventional levels and usages of language. He seemed to imply that all language is unconscious at least in a descriptive sense. Later he came to thematise this difference via his concept of *lalangue* as the language of the Real unconscious. The Real can only be expressed or brought forth by a different use of language and the Symbolic.

Thus, both the analyst's interpretation and the analysand's free association require a differential use of words to evoke something beyond conventional speech. The method of free association is similar to what was traditionally associated in religion with intuition and paralogical or transrational symbolic thinking within the reality of the body itself. Thus, both in spirituality and psychoanalysis the evocation of a transrational and non-conventional realm not only requires a different use of language but also a more essential and primary form of ideation not under the control of the conscious cognitive ego. Nevertheless, there are similarities and differences in how psychoanalysis and spirituality conceive of the Real.

The concept of the Real in Lacan, Zen, and Kabbalah

I have mentioned that Lacan defines the Real as that register of experience that escapes or is outside symbolisation or cannot be said by language. At other times, however, Lacan (1966b) refers to the Real in terms of the real of science: "everything that is real is rational and everything that is rational real" (p. 218). This statement goes hand in hand with the alleged rationalism of psychoanalysis and its emphasis on words and the Symbolic. The Real only becomes a phenomenological reality "to the extent that it becomes a word which hits the target" (idem, p. 71).

My thesis here is that the Real can be experienced in-itself, for example, through the practice of meditation, but that because it is a register outside language and symbolisation, its manifestation within the Symbolic requires a different use of language from that of formal logical language and the language of science. Moreover, following Ricoeur's definition of poetic metaphor as non-instrumental, one can also think of the use of the Symbolic by the Real as the non-activity of symbolic or linguistic activity. Such words do not have instrumental action as their goal or purpose. In this respect, the Chinese *Wu Wei*, or non-action (not no-action or inaction) can be considered as the quintessential characterisation of the Real.

A deviant, innovative utterance plays with the binary structure of formal language to make it say something that escapes the determining duality of the Symbolic. Classical Zen examples of this can be found in the following *koans:* a student once asked a Zen teacher, "What do you think in zazen (meditation)?" The Zen teacher responded, "Think not thinking" (*Hishiryo*). The monk asked, "How do you think not thinking?" The master said, "Non-thinking" (Katagiri, 1988). The Real is reached through thinking without thoughts, not thinking but thinking. Beyond rational thought returns as absolute intuitive thought. In another example, the Zen teacher asks: "What do you hit in order to get the cart to move, the horse or the cart?" The ordinary dualistic response would be the horse, of course! But the Zen teacher responds that you hit the cart instead! In other words, you have to do something with the practice if you want to affect the mind or the theory. Further Zen examples of peculiar non-dual predication would be phrases such as the sidewalk is walking me instead of I am walking on the sidewalk (the I is the ego, whereas the me stands for the true subject); or practice is practising instead of I am practising; or Who is me instead of who am I? or No-thing is All instead of the Lacanian nothing is All; or G-d is non-existence instead of God does not exist; and so on.

Within the Kabbalah of Abraham Abulafia (the master of the letter), structural language needs to be broken down in order to strive for an experience of ultimate reality. The fact that the Hebrew language is well known for its polysemous nature is intrinsically related to the twin fact that the study of Torah through the ages led to the development of numerous exegetical and hermeneutic devices aimed at plummeting and bringing forth the deepest level possible in the text. Techniques such as *gematria, notarikon,* and *temurah* are all aimed at both braking and elevating the order of conventional social language so as to have the Real be said by language. For example, *temurah* changes words by changing the order of the letters. Bakan (1958) cites the example of the *Sefer Yetzira* where "we have *oneg,* which means pleasure, and *nega* that means pain, the same letters in different order" (p. 267). In this instance, *oneg* and *nega* play with the signifier to match the non-dual use of language described above. The same word is used to describe opposite terms. A similar antithetical meaning and homophony can be found between the Sanskrit words *sukkha* (pleasure) and *dukkha* (pain).

This particular pair of opposites is significant for our purposes because both Zen and Lacan bring them into close relation to one another. In Zen, and Buddhism in general, Nirvana cannot be reached without overcoming and going beyond the duality of pain and pleasure (Freud's pleasure principle). Lacan developed his concept of *jouissance* to represent what lies beyond the pleasure principle and wherein pain and pleasure become the two sides of a single principle. Pain and pleasure always refer to one another although the pleasure principle wants to seek pleasure and avoid pain.

The word *jouissance* has been left in French because it describes an antithetical or non-dual meaning that cannot be captured by the English word joy, for example. Lacan (1974) distinguished between three forms of *jouissance* and explicitly associated what I and others have termed the Other *jouissance* with so-called mystical experience and female sexuality. Thus, in the Kabbalistic example the symbolic order of the letters (*oneg* and *nega*) is combined and permutated in such a way so as to access an experience and understanding of the Real (of *jouissance*). Conversely in a descending moment such experience (of the Real) is used to maximise the interpretation of the Symbolic since "knowledge of the inner aspects of the Torah, is conditional upon the attainment of the highest intellectual faculty, the prophetic intellect" (Idel, 1988, p. 237). The prophetic intellect would be the beyond thought in Zen which is revealed through intuition.

Two conceptions of metaphor: signifiers in place of other signifiers $(S_1$-$S_2)$ and signifiers where the signified is in the Real of jouissance $(S_1$-$S_0)$

I have spoken about the Real within the Symbolic as what allows for the emergence of new signifiers and prevents the Other from becoming a static and purely conventional or traditional/fundamentalist order. It is the Real as a *vacuum plenum* that turns the wheel of interpretation and begets/releases the sparks and light of new poetic significations. Poetry, just like dream-images or visions, has a navel that opens out on to the unknown, on to the empty kernel of being or parabeing. Turning and playing with words opens up a dimension of experience (the empty Real) that escapes the closure and circularity of discourse.

Key signifiers or what Zen calls turning words, with antithetical or non-dual meaning, gather the significations under a unifying principle that generates and transcends meaning at the same time. The *vacuum plenum*, is the unifying principle that generates and transcends meaning at the same time. From the wellsprings of the Real, words are reorganised to generate a new meaning beyond words. For example, when Zen ancestor Joshu was asked "What is the depth of the Deep?", he answered, "What depth of the deep should I talk about, the seven of seven or the eight of eight?". In this example, the innumerable is represented as numerable (the seven of seven), emptiness by form and the inside by the outside. Joshu is emphasising the aspect of "Emptiness is Form" or of the Real manifesting or appearing within the Symbolic. Another way of putting it is that since emptiness is emptiness (devoid of concept) and form is form, emptiness has to be revealed within the Symbolic world of words, ciphers, and knowledge. This is similar to Lacan's teaching that the unconscious is outside and not in the depths or is not a form of depth psychology. As Dogen puts it, the feet are walking in the bottom of the ocean while the mouth is speaking above the surface.

Furthermore, at the boundary between the Symbolic and the Real or as close as one can get to the Real within the Symbolic, the subject is a shout, the sound of the horn, the sound of a pebble striking a bamboo, the clapping of hands, a single senseless stroke of the brush, the lion's roar. Here the subject is a signifier without a signified or a case where the meaning is not in the words or the signified is within the Real.

But contrary to delusion or psychosis, the empty subject of the Real or the non-ego is precisely what establishes, forges, and supports the link between two signifiers and weaves together the net of the symbolic order and the symbolic and cohesive functioning of the subject. In psychosis, the opposite is true: the severing of the link between subjects and between signifiers renders the subject prey to the tyranny of the Imaginary.

The interaction between the Imaginary and the Symbolic can be understood in two ways or in two directions. First, there is the imaginary use of the Symbolic, and second, the symbolic use of the Imaginary. The language of the ego would be a good example of the first type of relation between the Imaginary and the Symbolic. The ego states, "I am, I speak", and misrecognises that the self-imputed statements are quotations or permutations of the words of the Other. This represents a case in which the Symbolic is subsumed or is operating at the service of the Imaginary.

In addition, by clinging to fantasy life and the objects of desire the ego can defend against the experience of lack or emptiness within the Symbolic. Fantasies constitute imaginary interpretations of the Symbolic or of the Real. For example, the fantasy and desire for a forbidden symbolic object. The subject could have just as well desired a permissible object, but no, it is the forbidden that is most fervently desired. Fantasies as imaginary interpretations of the Symbolic are to be differentiated from Symbolic uses of the Imaginary and the Real. Moreover, an imaginary interpretation of the Real refers to what Freud called the uncanny and to "phantasms" (imaginary ghosts) proper.

An example of the uncanny would be the experience of an analysand whom his mother involved in an incestuous sexual relationship beginning when he was nine years old. He then begun seeing a beam of light in his room projected unto the wall in the circle of which he would see the laughing face of a demon that he took to be the devil. In this example, the experience of the uncanny or of the Real appearing within the Imaginary can be distinguished from an incest fantasy located in the intersection between the Symbolic and the Imaginary. In addition, Lacan also linked the uncanny with unspeakable traumatic experiences that appear as ominous and hazardous intrusions from an inexplicable Real. Here the incest fantasy has become an uncanny incest violation that I locate within the intersection between the Imaginary and the Real.

Conversely, when the Imaginary operates at the service of the Symbolic to represent the Real, the metaphoric subject can be described, for example, as a flower or a pillar between heaven and earth. In this case, the subject is both a signifier and an image as a category of the imagination in the positive sense not of illusion or misrecognition but of facilitating the access to both the Symbolic and the Real. This, in my opinion, is to be distinguished from the negative category whereby the Symbolic is subsumed under the Imaginary. Paintings, for example, constitute symbolic uses of the Imaginary to represent the Real.

In addition, many scientific discoveries have often been described through the categories of the positive imagination as a kind of light-dawning experience. Einstein discovered the theory of relativity through a thought experiment where he visualised himself riding in a beam of light. When Darwin's theory of evolution hit him he said it seemed as if the scales fell from his eyes. Guttenberg described the idea of the printing press as coming like a beam of light. Another physicist was daydreaming in a London bus when he saw atoms falling into molecules. Finally, Newton got the idea of gravity from a falling apple. All of these visions, flashes of insight or great moments of discovery, constitute symbolic uses of the Imaginary to represent the Real.

It is the paternal function installed within the mother, as well as the participation of the symbolic father, that makes the Imaginary work for the Symbolic via the faculty of the creative imagination. The categories of the creative imagination are a function of the hole within the Symbolic to represent the Real. Creative images emerge out of the navel of the Symbolic that opens out into the unknown or the unseen structure of being. The unknown also refers to how the unsubstantial or dream-like quality of conventional reality is often ignored. Conventional knowledge takes reality for granted. We have to see with the eye of the Symbolic in order to correct the normal distortion of vision and use the creative imagination to arrive at new visions of reality via permutations within the symbolic structure. It is in this sense that the symbolic imagination can serve to access rather than distort reality or to reveal rather than conceal new dimensions or versions of reality.

The meaning of what remains unknown within reality appears as a hole, a mistake, or something missing within the conventional Symbolic order. Meister Eckhart underscored the importance of finding G-d in errors, mistakes, and forgetfulness. Replace G-d for the Unconscious, and we find Freud's ideas regarding the formations of the Unconscious. Out of the hole represented by something foreign or unknown within known territory, arises a new vision or image of reality, a non-conventional, evolutionary leap beyond the established uses of language and ideology. The Real as the unknown w/hole or emptiness performs a useful function for innovations and renewals of the Symbolic via the Intermediary of the Imagination.

The complex relations among the three registers and their function in the production of various psychical phenomena are a helpful paradigm to distinguish the differences and similarities between various phenomena. Freud and Jung, for example, could not agree on the question of images and the Imaginary, because when Freud spoke of images he was thinking of imaginary interpretations of the Symbolic and the Real (fantasies and the uncanny), while when Jung spoke of images, he referred to symbolic interpretations of the Imaginary and the Real (poetic visions of emptiness). Both were right and yet both were wrong in that they were talking about different although related things. The relations among the different phenomena in question can be represented according to the following depiction of the Borromean knot.

Symbolic images and the deviant or poetic use of language reveal something unknown within being situated in a (core-the *objet a*, to be precise) region beyond the understanding of the small, analytical

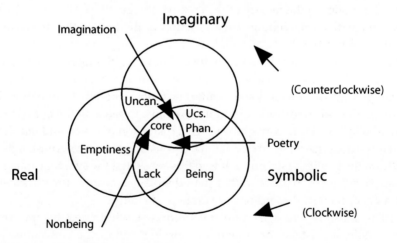

Figure 1. The Borromean knot.

ego-intellect. Moreover, both the symbolic imagination in the spiritual sense and key linguistic signifiers are efficacious and capable of working and causing effects within people. Both the construction and deconstruction of psychical symptoms have depended classically on this principle. According to Jung, for example, an archetype responds more to the organisation of an image or imago that he describes as being something in-itself. In Lacanian terms, such an image would not refer to any signifier outside itself; it—the image—is its own signifier and signified. For Freudians, Lacanians, and Kabbalists, however, the dream image needs to be broken down into its constituent elements, letters or dream thoughts. Just like with conventional reality, the objects that we see through the eye or sense organ are psychical or mental representations of the symbolic structure. However, the signified for such signifiers could very well lye within the Real rather than the Symbolic. But what is extra-mental or extra-symbolic is not the objective quality (symbolic) of the objects but the mystery of things beyond the categories of reason and language.

Consider the example of the dragon image. In Zen Buddhism, the dragon symbolises hidden wisdom and the playful authority that this wisdom conveys to a Buddha or enlightened being. If the word dragon were conceived as a signifier instead of an image, the signifying chain, by homophonic association, would lead to such vernacular expressions as being a drag or a subject being dressed in drag.

An ordinary non-Buddhist person might dub a Buddha a drag, too serious and austere. An old Abbott of a monastery or temple can be seen as a fuddy-duddy, an old-fashioned, fussy, grumpy elderly man who is extremely conservative and dull. "Fuddy" is also another slang term used for male or female genitals. Thus, the fuddy-duddy is defending or reacting to sexuality, genitals, and sexual difference. A man dressed in drag also reveals the opposite meaning (to being a drag) of a male being out-going, party-loving, and effeminate. Nevertheless, both antithetical meanings are condensed within the word "drag". Although it is true that the second sense of the word "drag" could convey a glimpse or semblance of a liberated attitude (mystics are often associated with a passive, feminine, receptive position), neither of these partial dual meanings reveals the realisation of non-duality.

The "drag" of symbolic castration within masculinity (serious and austere) and the void represented by femininity that can be revealed/concealed by different garments (drags) are both simultaneously conveyed through the dragon image. In this regard, the utterance or enunciation of the antithetical signifier "drag" could have the same effect as the presentation of the dragon image. Like the metaphor of the sound of the lion's roar, the visual image of the dragon or the acoustic image of the lion or of the word drag are senseless letters either where the signifier and the signified cannot be divided and separated or where a wordless S_1 is used as a sign of the realm.

The visual and acoustic images are beta sense elements (in Bion's theory) that can also be understood as letters or S_1 as a distinguishing mark or markless mark that is not yet a discreet value within a system of differential elements or a battery of signifiers (language). S_1 has not linked up with S_2 to constitute the phoneme as an elementary unit of the signifier within language. It in this sense that the *objet a* (a voice, for example), although an object rather than a signifier, can be linked up with a senseless letter (as an elementary unit of the signifier) as a signifier degree zero.

The image of the dragon or the sound of the lion's roar is given as a signless sign of an experience of realisation that escapes capture by the logical net of the signifier. However, some Zen teachers would quickly point out that the image is only the finger pointing at the moon but not the moon (Real) itself. On the other hand, other Zen teachers also point out that the moon is in the finger itself or the Real is within the Symbolic not outside of it. It is also feasible that the dragon image as a word or a dream-thought could occupy a place within a signifying chain for a subject in a dream or in a conversation. Here the Symbolic enters into the Real and acquires individual meaning for a desiring subject but no longer functions as a manifestation of non-duality.

There are two different conceptions of metaphor at stake here. In the case of the symbolic metaphor or of a metaphor operating within the register of the Symbolic, a signifier (S_2) is linked to another (S_1). When the Real enters the Symbolic, the signifier (S_1) is not a replacement for another repressed/opposed signifier but is in a state of erasure or senselessness that I denominate S_0. In the example above, S_0 stands for an Other *jouissance,* the non-duality contained both within symbolic castration in masculinity (the drag of the law: form is emptiness) and within feminine forms (the law is a dress/robe: emptiness is form).

Both types of metaphor are polyvocal and cannot be reduced to a single signification, but for different reasons. In the former, the signifier can always mean something else, other or its opposite by virtue of its connections within the signifying chain and the symbolic order. In the latter, since S_0 is outside the logical net of the signifier (although intersecting the Symbolic), S_0 also means something Other but what will be defined here as the Other of the Real not of the Symbolic (the Other within the Other rather than the Other of the Other). The *objet a* is the Other of the Real within the emptiness or lack in the Other.

What I am calling the Other of the Real does not mean, however, a Real unlinked to the Symbolic, but quite the opposite, the Real as it appears within the Symbolic as a senseless signifier that represents the Real or empty quality of an object. Thus some special symbol does not signify something in itself in contrast to what Jung calls a semiotic sign that always refers to something else. The Other in this instance signifies an experience or realisation of the Real as a horizon beyond language yet made possible by language. A symbolic something that could be anything (and not solely an archetype) is being used to reveal a No-thing that is an experience within the register of the Real.

In his essays on general linguistics, Jakobson (1974) used the example of pointing with the index finger to examine the function of language and communication. He considers the possibility of needing to explain to a non-English-speaking indigenous person what a pack of Chesterfield cigarettes are. If he points at the cigarettes, he thinks that the native person will not know whether he is pointing at this particular pack or to cigarettes in general, to something that is to be smoked or smelled, or whether he is trying to sell or prohibit the cigarettes. Rather than by pointing with the index finger, what the pack is or is not is determined by a battery of other signifiers that function as signified for the object/signifier cigarettes.

However, in this example Jakobson only examines the communicative/instrumental but not the evocative function of language. The evocative function of language is at play in pointing to something beyond language the meaning of which is not dependent on other interpretant signifiers.

In the Zen example of the finger pointing at the moon, the moon is a One luminous planet that helps human beings to see at night or in the dark. The dark here represents the unknown and the moon is the light of the night that illuminates what the light of the intellect can make dark. The moon also has the function of controlling the ocean tides although this is not immediately apparent. In addition, to the natural and concrete meaning of the moon affecting the ebb and flow of tides, human beings have added the construction of the moon as a symbol of maternal feelings, love, and emotional life. The mediating link between the two is water, the intrauterine amniotic sack, and feelings being linked to the water element as revealed in tears and the wetness around the eyes. The link between birth and water has already been made by Otto Rank (1909). Finally, ever since the landing on the moon, the moon nowadays has also acquired the meaning of the conquest of space.

The natural world represents a form of experience that pre-existed the realm of human culture and is shared with other species. This is an aspect of the Real or of *das Ding* that is shared with the relationship to the archaic maternal object that also pre-exists the acquisition of linguistic signification. However, feelings themselves, although they are closely linked to the body and physiological states, evolve within the context of language and do not pre-exist the words that we have for them. Only the pleasure-pain continuum aspect of feelings, included under the phenomenon of *jouissance*, is linked to the Real or to a dimension beyond language.

Now there is, however, an aspect of linguistic signifiers themselves that are also linked to the Real. The Real within the Symbolic refers to the unsubstantial and vanishing characteristic of language. Language can represent objects in their absence, and words themselves are not objects but simply sounds and ideational representations that do not occupy any place in space and both are and are not, here this moment, gone in the next. Paradoxically, only feelings and human objects remain as inscriptions of language within the body and the material world.

In a now classical illustration, Laplanche and Leclaire (1966) described a dream of an analysand wherein the central element was the image of a unicorn. The analyst interprets the meaning of the image by decomposition of the French name for the mythical animal: *Li-corne* is composed of the words *lit* (bed) and *corne* (horn). Thus, the unicorn is a signifier for a phallic object of desire or for a phallic *jouissance* or the Real of sexuality caught in the net of the phallic signifier.

It is interesting to observe that the unicorn was used by Zen teachers to describe the transmission of the Buddha mind from teacher to disciple. The magical animal represents a sublime form of life and desire with the horn representing the One and the determination and penetration of wisdom. Like the use of a staff as a symbol of authority by a Zen teacher, the horn could be conceived as a signifier of the imaginary phallus. Yet like a unicorn, the imaginary phallus in reality does not exist. In the late Lacan, the S_1 of the imaginary phallus and the master's discourse can be differentiated from the One of the Real.

In Zen, the staff is a signifier of the wisdom of emptiness or the emptiness of wisdom. For an analysand, the unicorn may represent a signifier of phallic *jouissance* (S_1- S_2 or horn-bed) while for the analyst the unicorn stands as signifier of a lack or of a knowing about unconscious sexuality or sexuality in the Real unconscious. For the analysand, the unicorn is a phallic fantasy or an imaginary phallus, while for the analyst the unicorn is a symbolic phallus absent by its very definition. It is via the symbolic function of the phallus, that the phallus and the unicorn can signify a knowing and an Other *jouissance* (S_1-S_0 or horn-emptiness) beyond language and sexuality. This point is examined herein later on.

The Symbolic and the Name of the Father

The image or imago, the braking down of the signifier, the associative signifying chain, symbolic forms such as the lapsus, the joke, a mistake, the sudden action, the sparkle of wit in artistic or scientific creation, all have in common the shattering of the imaginary homogeneity of conventional social consciousness. According to the Kabbalah, the creative process requires that the small ego-intellect be pacified and made passive (symbolically castrated) in order to prepare the larger psychical being to receive and become symbolically inseminated by the divine influx, the *Ruach Hakodesh* (holy spirit) emanating from the active intellect, as the source of knowing and understanding.

The metaphor of divine insemination symbolises not the imaginary but the symbolic phallus. It is the lack of an ego or an imaginary phallus that opens the gates of the metaphoric process. Thus, pacification represents symbolic castration more than a repressed desire to be penetrated by the imaginary phallus/father. However, in some cases the latter could also be an accurate interpretation.

Abulafia referred to the practice on the "path of the names" that one develops by permutation of the ordinary language "until you arrive at the activity of a force which is no longer in your control, but rather your reason and your thought is in its control" (quoted by Idel, 1988, p. 235). It is interesting to note the similarity between the importance given in classical Kabbalah to divine names (in plural) and particularly to the permutations of the name of G-d (the Tetragrammaton) and the central place occupied by the Name of the Father as a key signifier organiser of the symbolic order in Lacanian theory. Consider the following quote from the Zohar (the "bible" of Jewish mysticism):

> How assiduously should one ponder on each word of the Torah, for there is not a single word in it which does not contain allusions to the Supernal Holy Name, many aspects, many roots, many branches.
>
> (quoted by Bakan, 1958, p. 263)

The Zohar points to a connection between the Name of the Father and the symbolic tree-like structure of language; between the paternal metaphor and the symbolic play between hidden or latent and revealed or manifest word elements, the associative roots and branches of the signifying chain. The very scroll of the Torah is written without vowels to allow for the polyvalence of meaning of every word. In Kabbalah, however, the Name of G-d is permutated in order to disintegrate and transform ordinary language into a vehicle of the Real, while in Lacanian theory the paternal metaphor is supposed to give organisation and formal meaning to the symbolic order. How to understand the contradiction between these two views?

Take, for example, the name of the Absolute within Judaism. Conventional Judaism conceives G-d as male and as such He is daily addressed. The High Holy days prayers also address Him as "our Father, our King." The most common name that can be used but not falsified and called in vain is *Adonai* (Lord). However, it can be argued that *Adonai* is only a conventional symbolic rendition of the Real name or the name of the Real that is *YHVH*. Nobody knows exactly what this Name means. But while *Adonai* is a masculine name, the name of the Real includes both the God and the Goddess and I would argue even God and no-God (true G-d is no-God). The Real (*YHVH*) is symbolised as the Name of the Father (*Adonai*) in order to organise conventional patriarchal social reality as a differential symbolic binary order. But in order for reality to emerge from the Real (rather than from the Imaginary or Symbolic), the Real needs to be re-linked (*re-ligare*) to the Symbolic, and the symbolic name of the One (*Adonai*) needs to be dissolved back into its Real formless, meaningless form (*YHVH*). Thus, Kabbalah contains a practice of disintegration and dissolution of conventional reality in order to manifest the Real without its (thought) coverings or in order for the ordinary coverings to become semblances of *jouissance* rather than of conventional meaning.

A similar case occurs in Zen Buddhism. *Tathagata* is the Buddha-name which stands for the Real and which is used without knowing exactly what it means. It is most commonly thought to mean "reality as it is" or "the way things are" or "how they go". Reality here includes conventional everyday reality and the non-dual Real, form and emptiness. A translation by homophony into Spanish and English would render: gate of the Father or grandfather. Tata is the sound-word that infants may use to designate the place of the father prior to the acquisition of language.

In many Latin American countries, "Tata" remains an affectionate and respectful way of addressing a grandfather. However, *Tathagata* is clearly and primarily meant in Buddhism to describe a Buddha as an enlightened being who has realised the Real of Buddhahood. In this sense, *Tathagata* would signify the source of fatherhood or fatherly authority within the Real. But within the Real, Buddhahood, reality or emptiness are not conditioned by any fixed meaning, name, rule, or form. True Buddha is no-Buddha, and true name is no-name. Again, it is the no-name of the father that forges the link between two signifiers and weaves together the net of the symbolic order and the symbolic and cohesive functioning of the subject. The Aleph is the silent letter by virtue of which the others function.

Examination of the relationship between the Name of the Father and what Lacan calls the lack in the Øther may also be helpful in addressing the problem currently under discussion. According to Lacan, language appears to be haunted by a lack in the Symbolic. What does this mean? That within the symbolic order itself there will be a $S(\emptyset)$ signifying the castration of language (Øther) or that which "the signifier is impotent to pinpoint" (Patsalides, 1997). Lacan gives the Freudian castration complex a more abstract interpretation. The absence of the phallus refers to a lack within the Symbolic. The Name of the Father or the paternal metaphor as a signifier $(S_1\text{-}S_2)$ is used as a stopgap for this hole or missing place within the Symbolic. The following "matheme" would represent this state of affairs: $S_1\text{-}S_2/S(\emptyset)$.

To go beyond the paternal symbolic order, to go beyond the binary duality of language, signifies accepting the impotence of language to represent the Real and to face this emptiness or lack of the symbolic without a fixed signifier of the symbolic father. The spiritual name of the father, *Tathagata* or *YHVH*, reveals the emptiness of language and of the subject. In contrast to this, the conventional names of the father conceal or cover over emptiness and give reality its fixed, substantial, and illusory appearance.

Since *jouissance* is the unthinkable/inconceivable being which language cannot designate, in a Lacanian and Judaic interpretation, the Name of the Father functions as what links the registers to one another and particularly in the intersection between the Real and the Symbolic. The Other *jouissance* operates out of a lack in the Symbolic to represent the Real.

Thus, there are two terms: the lack in the Øther or the lack of the Symbolic that in another register really means the *jouissance* or experience of the Real. In addition, a third term would mediate between these two: the Name of the Father with two faces; one turned towards conventional reality and functioning as a stop-gap and support of metaphoric expression, the other leading through the hole of the Symbolic to the source of reality in the Real. The Kabbalistic teaching of the different faces of the Name can be understood as how the Name operates within the registers in the process of linking them together. The imaginary function of the Name generates the illusion of a whole or a complete system that underpins the consistency of the visual world and language, between identity and culture, the individual and society.

However, the world is not really sustained by visual reality. We only need a blind person to remind us of this and of the normal distortion of vision. The symbolic order of language and culture is held together by the mystery of things unseen. When the system brakes down then we can discern what it is made of, or when we find out what it is made of then we also acquire the power to destroy it. This is the lack in the Other and the vulnerability of the world and creation. The entire enchilada can disappear as quickly as a puff of smoke.

The hole within the Symbolic, which functions as a connection between the Symbolic and the Real, is both a breaking point and a vanishing point, a point of disorganisation/breakdown (of the binary paternal order) and a point of breakthrough and enlightenment (beyond the binary duality of language).

The Real and the (No)-thing

Clearly, the originality of seeing in Zen and the divine influx emanating from the active or prophetic intellect in Kabbalah reveal a non-dual Real through a permutation of conventional dual language different from the play of the signifier and free association in relationship to the Real of sexuality and aggressiveness in the Freudian/Lacanian Unconscious. One refers to spiritual enlightenment or a realisation of ultimate Reality (that things in their own being are empty), the other to a knowing based on *lalangue* revealing the Real of unconscious desire and sexuality. They both refer to an "It", but the "It" symbolised in each conception differs.

In Zen, the "It" is the No-thing that simply means the inconceivable nature of the sacred. The sacred is empty or holy in the sense of empty yet it manifests in the form and letters of wisdom and the empty heart of compassion. The id is the Real of the drive, the place of the *objet a* cause of desire or of the subject's *jouissance*. *Jouissance* always asks for more and evades complete satisfaction. An arrow always flies by its target even when the target is hit or precisely when the target is hit. *Jouissance* has to be left open and unattained or unknown for it to manifest and flow in ordinary circumstances.

The Real of sexuality is the desire of lovers which cannot be fully conveyed by words and which disappears and is extinguished once love is consumed and/or consummated. Conversely, the real of sexuality can also be expressed in the opposite direction as the longing that remains and is not extinguished once intercourse and orgasm has taken place. Romantic love will move from imaginary fantasy, to symbolic vows and commitments, to the emptiness and impermanence of the subject and the Other.

Moreover, it is a well-known affirmation within Buddhist Mahayana and tantric sutras that during sexual activity people who do not practise meditation may have glimpses of Nirvana. The tantric Buddhist tradition remains as a testimony of this understanding. The Real of the drive or of desire can be reached either by frustration or gratification (it was not about that). Similarly to the tantric tradition, Jewish tradition appears to have attempted to join both senses of the Real It as revealed in one of the most famous parables of the Zohar.

A beautiful damsel secluded in a palace hints to her lover to approach her, and after a sequel of disclosures and discussions, he becomes her husband. This state is seen as tantamount to his possessing the palace and all its beloved secrets. The significance of the parable is offered by the Zohar itself: the damsel is the Torah, which is dressed in four, or perhaps even five, levels of meaning that must be penetrated by the perfect student of the Torah in order to reach its ultimate layer, the Kabbalistic meaning—a state portrayed as having overt sexual overtones.

(Idel, p. 227)

The Real is at work in the wisdom/knowing of emptiness and the realisation of the prophetic intellect (in the Kabbalah) contained within the side of the Name of the Father (*Tathagata/YHVH*) that is turned towards or emerges from the Real. The Real is also at work in the *jouissance* and mystery of sex associated in Kabbalah with the presence of the *Shechinah* or the supernal, mythical body, Mother of all delight. In either case, direct experience beyond the Imaginary and the Symbolic will be required for "entry into" the dimension of the Real. Symbolic words and images direct the subject towards the Real that is the source of all "conception" and "creation" (gestation). It is the immersion in the Real that reveals the lack and mysteries within the Symbolic.

In the Genjo koan (mentioned in previous chapters), Dogen writes: "When Dharma does not fill your whole body and mind, you think it is already sufficient. When Dharma fills your whole body and mind, you understand that something is missing." Once the immersion in the Real has taken place and the water of Dharma fills our body and mind, then we realise that our symbolic ideas and understanding are insufficient. Whatever ideas or letters brought us to practice will now prove to be not enough or lacking.

I have mentioned that Lacan (1959) gives contradictory accounts of what he means by "the Thing" just as he gives differing accounts of the Real. On the one hand, his understanding is very close to Zen when he defines "the (no)Thing" as emptiness or void that can never be captured by the signifier. There always remains an aspect of things-in-themselves that is left out and that escapes incorporation into the Symbolic. But in other places, Lacan argues that religion can never give us the Thing because it can only be found within the pathways of the signifier or the symbolic register—the Thing becomes the object, the fetish, or the archaic mother, instead of the emptiness that the subject is looking for in the object. Lacan also says that religion consists of all the different ways of trying to fill away (deny/conceal) emptiness and that only psychoanalysis accepts it the way it is. This certainly would not be true of Zen Buddhism,

Jewish Kabbalah, Vedic thought or the Christianity of Meister Eckhart. The notion of benevolent emptiness is present in all of these traditions.

I follow Lacan from the place where he defines the Thing as what the desire of the subject is seeking to re-discover in the object (the Agalma, or the non-object quality of the object). Psychoanalysis is the discipline and field that seeks and appears to find the letters of the Real within the pathways of sexual signifiers in the unconscious. Such letters are conveyed through *lalangue* and free association as symbolic forms beyond both grammatical language and the formal logic of the analytical ego-intellect.

The differing definitions of the Real may be understood in the light of Lacan's characterisation of sublimation as what elevates an object to the dignity of *das Ding*. However, I would dare to improve on this definition by advancing the thesis that the Sublime or *das Ding* is the emptiness at the core of the object which allows for the object to be satisfying or fulfilling but which also drives the drive or desire to seek for the Real beyond the object and the signifiers of the pleasure and reality principles. The Sublime or Nirvana is the empty Real without an object and yet also within the object. In this context, the Sublime within the Real can be defined as the It of the id.

For Freud, sublimation involved a change in the aim and object of a drive; going from an exciting pleasure to at least an initially frustrating reality, and from a sexual object to an object of social utility. In clinical practice, such definition presupposes, for example, that once Oedipal signifiers are reconstructed, these need to be sublimated or at least used for other purposes.

Objects of social utility are emblematic of the social construction of reality but not of the Real of sublimation. Objects of social utility provide substitutive or indirect forms of satisfaction. In contrast to this Freud defined sublimation as a direct satisfaction of the drive. Satisfaction represents a form of pleasure and at the same time *satis* in Latin means enough or good enough. Enough can mean the drawing of a limit (you've had enough, be content with that for now) or it can mean: "Oooh! that is good, that feels good, that hit the spot. Now I am satisfied and can rest from the constant pressure of the demand of the drive." Satisfaction here is often contra posed or differentiated from the death drive or *jouissance* that always asks for more.

The question here is whether *jouissance* represents an infinite and ever receding horizon or that simply the ultimate event horizon has not yet been reached. Paradoxically, the aim is reached by not reaching it, yet this not reaching the aim does not represent an abandonment of the aim. Reaching is not reaching and not reaching is reaching. Circling around the object but without aiming directly towards it provides a direct satisfaction. If you turn towards it, you turn away from it. The object is there and yet it is not. The aim of Real sublimation is aimless and yet this aimlessness or emptiness is precisely its goal. Freud says that the reality principle represents a temporary delay or stop in the long road towards pleasure. In the end the reality principle still works for the pleasure principle and in this way happiness is linked to both virtue (forbearance) and pleasure.

As earlier stated the lack in the Øther or the lack of the Symbolic in another register really means the *jouissance* or experience of the Real. The distinction between S_1 or a repressed sexual signifier and S_0 as a signified beyond language, both of which allude to unconventional uses of language to evoke the Real of the unconscious, is also related to another distinction that I formulated between the id and the It. The gaps and absences within language produce metaphoric permutations within the structure of conscious and unconscious language that invoke and reveal a Real of the sexual drive. *Lalangue* or the language of the unconscious (S_1) reveals an id of sexuality which remains concealed due to censorship and which chases after a lost and elusive object cause of desire.

In the case of the It, the permutation of conventional language and of the Name of the Father precisely has the function of bringing forth the experience of the Real as a plenum (S_0) without an object rather than as a lack or a missing object within the Symbolic [S(Ø)]. The Real non-object differs from a missing object (Symbolic) and from a fixed imaginary fantasy object that could complete the subject. The *objet a* that at the end of analysis has been separated from the image of an object or a subject precisely corresponds to the unary trace, the markless mark, or the presence of an absent object or a non-object.

Because desire is chasing after or clinging to an object or an experience that could close the lack or gap within the subject, master signifiers of religion, of Buddhism, of psychoanalysis, science, etc., hold the promise of completing the subject or the Other. However, once the experience or beyond experience of the Real has taken place, as Dogen says, the Symbolic itself will also be realised as having something missing. The Zen teaching of enlightenment itself is impermanent and subject to the changes, vagrancies, and inebriations of delusion, although the light itself is basically incorruptible. Enlightenment as an object is delusion and the object of delusion is enlightenment.

The difference between the Real as a plenum and reality as a lack in the Øther is equivalent to the difference between a negative emptiness of absence (of an object) and a positive emptiness of w-holeness. Finally, these two forms of the Real do not exist as mutually exclusive orders since I also begun to pinpoint the bridges and connections between them. Building on Freud's notion of sublimation as a non-defensive vicissitude of the drive and Lacan's characterisation of sublimation as what elevates an object to the dignity of 'the Thing', I propose that is the emptiness at the core of the object which allows for the object to be satisfying or fulfilling but which also drives desire to seek for the Real or for a realisation of the emptiness of being.

CHAPTER SIX

The Tetragramaton, the Borromean knot, the four worlds, and the Tetralemma

I will begin this chapter by building two conceptual bridges between Lacanian psychoanalysis and Jewish Kabbalah. The first links the fourth dimension (*sinthome*) of the Borromean knot (in the later Lacan) and the four letters of the Tetragrammaton, while the second links the Kabbalistic teaching of the four worlds with the four dimensions of the Borromean knot.

I will delete the o in the word G-d not out of some orthodox zeal but to make the word and the concept compatible with Zen and Lacanian thought. The o is similar to the small o or *a* (from *a-utre* or other in French) of the big Other (I keep the O [of big *A-utre*] in English to make it consistent with Other in English). The *a* is the letter that falls off the big Other (of the Symbolic: G-d) and represents the Real as the Other *in* the Other or the empty object that the Other is missing and that constitutes the desire of the Other rather than for the Other. The *a* is the little that holds the great.

When Chinese Emperor Wu asked Bodhidharma (the Indian ancestor who brought Zen into China) whether there was any merit in building temples for Buddhism, Bodhidharma answered: "No merit". Then the emperor asked him, "What is the highest meaning of the holy truths?" Bodhidharma answered: "Emptiness, nothing holy". Temples and holy truths were the objects of the Emperor's desire, the things that drove his will and desire, what he thought he and his people were missing or lacking, and what he thought would compensate for China's past losses and shortcomings. Emperor Wu wanted Bodhidharma to demand temples from him. However, Bodhidharma broke the news to the emperor: the object, the *a*, and the Other (the Other here stands for the cultural Other as well as for the scriptures) are empty. The small *a* represents the hole within the whole.

Similarly, the first of the Bible's Ten Commandments represents G-d as a jealous god that demands: "You shall have no other gods before me." It seems as if G-d wants some attention and has a desire to be the One or the only One. G-d appears to be missing the *a*, or the cause of his people's exclusive love and devotion. In actuality, G-d is empty, and the object of his/her desire is emptiness, and humans demand that G-d demand loyalty from them. Humans posit the Other as desiring and lacking. In the Real, G-d is a plenum and does not need to be worshipped over and above his competitors. But the commandment also implies that if a subject is not before G-d then perhaps it is acceptable to have other manifestations of the One. Standing before G-d the subject is expected to be present and faithful. When the subject is a Jew then the subject has to be a Jew. Buddhists are faithful to Buddha and Christians are faithful to Christ. Don't call Buddha Christ or Christ Buddha, but whether devoted to Buddha or Christ, in the empty act of faith one is always before the One.

The empty *a* of the Real is not unlike the silent letter aleph of the Hebrew alphabet, or the no-thing aspect of the Real in the Other of language. This form of re-presenting the *a* and the Name also keep the term G-d from turning into an imaginary or symbolic object and preserves the mystery and subjective nature of the Name and word G-d.

The Name of the Father ➜ YHVH (four-lettered Name of G-d)
Four Worlds ➜ Name of the Father/Real/Symbolic/Imaginary

The Kabbalah is considered the spiritual or mystical teachings of Judaism or the teaching that expounds the hidden mysteries of the Torah or Jewish Bible. Torah means the same thing as Dharma in Buddhism. It means Law, Teaching, and phenomena. In addition, Dharma in Buddhism ultimately represents the Law of emptiness. The Kabbalah evolved out of Spanish and French culture in the

Jewish communities of Gerona and Provence during the Golden Age of the Jews in Muslim-occupied Spain. The main book of Kabbalah is the Zohar, or the Book of Radiance. It was written by Rabbi Moses de Leon, although orthodox Jewry attribute it to the Talmudic sage Rabbi Shimon bar Yohai.

According to Kabbalah, the mind and the human world are actually composed of four worlds: emanation, creation, formation, and action. Emanation is the world of the spirit or Being proper; creation corresponds to the world of thought; formation to the world of feeling, while action is the world of ordinary everyday activity.

Classical Kabbalah has already linked the four worlds and the Tetragrammaton. Using the Lacanian concept of the Name of the Father as a letter (YHVH), it is also possible to understand the link between the four worlds and the Borromean knot. Lacan says that the Name of the Father (that emerges from the Real) is what ties the other three together (Real, Symbolic, and Imaginary). The latter three dimensions (RSI) can be understood as linked together by the aspect of the fourth dimension that is in each of them, or how the One is in the four and the four in One.

The Real corresponds to the world of emanation, the Symbolic to the world of thought, the Imaginary to the world of feelings, and the *sinthome* to the world of action or everyday activity. The Imaginary is the world of feelings because human beings usually either ignore their feelings, or don't consider how thoughts determine feelings, or mistake the objects involved in feelings. The fourth world, or the world of action, is the One that ties the other three together. The world of action is where "the rubber hits the road", "the proof is in the pudding", or as a classical Chinese Zen saying puts it: "Ordinary mind is the way". The fourth world/dimension in Lacan is both the Name of the Father and the *sinthome*.

Buddhism also has a teaching of the three worlds: the world of desire, the world of form, and the world of emptiness or formlessness. The world of desire corresponds to the Imaginary world of feelings; the world of form is the world of thought; while the world of emanation is the world of emptiness or formlessness. The fourth world is missing in early Buddhism but can also be found in the later Mahayana teaching. The wisdom of everyday activity is one of the four Mahayana wisdoms. In addition, Zen or Chan monastic teaching in China survived imperial persecution of Buddhism (due to being viewed as parasitic to society) by monks working in the fields, a practice that was formalised in Pai Chang's maxim of "A day of not working is a day of not eating". From Pai Chang's maxim to Joshu's "Ordinary mind is the way" is only a small step. Buddhism had to evolve and come a long way from the ascetic practice of leaving the world to realising the Dharma or Nirvana in everyday life and activities (including ordinary attachments and afflictions).

For the Name to be helpful, it has to be put to good use especially if one intends to disregard or ignore it (doctoral ignorance, atheism, etc.). The *sinthome* in Lacan represents what we do with what we are made of, with the traits, symptoms, and behaviours that trouble or afflict us. An act entails taking responsibility for choices and desires, and for acting either intentionally or without thinking. Non-thinking does not mean acting out or not-thinking (although in character disorders, it does), but rather trusting and having faith in clear mind and the clarity of thinking and non-thinking. Such trust is predicated on symptoms and traits becoming ego-dystonic and known to the subject. In my work, "ego-dystonic" refers to that area where the subject becomes large enough to include what falls outside the zone of ego-comfort, or the likes, dislikes, and predilections of ego defences. In contrast to this, ego-syntonic refers to the small self of the defensive ego. There are also defences that are not ego-based and that are rooted within the forms and formations of language, but this question is outside the purview of this book (see Moncayo, 2012).

In Lacanian theory, the word *sinthome* is used to describe a new relationship to the symptom and to underscore that the unconscious is worked over within the unconscious and not outside of it. This differs from the notion of making conscious the unconscious (in psychoanalysis), or enlightening delusion (in Buddhism), as if we could ever be rid of the unconscious or of our dream life. Dogen taught that we have to wake up from a dream within a dream. In addition, the Name of the Father as a *sinthome* also points to the function of the Name and of the father as an expedient rather than as a substantial essence. Despite the fact that names and fathers are not without posing problems for human beings, we have to use them in order to go past them or beyond them.

In Kabbalistic and Zen language, the world of emanation (*Atzilut*) is moment-to-moment experience as a function of essential emptiness or the emptiness of essence. The flow of *Samadhi* or of the Sabbath (*samedi* in French), as a mindful/blissful and concentrated state, otherwise known as the radiance and effulgence of the divine light, moves and manifests within Real experience. The essence of emptiness or the wind of the spirit manifests within a non-representational or non-perceptual realm that is a source of faith and dread as well as the pivot where thought, feeling, and action are transformed. Emptiness is the hole/emptiness in the middle of the wheel of action, or the space and air inside the tube of a tire, and on the basis of which the different worlds turn.

What prevents the hub of the wheel from functioning (in emptiness) is the belief and clinging to a personal sense of self. The jewel in the Jew is the emptiness of the wind of the spirit (*ruach*), of the heart, and of psychical rest in the awakened state of the Sabbath. The jewel is covered over and the Sabbath state compromised when the mind is restlessly preoccupied with thoughts of me, mine, and us against them. The Hebrew language already knows this as reflected in the relation between *Ani* and *Ayin*: self is emptiness and emptiness self. We build a bubble of self in lieu of the emptiness of the hub of the wheels of the divine chariot/vehicle. When the hub is left empty, then the world can turn on its axis unhindered.

The Hebrew word for prophet also points in the same direction. The root for *Navie* is *Navuv*, meaning hollow, and both Job and David enunciated teachings about the hollow ventricle of the heart. "A hollow (*navuv*) man will gain heart" (Job 11:12) and "My heart is hollow within me" (Psalms 109:22). On the other hand, the place of emptiness can also be a place of fear/anxiety/loss for the mind that is holding on to or being held back by a belief in a personal self. In this case, the emptiness of self is felt as a threat and a source of anxiety.

The world of Atzilut may have awareness but does not have self consciousness or memory as usually understood. Atzilut is like the enlightened aspect of the *Alaya vijnana* consciousness (unconscious for all practical purposes) in Buddhism that receives impressions while not having an impression of its own. Like the Real, the *Alaya* of Atzilut is a register without a registration book or a code. We unconsciously and unknowingly know that Atzilut is the emptiness of being and a traceless trace without beginning or end. In itself, the essence of emanation is precluded from thought or from self-consciousness. Within the world of Atzilut, the essence is revealed as a pure experience/awareness concealed from concept.

According to Zen's first principle, there is a difference between the concept and the experience of emptiness. The concept of emptiness is empty of content. Emptiness is an experience beyond experience. According to Suzuki Roshi, emptiness means to have direct, pure experience without relying on the form or colour of being. Emptiness is experience empty of preconceived ideas of big or small, round or square. For Suzuki Roshi, the latter don't belong to reality but are only ideas. Emptiness is a form of pure experience without a concept of emptiness.

As soon as a thought arises and the world of Atzilut or the Alaya becomes a purpose, intention or object, then a second world is born/created and woven into the first. The flow of Atzilut is interrupted although it remains present like a still pool within the world of thought that has been created. The second world is consistent with what Zen calls the second principle.

However, for Dogen (fascicle Bukkyo of the Shobogenzo), the second principle is the universe itself.

> What we mean by sutras is the entire universe itself. There is no space and time that are not the sutras. They use the words and letters of ultimate truth and the words and letters of wordly truth. They employ the language of gods and the language of human beings. They use the words and letters of beasts, those of *asuras*, and those of hundreds of grasses and thousands of trees. For this reason, the long and short, the square and round, the blue and yellow, the red and white—all of which marshall on in a dignified way throughout the universe in the ten directions—are undeniably the sutras' words and letters and faces. These words and letters are all regarded as the instruments of the great Way and the scriptures for Buddhists.

> (translated and quoted by Hee-Jin Kim, 2007, p. 60)

For Jewish Kabbalah, it is the essence of emptiness, or the emptiness of emptiness, that unites speech, words, and thoughts. The latter are not some illusory world, disconnected from reality as if reality could exist without them. The illusory world is made up of our fantasies about what the worlds are actually made off. According to Bodhidharma, meditation emancipates the subject from being enslaved to the letter of the scriptures, from fantasy and discrimination, while leaving the creative imagination intact. Being emancipated from conceptual discrimination does not mean a rejection of scripture but rather having experiential understanding of the scriptures. It is the latter that allows for a higher form of intellection or intuition to emerge. Scripture here means not only words but also the interdependent structures that make up the world, including our bodies. For Kabbalists, the mysteries of the Torah were not revealed through the intellectual faculty, but by means of the divine influx emanating from the *Ein Sof*.

From this perspective, according to Dogen, belief is able to follow circumstances completely. The different worlds are linked together. There is no experience in the moment without prior experience but past experience does not determine the experience in this moment. How do we know about a reality that is not based on ideas without appealing to words or gestures that tell us about a reality beyond words and ideas? This is the function of practice/realisation. As Dogen wrote:

> Belief as a root is beyond self, beyond others, beyond intention, beyond our contrivance, beyond outside influence, and beyond independently established criteria; thus it has been transmitted intimately between east and west. Belief demonstrated with the whole body is called belief. It follows inevitably from the condition of Buddhahood, following circumstances completely and following itself completely. Unless the condition of Budhahood is present, the belief is not realized. For this reason it is said that "The great ocean of Buddha dharma is entered by belief itself." In sum, the place where the belief is realized is the place where Buddhist ancestors are realized.
>
> (Fascicle 73 of Shobogenzo, Book Four)

The kind of belief Dogen is speaking about differs from the belief that hinders realisation or from the realisation that hinders or excludes beliefs. Dogen's words are letters of emptiness that are themselves the moon of realisation. Here, there is no gap between the second principle of concepts and the first principle of realisation within pure experience.

Just as a hand cannot grasp thought, thought cannot grasp non-thinking. The essence of a human being remains invisible and concealed to the other and to the materiality of language and the signifier. Essence is revealed in-between words or on the blank scroll that words are written on. Science, for example, does not know what thought is. So far thought fails to show up in an electroencephalogram. Because of this in Western philosophy metaphysics has been associated with the world of ideas that lies behind the world of appearances or material forms. Thought however, and the thought of enlightenment in particular, is different from ideas. Thought is Real, while ideas and thinking are Symbolic and Imaginary.

Ideas are what determine us without our knowledge or awareness. According to Zen, we need to be freed from the thoughts that bind us and cause our suffering. Thinking here is tantamount to delusion and the main delusion is the thought of self that does not correspond to the way things actually are. Uchiyama Roshi speaks of opening the hand of thoughts. Thinking is like a secret aggressiveness bound to a false idea of self that we need to defend and protect. Our thoughts are like a clenched fist that we steadfastly hold behind our back so the other cannot see our intentions/motivations.

But in the world of *beriah* or creation, thought has a different meaning. It is something spiritual rather than material although not separate from materiality (the naught of thought or the spirit of reason according to Hegel). In the teaching on the eightfold noble path, the Buddha spoke of right thought, and Buddhism in general teaches the importance of raising the thought of enlightenment.

In the *Gakudo Yojin-Shu*, Dogen urges practitioners to arouse the thought of enlightenment:

> The thought of enlightenment has many names but they all refer to one and the same mind. Ancestor Nagarjuna said, "The mind that fully sees into the uncertain world of birth and death is called the thought of enlightenment." Thus if we maintain this mind, this mind can become the thought of enlightenment.
>
> (Dogen, 1985, p. 31)

The thought of enlightenment opens the closed hand of thought. The opened hand of thought is another name for what in Zen is called "the original face before your parents were born". The original face is represent in the following painting of Bodhidharma by Hakuin (Tanahashi, 1984).

The thought of enlightenment represents the reality of the unborn and undying akin to the unborn subject of the Real in Lacan. This thought is the "ought" or ideal of awakening to our Real nature or what Heidegger, Lacan, and Bion call *das Ding*, or the thing-in-itself. In addition, in Mahayana Buddhism thought is also the thought of awakening with all beings. The thought of enlightenment is not the

Figure 1. Large Daruma scroll by Zen teacher Hakuin Ekaku (1685–1788).

thought of a personal enlightenment but rather the thought of an enlightened humanity or the thoughts that benefit beings in general and not just yourself.

For the Kabbalah, creation (the universe) is a thought that is taking place in the mind of the Godhead. This teaching coincides with the thought that Buddha had upon his enlightenment. He realised that he had attained enlightenment with all beings and that the world was already enlightened. Creation or the universe is a single enlightened thought or an inclusive enlightened singularity. In the writings of Isaac the Blind (Scholem, 1978), there is a "Thought which has no end or finality". In Zen, this corresponds to the intention of practising without a gaining idea, which is another way of understanding the thought of enlightenment. For the Kabbalah, the domain of pure thought is a domain impenetrable to the closed hand of human thought. Instead, pure thought is revealed in *Kavana* as attention, devotion, and intention.

In this sense, emptiness is a wall of incomprehensibility confronting the mind. Emptiness is incomprehensible because of being devoid of concept and therefore perplexing to the human intellect. Emptiness is a realm of manifestation or emanation without differentiation or discrimination. For the Kabbalah (Scholem, 1962), emptiness is the first formless form or the "image" or "likeness" of the Infinite (*Ein-Sof*). More than an image, we could say that it is the possibility or potential for an image, just as light conditions the possibility of seeing a world of form and colour. Conversely, the same thing could be said in the opposite direction. Because there is a light that is not conditioned by darkness or light, light, therefore, is not obscured by darkness and is not revealed in the light.

In the phenomenon known as Saturnalia, or the dark sun of high noon, the light of the mind remains dulled or covered when the actual sun is at the highest point in the sky. This is also the point when the depressed feel their depression most acutely and remain indoors and in bed with shades closed during the day instead of sleeping at night. Depressed people live their life upside down: dark during the day and light during the night. The infinite light is another name for the infinite empty mirror in which the image of all things is revealed. Yet the infinite mirror itself is not a clear mirror: "It" does not have an image or form, yet makes all images possible.

The open hand of non-thinking, or what Dogen calls thinking-non-thinking, is what can grasp the pure thought of creation and enlightenment. In zazen or Zen meditation, the thought of enlightenment is held by the hand of non-thinking. Out of non-thinking emerges the hand of enlightened thought and creative thinking outside the box. Non-thinking is like a box without a lid or what is empty about thought that links and re-links thoughts together.

The Tetralemma

Non-thinking, the Real, or the inconceivable in Zen does not in fact amount to a denial or negation of logic or reason. It simply points to a dimension of reality that is beyond reason and words yet is entangled and intertwined with them, nonetheless. Zen is not illogical nor should Nagarjuna's Tetralemma (described below) be interpreted as an attempt to deny reason or logic altogether. In this, Nagarjuna's dialectical method is similar to dialectical logic in the West that also seeks to find rationality beyond formal Aristotelian logic. Dialectical logic does not seek to deny formal logic but simply to discover its legitimate and proper delimitation.

Formal logic is the logical type appropriate for the natural sciences and for instrumental rationality and statistical studies (propositions are either true or false despite the fact that statistical facts are in fact probabilities). Dialectical logic is the logic necessary for the theoretical social sciences wherein things can be both true and false, fiction and fact at the same time. Finally, there is another logical type comprised of what Adorno called negative dialectics. The latter corresponds to the Sanskrit *neti*, *neti*, where things neither are nor are not. This is the logic necessary for approaching the Real leading to what Lacan called the logic of the not-all. For example, Zen teaches that the flavour of the food cooked in the Zen kitchen is not in the food and not not in the food. To approach the Dharma or the flavour of emptiness requires going beyond the instrumentality of gourmet cooking. The taste of the food is a thought without end.

TETRALEMMA	
Proposition regarding the flavour of Zen food	
The flavour is in the food.	Formal logic. One is true and one is false or one may be true for some food but not for others. Imaginary.
It is not in the food.	
It is in the food and is not in the food.	Dialectical logic. Symbolic.
Neither is in the food nor not in the food.	Negative dialectics. Real.
The flavour *is* not not in the food. The positive is in the negative but devoid of concept. The Real is wondrous emptiness.	

The naught of thought cannot be turned into a positive category. It is not-all positive nor not-all negative either. The positive Real is found in the double negative that differs from the negation of the negation that results in a positive concept or judgement.

You cannot say the flavour of emptiness can only be found in Zen food, as a particular affirmation, because it would deny that the flavour could also exist in non-Zen food or that it could be absent from what appears to be Zen food. But then where is the flavour if it is neither in the food nor not in the food? The flavour is not-not in the food. The positive is in the negative, or the Real is in the negative but devoid of logical categories.

In the grid above, I have collapsed the first two categories of the Tetralemma into one and placed them under the heading of the Imaginary. This reorganisation opens up the fourth category of the quartet for a dimension made possible by negative dialectics yet beyond it at the same time. In addition, this reorganisation makes the Tetralemma line up with the Borromean knot.

Another example of the Tetralemma resides in the differences among Buddhas, priests, or saintly persons and ordinary human or sentient beings. The Mahayana teaches that saints and snakes intermingle or the non-duality between the two, and Zen teaching, for example, sets a non-dual standard for both Buddhas and sentient beings. The teaching of Zen mind beginners mind points to the non-duality of the beginner and the advanced practitioner and how both are to practice without ulterior motives or gaining ideas. There are material but also spiritual gaining ideas. The latter is what Trumgpa Rimpoche called spiritual materialism. A spiritual gaining idea is thoughts of status and self-importance and wishes to attain enlightenment that generate a duality between delusion and enlightenment.

The Therevada teaching has no problem in presenting a persuasive dual teaching of using the practice of meditation to transform delusion into enlightenment, hate into love, or greed into kindness. Here we find spiritual ulterior or dual motives. This would be the equivalent of formal logic: things are either enlightenment or delusion, and the aim is to transform one into the other.

In Jewish teaching, the dual or ordinary teaching (the commonsense or normal tendency, for example, to avoid heat and cold and seek coolness and warmth instead) is permissible for the people but not for leaders. An example of this in the Bible is the case of the ashes of the red heifer used to purify the people and yet at the same time the ashes render the priest impure. It is permissible for people to engage in practice with gaining ideas, defensive, or dual purposes because eventually they may let them go. However, these same motives are not permissible for the priests or teachers. The dual teaching is a preliminary teaching that eventually has to be replaced by the non-dual Mahayana mind.

There is the wine of delusion but then there is also the wine of enlightenment. In evolved Zen teaching, not only is the teaching of enlightenment abandoned but also the teaching of not teaching is also abandoned. When no targets are set up, then no injuring arrows are forthcoming. There is nothing to argue or not argue about.

TETRALEMMA	
delusion	Formal Logic. One is True and one is False, or one may be true for people but not for leaders. Imaginary.
enlightenment	
There is delusion in enlightenment and enlightenment in delusion.	Dialectical Logic. Symbolic.
Neither delusion nor enlightenment. Nothing to teach.	Negative Dialectics. Real.
No positive teaching of emptiness or of negating the non-dual teaching. There is emptiness in both delusion and enlightenment. Awakening from delusion within delusion or from enlightenment within enlightenment.	

Jacob's ladder and the four wisdoms

There is a classical Midrash that connects the four steps of Jacob's ladder (Genesis 28:10–19) with the four-lettered Name, and the four worlds. The four worlds can also be linked with the four wisdoms of Buddhism. There is the wisdom of the infinite mirror of seeing everything as it is from the perspective of both form and emptiness. Then there is the wisdom of thought, creation or of discerning the differences among things. The third wisdom is the wisdom of compassion and of seeing things from the perspective of the One (sameness). Finally, there is the wisdom of action or of manifesting/realising Dharma/Torah in everyday activities. The noumena is found in phenomena.

The four worlds are One, in the sense that each One is One but also in the sense that each One both conceals and reveals the other three. The One conceals the Other and the Other reveals the One. Universe in Latin

points to the revealed universe, the One turning verse. The word *Olam*
in Hebrew points to the aspect of the world that is concealed. Latin
ignores what Hebrew knows as well as vice versa. When one dimension
of the world is revealed, the other is concealed. The universe conceals
the multiverse, or the One conceals the Other, while the multiverse
reveals the One, or the principle of the One in the Other. The One is
always meeting the One in the Other. This principle can also be described
as "Japanese prime minister 'Uno' (One in Spanish) arrives in Jerusa-
lem". The traditions of India meet the traditions of Israel, or the I meets
the I, and Ishmael meets Isaac. The One sees eye to eye with the One
and with the Other. The gaze of the Other is the look of the One and the
look of the other is the gaze of the One.

The first principle conceals/reveals the second principle, and the
second principle conceals/reveals the first principle. Differences con-
ceal/reveal similarities and similarities conceal/reveal differences.
Wisdom conceals/reveals compassion and compassion conceals/
reveals wisdom. Speech conceals/reveals thinking and thinking
conceals/reveals speech. Speech and compassion conceal/reveal action
and actions conceal/reveal compassion. And so on and so forth in all
possible combinations.

Inspired by the Midrash, as much as direct experience, I propose to
consider the four steps of Jacob's ladder in the following way:

1. The letter Yud corresponds to non-thinking. The experience of non-
   thinking is the experience of resurrection/redemption, of being
   reborn and of psychical death and self-transformation while still
   alive. In Buddhism, this corresponds to the clear round-mirror
   wisdom and according to the Kabbalah prophecy and vision come
   through a mirror (the infinite mirror). Things previously unseen or
   understood can now be clearly realised.
2. The letter Hei or "G-d's hand" as the thought of enlightenment
   without end. The thought of impermanence and creation within
   birth and death. The wisdom of discernment: "I sat alone, because
   Thy hand was upon me" (Jeremiah 15:17).
3. The letter Vov or "G-d's arm" or the Bodhisattva of one thousand
   arms. This is the bridge of communion and of compassion and right
   speech. Blessings require a benediction, or that right thoughts be
   uttered and said to the other. This is the wisdom of compassion. In the
   Torah, G-d speaks to the prophets in enigmatic dreams and visions,

but to Moses he speaks mouth to mouth and in the awakened state. Wisdom is revealed not only in enigmatic speech or non-duality but also in simple benedictions and enunciations within the world of duality.

The Book of Job (19:26) states: "from my flesh I see God". This refers to the body and to the world of feelings in relationship to thoughts. The interaction between the mind–body *jouissance* of Atzilut (Other *jouissance* in Lacanian theory) and feelings leads to the four divine abidings: loving kindness, joy, equanimity, and compassion. Benedictions are uttered out of the four divine abidings.

4. The letter **Hei** or the human hand that receives (kabbalah) and that acts beyond thinking. Enlightened action or activity: symbolic acts that bring the four worlds together. This is the wisdom of action. When you act beyond thinking then space and the essence moves with you like a bird flying in the sky or like a swan swimming in a lake. In this case, there is no difference between thought and creation: bird and thought is One and the same thing.

The Name of the Father and sexuation

The Tetragrammaton in classical Kabbalah is also used to describe the masculine and feminine attributes of G-d. The concealed aspect of G-d is masculine (YH) and the revealed aspect is feminine (VH or *Shechinah*), the reverse of the anatomical characteristics of human genitals (revealed for the male, concealed for the female). This use of the Tetragrammaton can be linked to how the Name of the Father concept in Lacan is used to explain sexual difference. Sexual difference is given by the father rather than by the mother or her desire. In relationship to the mother, both sexes are the same; while in relationship to the father, they are different.

The Lacanian concept of the Name of the Father allows for a different interpretation of the mystery surrounding the difference between the sexes. Sexual difference cuts against the grain of the symmetry and alleged harmony between male and female, Ying and Yang, that is commonly cited in spiritual literature. The usual Jungian anima and animus simply points to bisexuality or androgeny as the optimal solution for the conflict between the sexes and does not adequately address the serious problems associated with sexuality and sexual difference. Bisexuality does not eliminate difference, because if the male becomes feminine and the female masculine, there is still a difference between the biological male and psychical femininity, and between the biological female and psychical masculinity.

I mention the serious problem of sexual differences because beyond the ideological struggles for equality between the sexes (necessary in education, employment, politics, etc.), the conflicted relationship between the sexes in sex and marriage does not seem to be helped by any spiritual or egalitarian ideology as reflected in the increased rate of failed relationships in Western postmodern culture.

To the credit of Torah and Judaism, the sexual relationship and the relationship between the sexes is never excluded from any discussion of spirituality or the gender of G-d himself/herself. This fact is seen by many as consistent with the Jewish origins of psychoanalysis.

But then how to understand sexual difference from a combined Lacanian and Kabbalistic perspective? To begin this effort, I will insert Lacanian mathemes into biblical text regarding the sexes.

God created man (\$) in his image ($\emptyset$), in the image of God he created him (Φ), male and female he created them (φ/a) (Genesis 1:27).

Rather than understanding the masculine bent of the text as a sign of patriarchy and of masculine domination/supremacy, the text can also be reframed as a reference to the function of the Tetragrammaton and the Name of the Father as a structural operator in generating the differences between the sexes. This asymmetry with regard to the sexes, which appears to be resolved on the side of masculinity, needs to be understood against the background of the symmetry between the sexes in relationship to the desire of the mother. The asymmetry between the sexes places the problem of equality in relationship to a loss or emptiness rather than in terms of a symmetrical net gain for masculinity and/or femininity. There is symmetry with regard to having and not having, but asymmetry with regard to the registers in which the loss and gain takes place, and whether the loss takes place at the point of exit or entry into Oedipal/family structure.

Patriarchal and egalitarian discourses are mirror images of one another. The problem for egalitarian discourse is not that the masculine has something that the feminine is deprived of, but that the feminine wants the same power that the masculine is perceived as having. The first mistake is the perception that the masculine somehow is not subject to symbolic castration. Symbolic castration itself is confused with imaginary castration as a kind of dispensable damage that society or patriarchy has inflicted upon men. Matriarchy in turn is conceived as a purely supportive, gratifying, and permissive society or social organisation.

The second error, which follows from the first, is thinking that the solution is for women to aspire to the same kind of illusory masculinity, rather than making men accountable to the loss that society extracts from the individual. Femininity and feminism, therefore, are conceived in the image of imaginary masculinity. In turn, femininity is also conceived in imaginary terms as a form of powerlessness or oppressive kind of emasculation. It is this kind of interpretation of the biblical text that is responsible for the very prejudice that the text is perceived as embodying. Truth is in the eye of the beholder.

"G-d created man" needs to be interpreted as the creation of sexual difference within the world of thinking (the sexual theories of children, according to Freud). The boy fears losing what he thinks he has or that his father has given him (φ), and the girl fears not having ($-\varphi$) what she thinks the father and the boy have. The image of the father/G-d in this case is an emptiness of absence ($\emptyset$) rather than a presence. YH as the masculine side of the Name is the concealed face of the supernal image (dark mirror) and the shadow or dark light that this absence casts on both sexes.

The narrow path/pass beyond the rock of castration involves both sexes having to come to terms with the loss of the imaginary phallus in themselves and in the Other. This represents a structural loss that can be symbolised by the symbolic phallus that is missing by its very definition (Φ). If the boy can accept the loss of the imaginary signifier he thought he had, then via the loss of loss he will be able to use the object that he has and gain access to phallic *jouissance*. If the girl can accept what she does not have, then she will also gain access to phallic *jouissance* with a man, and to feminine *jouissance* or a primary form of femininity (*objet a*) not available to masculinity (as distinct from biological maleness) at least at a sexual or gendered level.

The graph or grid below combines Lacan's thought on sexuation and *jouissance*, Freud's ideas on religion, and Kabbalistic thought regarding the sexes. I place the imaginary axis for both sexes in the middle to show how both sexes identify imaginary femininity with the absence of the imaginary phallus and how both sexes identify imaginary masculinity (in males or females) with the presence of the imaginary phallus.

Masculinity	Femininity
Dependence on a Providential Father. The Name/Phallus that conceals the gap of the subject. Imaginary/Symbolic Law.	Symbiosis with mother. *Jouissance* of the Other. Imaginary/Real version of the oceanic feeling or dual unity.
φ and –φ (Imaginary Phallus)	
$\exists x\,\overline{\Phi}x$ There does exist a man (male or female) not subject to castration. Primal Father. Phallic female.	$\overline{\exists x\,\overline{\Phi}x}$ There does not exist a woman not subject to castration.
Phallic *jouissance*	
$\forall x\,\Phi x$ **S(Ø)** All men are castrated. If used, the Name of the Father can be dispensed with. Name of the dead father that reveals the lack in the Other and the subject of the Real. *Yud Hay*. Other *jouissance*. Symbolic/Real. The Name is the Signifier of a lack/emptiness. Phallic function.	$\overline{\forall x}\,\Phi x$ Not all of a woman is subject to castration. Feminine *jouissance*. *Vov Hay*. Symbolic/Real. *Objet a*. *Chaya* or Infinite Life. *Shechinah*/ Primary Femininity.

Finally, and to conclude, I offer a supplemental grid of "Zenxuation" to represent the graph of sexuation within a Zen framework.

	Femininity	Masculinity
Imaginary	Selflessness as low self-esteem, as an absence of ego rather than as the emptiness of no-self.	Narcissistic and aggressive idea of perfection. The ideal ego and the imaginary phallus.
Symbolic	In no-self the myriad things advance and confirm the self.	No-self as a negation of ego. Ego-death and no-self as an ego-ideal.
Real	The signlessness of the Real. Infinite Life.	No-Buddha and the no of Buddha. The Infinite Mirror.

Many women, especially in the United States, feel hurt by the teaching of no-self because it seems to reinforce the selflessness and powerlessness that women already experience in patriarchal society. However, I propose that this perception mistakes two kinds of powers and two different registers or aspects of self-nature. There is the power of domination and then there is the power of renunciation. From the point of view of domination, the power of renunciation appears as weakness, but from the point of renunciation, the signs are reversed. Brute power or force is a form of ethical weakness, and renunciation represents great character strength and virtue. This explains why there is so much controversy in the political left and right as to whether traditional femininity represents a form of weakness or strength. The same goes for the power of domination.

Thus, I address the paradox of power and gender by placing them within the context of the registers of experience. In the Imaginary, domination and lack of self represent strength and weakness respectively for the masculine and the feminine; while in the Symbolic, the values are reversed. Femininity gains access to the self-confirmation and mirroring given by things, situations, and cultural forms (such as education). Masculinity has to experience a negative moment of losing what men thought they had in order to gain access to the Symbolic proper (legitimacy rather than domination). Symbolic masculinity differs from the imaginary masculinity represented by patriarchal culture. It also differs from the emasculated man of postmodern culture or first-wave feminism as commonly understood. Both patriarchy and matriarchy are two sides of an imaginary construction. In the case of patriarchy, for example, the right of men in traditional cultures of marrying prepubescent girls, and having sex with them once they can bear the weight of older men, cannot but be seen as a perverse form of the archaic and brutal imaginary father.

Because the symbolic loss of the imaginary phallus is first experienced in the Imaginary, masculinity is prone to reifying the legitimacy of the Symbolic. The superego and the ego-ideal are forms of the ego, and therefore subject to narcissistic distortion whether in patriarchal or matriarchal organisations. This danger is corrected in the dimension of the Real via the negation of Buddha (true Buddha is no Buddha) and the practice of beginners' mind. The phallic function of symbolic castration also gives both sexes access to phallic *jouissance* and to a supplemental *jouissance* in the case of femininity. Finally, femininity remains Real so long as the self-confirmation provided by things remains traceless and this tracelessness is continued forever, as Dogen says in the Genjo koan.

Symbolic loss and the breaking of the glass and mirror

Glass is a wonderful human creation. A drinking-glass has the wonderful function of holding water and a looking-glass reflects the light. A glass holds water and a mirror reflects everything as it is while being empty and transparent of self-nature. Yet glass is a fragile thing and can easily break. When it breaks, it breaks along the lines it was made of. The glass, like everything, has a structure, but once the structure is put together, the structure vanishes into the phenomenal world and is revealed as a single event (the glass). In a Zen story, Manjusri, or the bodhisattva of wisdom, is showing a visiting monk a transparent glass and asks him whether they have glasses like this at the monastery where he comes from. The monk takes a good look at the glass and when he turns around to answer the question, Manjusri has already vanished. The question about the glass was not only about the glass but about self and no-self, perception and non-perception.

In another story, a disciple asks the teacher: "What should I do with my mind once it has become like a clear mirror that reflects everything?" (one of the four wisdoms of the Buddha). The teacher answered: "Break it into a thousand pieces."

In contrast to the Kabbalistic Lurianic myth of the breaking of the vessels, the mirror does not break because the light was way too powerful to be contained by the form of the looking-glass or clear mirror (vessels). This assumption reveals a duality and a hierarchy between emptiness and form (with the former being more powerful than the latter). It is the function of the mirror to break because a mirror does not exist without the things that it reflects. Mirror and reflection arise together. The mirror is in the reflection and the reflection is in the mirror. When the mirror breaks, the mirror vanishes into the pieces and the peace of the things that it was reflecting. In addition, all mental and material formations are in a process of dissolution, of breaking up like fine glasses smashing.

Sometimes, a person gets up early in the morning to build a mirror that will reflect everything in the universe. At other times, the same person has to rest and sleep in, and the mirror lies covered or darkened by sleep, tiredness, and aching muscles.

The universe itself has a built-in defect in the purity of the mirror ($\emptyset$). The still clear mirror is broken in one big bang, in one fell swoop. If the mirror did not break, there would be no activity or universe to speak of. There has to be activity, and for speaking beings there have to be things to speak, commune, and communicate about. This is the so-called defect in the purity of emptiness. Stillness is replaced by a noisy conversation in the middle of a noisy street. Yet it is all taking place within perfect stillness. The landscape stands still although the earth and the universe are accelerating at amazing speeds.

But in the course of things, we become afraid of the activity and anxious over the breaking apart that comes with impermanence. We don't understand why or how things fall apart or are put together or come together once again. We become anxious over the presence or absence of subject and object, over the things that appear when the mirror disappears, and over the empty mirror that appears when things disappear or cease in their function.

This is similar to the breaking of a glass at a Jewish wedding. Right at the moment that the mirror shines bright, the glass is broken to remind us of the ordinary and everydayness that will constitute the basis for the marriage. Weddings are wonderful, but the greatness of a wedding is in no way a reflection of whether the marriage itself will work. Just like two bodies will become one flesh, particles in the universe are merrily going their way, matter and anti-matter jostling and clashing, positive and negative electrons interacting, sometimes coming together, and sometimes growing and pulling apart.

Eigen (1998) points out how in Winnicott's notion of primary unintegration, pattern-making or structure is secondary. Unintegration may even be antistructural or poststructural. Unintegration represents the breaking of the mirror or of the vessels, like a bull in a china shop. Formlessness, chaos, or nothingness prevails. Similarly, anthropologists have discovered rites of passage or liminality, times to rest from structure, hierarchy, and the press of the structure of society, or the demands of the Other. What a relief not to have to shape up or wake up at a certain time. But when we rest from one set of demands, we don't exchange this for no demands at all, but rather for a different set of demands altogether. When not responding to structural demands, we are responding to the demands of anti-structure or unintegration. There is a Jewish joke (perhaps a serious joke) about the devil telling a person not to get up in the morning at the appointed time. The devil says "Come on Joe, you are way too old to be getting up this early." Joe responds to the devil: "But you are way older than me, and you are already up."

Non-structure represents emptiness rather than form, or impermanence, change, and free energy rather than a stable homeostasis or quiescent energy. Free energy also comes in different forms. For Breuer, before Freud, it was a state of stability and clarity. For Prigogine (1984), as for Freud, energy is unstable and subject to flow and motion. Free here means primary rather than a secondary process. But primary process or instability is not a stable unstable state either. Things are in flux until there is a paradigm change; things are unstable for a while until a new order emerges out of chaos or emptiness.

For Kabbalah, the conventional order of the signifier needs to break down, disintegrate, and dissolve in order for a new order to emerge from the ashes of the great fire of liberation. The same is true in Zen. A practitioner temporarily withdraws from ordinary life in order to practise meditation, and this may cause a crisis in their life, in their family, or their livelihood, if the latter three had not happened already. But once the Real is realised, then the Real can be inserted right back into the symbolic order and the ordinary becomes the true ordinary, emptiness becomes form and form emptiness. Ordinary is related to order not disorder.

You might as well enjoy the senselessness of it all, the confusion and loose associations between theories and registers, men and women, self and other, life and death, pleasure and pain, because it won't last either. Pretty soon, a new regime or order will be set in place, a new cookie will be baked, until the new upheaval or until the cookie crumbles once again and a new universe is born, and so on and so forth *ad infinitum*.

Eigen, following Winnicott, points out how unintegration corresponds to analytic free association within a session as a time for aliveness and play. Unintegration has a definite positive role to play in the life of the psyche. From this perspective, an integrative approach has similar problems to a holistic approach, if by holism we mean a whole that does not have a hole or emptiness in it. As soon as we call something integrated, the spectre of disintegration or dissolution becomes a real living possibility. In analysis, an old characterological order needs to be broken up and the pieces reassembled or the strings re-knotted. The unconscious emerges piece by piece like pieces of a puzzle that at first appear to be random and chaotic and yet over time end up forming part of a coherent structure.

The fragmentary nature of the psyche is produced by two elements in constant conjunction (an acausal or anti-causal concept that Bion (1965) borrowed from Hume): the displacement of the object of desire, from one object/signifier to the next, in an infinite attempt to find the same elusive object; and the defences taking place within language forever vigilant in their attempts to reveal and conceal disturbing beta or rogue elements of the psyche. Beta elements include internal and external objects, physiological states of hunger, imaginary hatred, and *jouissance* surrounded by the actions, traits, and partial objects of the other: a noise, a grunt, a smell, a nose, a cough, a voice, gaze, and so on.

The Borromean knot, as a topological theory, is a theory of non-equilibrium, because far from equilibrium, oppositions, contradictions, repressions, divisions, misunderstandings, fluctuations, and bifurcations are the norm. The registers are both One and Other to each other. The three registers say "I am One" at the same time, thereby instantaneously becoming Other for each other. Chaos is a type of unstable order. Order functions across different dimensions of time and across different worlds. Multiple, variable activities are required to produce order in nature, and yet everything is reflecting everything else in perfect and stable stillness. The more it changes, the more it remains the same. The Other is also One and the One Other.

Breaking points are predicted by the structure. Breaking points are vanishing points where the structure dissipates or evaporates and reveals itself as discontinuous. The place of connection or intersection is also the place of emptiness or formlessness, the point where the structure folds on itself. However, pretty soon, once dissipated, the structure or form will emerge once again as if by magic, like a bubble or a dream.

In another place, Eigen links unintegration to the experience of dread that comes with change:

> Bion tends to emphasize negative aspects of experiencing in O in his explicit "descriptions" (analogical evocations). For him impact of O tends to be dreadful: "The emotional state of transformations in O is akin to dread …. To let go of usual modes of being and knowing is frightening.

(p. 77)

The place of connection is also one of disconnection. Either connection or disconnection, binding or unbinding, can lead to life or death, and life and death can also lead to one another. The analysand connects with the analyst yet has to disconnect from aspects of their own psyche, from defences that have provided equilibrium, and reconnect with parts of themselves that they have disowned or rejected. Breakdown and break-through, form and emptiness, stability and change, are interrelated. The unconscious and undoing of defences can be scary. Malevolent deper-sonalisation is awful while benevolent depersonalization is awesome, but the two often happen together in varying combinations. To undergo personal transformation can be pleasant and painful, awful and awe-some, at the same time.

There are positive qualities of the unconscious that are not simply functions of the ego, since the ego tends to be threatened by non-being and reactive to processes beyond understanding or rational formal description. Examples of positive qualities of the unconscious include the Real unconscious of the unknown, enigmatic or unknown-knowing, the Other *jouissance* as a manifestation of the drive and *das Ding*, the creative imagination, free energy on the basis of a primary secondary principle, the unconscious of the lack or of the void that includes the concept of the lack and the lack of a concept, and so on.

As Bion taught, to accept the unpleasure or pain that comes with transformation and growth requires modifying the pleasure principle but also the usual ways of defining or thinking about the world and others. Undoing defences in a session or in a conversation and work-ing with the feelings evoked may be unpleasant and even traumatic, something to be avoided or at least not repeated. However, sooner or later, the same place will have to be revisited once again, if not in this session, in the next; if not with this analyst, with the next; and if not in this period of life, in the next.

Bion tends to think of the processing ability of the psyche in the image of the secondary process or as a process of defence against trauma. However, the processing function includes both primary proc-ess and secondary process and both include an entanglement of desires, drives, and defences. Processing creates chaos and order, construction and deconstruction, expression and repression.

The processing ability of the psyche is both expressive and repres-sive. The primary process manifests the drive and reveals desire at the same time that it looks for the next satisfaction or image/representation to avoid the dissatisfaction associated with the first one. Defences not only help recover from old trauma but also lay the foundations for new ones. Within development, frustration emerges from the ashes of privation only to have future castrations to look forward to. Deficient processing takes place not because of earlier or original traumas (of the embryonic psyche or the birth trauma), but because old defences create new problems and desires that continue to overwhelm the current defensive capacities that will soon be replaced by new formations of desire and defence.

CHAPTER SEVEN

Mindfulness of breathing and psychoanalysis

This chapter is dedicated to Wilhelm Reich, who is generally considered the father of character analysis (within psychoanalysis) and of somatic psychotherapy (outside psychoanalysis). Reich was a brilliant and tortured soul who had experienced the object matter of psychoanalysis in his own personal family history. He witnessed his mother's infidelity at a young age and both parents died under tragic circumstances. Unfortunately, he was not able to find an analyst with whom he could have carried an analysis to its logical conclusion. Nevertheless, despite his personal difficulties, Reich raised important questions at the intersection of the mind and the biological, libidinal, and social body.

The organism self-regulates according to the homeostatic function that Cannon (1932) called the "wisdom of the body". At the same time, the organism is also not without organ or system weaknesses leading to illness or imbalance within the homeostatic function or the immune system. Structure and anti-structure are found in steps across the subatomic, atomic, cellular, and organ levels of matter: electrons work within atoms, atoms fall into molecules, molecules form into cells, cells combine into organs, and organs work within systems, and systems are regulated by the brain. All in all, there are 200 trillion atoms inside a human cell and 100 trillion cells inside a human body.

The autonomic nervous system controls respiration, urination, sexual arousal, and maintains homeostasis. Etymologically speaking, "homeostasis" means "similar stasis" or "similar standing (or sitting) still". The word represents the function/concept of maintaining a stable constant condition within the internal or external environment.

Homeostasis (under the ANS) regulates body temperature, sugar levels, and pH levels in the blood. The autonomic nervous system is divided into two subsystems: sympathetic and parasympathetic. The sympathetic nerve cells mobilise energy for the "fight or flight" reaction during stress, causing increased blood pressure, breathing rate, and blood flow to muscles.

Conversely, the parasympathetic nerves have a calming effect; they slow the heartbeat and breathing rate, and promote digestion and elimination. Thus, stasis or constancy has different or opposite meanings in the sympathetic and parasympathetic systems. In the first, stasis represents arousal, while in the second, it means quieting and calming. This does not amount to a formal contradiction because we are speaking of two subsystems within a system (the contradiction is not happening in the same place in the same respect).

The same is not true when the concept is applied to more general psychosocial phenomena. Homeostasis or stasis can mean the elimination of conflict when opposing forces cancel each other out or are otherwise reconciled. Here, stasis points to a state of psychological and social peace. But stasis can also mean a set of symptoms indicating an internal disturbance and high stress in individuals and groups.

In this way, the biological mechanism of homeostasis needs to be differentiated from the phenomena associated with mental, psychical, family, and social group defences. For example, Lyotard (1989) has pointed out that within academic, professional, political, or religious organisations and hierarchies, the *status quo* is maintained by disregarding ideas that disturb prevailing views and structures. According to family systems theory, the stability of the family is maintained when a family illness, problem, or secret is denied or defended against by having a scapegoat onto which the illness of the family can be projected and thereby disowned. In both of these examples, stability is maintained despite it being detrimental to those involved.

Within psychosocial phenomena, not "rocking the boat", or maintaining homeostasis, can have either positive or negative consequences. Within physical phenomena, not rocking the boat, or homeostasis, has only one beneficent meaning. However, when a physical phenomenon is used as a metaphor within a different human context, the meaning changes accordingly and becomes polyvalent. This is a good example of how different kinds of logic are necessary to understand natural and psychosocial phenomena. Formal logic may be sufficient for natural phenomena, but dialectical logic, and negative dialectics or what I call the logic of contradiction, is fundamental to understand psychosocial phenomena.

Breath awareness differs from automatic breathing within the ANS. Breath awareness would seem to be a function of the central nervous system (CNS). In meditation, breath awareness can range from following the breath to leading the breath from the chest to the belly, or *hara* as it is called in Japanese Zen. Once the breath is circulating from the nostrils to the stomach and back at a slow rate, then breathing once again can happen in an automatic, autonomous, natural fashion (ANS).

Now, how are body and mind linked in this case, what makes the transition from the homeostasis of the ANS to the homeostasis that takes place within psychosocial phenomena and according to a different logic?

According to Buddhism, human beings are self-created, but the self in this case is Big self or Big mind and not the small self of the ego. For example, the CNS gives human beings voluntary control of motor activity, but this is something that for most people is found already there, it is a given that is taken for granted. The CNS does not appear to have been designed by any particular human being. Nonetheless, the CNS is something that evolved from the activity of organisms over many generations. Big mind is this activity over a long period of time and that includes a collectivity of species being.

Much like the nervous system, language evolved from speech and writing and human culture over many generations of human activity. Now we find language already there as our own activity that speaks to us and regulates our interactions in a similar way to how the ANS regulates many functions of the organism. Nonetheless, like with the CNS human beings also have control over speech and writing.

The Lacanian psychical or psychosocial Other represents how language operates and manifests within human subjectivity and intersubjectivity in an automatic, autonomous, machinic-like structure that is not without lack, inconsistencies, chaos, contradictions, or breaking points.

Language as a mental function emerges from an interaction between biological brain and human culture. The laws of culture interact with the natural laws of the brain/body, producing what we know of as mind. Language represents things that are absent and that became a part of human culture through a series of sensory mediums and cognitive mediations. Cultural rules or laws co-arise with the laws of language to conform what Lacan called the Other or the register of the Symbolic. It is the mind, in the sense of language and culture, that in turn programmes and wires the thresholds and action potentials for the inhibition and facilitation of substances involved in the transmission of impulses within sensory or motor nerves of the brain.

The Other is a better term for a social or cultural environment that reaches deeply into the inner recesses of the mind and the body and from there conditions or determines the functioning of the mind and the body, at least to some extent. It is difficult to say which part of the brain responds to the organism and the natural environment and which part interacts with the cultural and psycho-familial environment. Many mental functions such as thinking, attention, and desire may constitute emergent synchronised brain waves combining different areas of the brain. It is still unknown whether the different complementary causal series (cultural and psychical factors) are based in areas of the brain or constitute different types of brain waves emerging from the combined action potentials of several areas of the biological brain.

Breathing and the objet a

Psychoanalytically speaking, breath awareness is a function of the Real subject that is devoid of content and lives between ideas and words. A world linked together by the invisible network of language provides some breathing room for the subject in the spaces and silences between words.

A Real awareness is Real in a double sense. First, because it is linked to the Real of the organism (the breath) that functions independently of the ideas or concepts we may have about it; and second, because it differs from the phenomenological consciousness that is tied to the Other's gaze and recognition.

The Real in Lacan is linked not only to the organism but also to the drive in the form of *das Ding* or the no-thing or emptiness. Furthermore, breathing is linked to emptiness in two ways. Emptiness has an intimate association with space and air (Shakespeare's "airy nothing of heaven"). Both air and space seem to be like nothing yet there is something living in it (for example, particles, molecules, and dark matter and energy).

To the naked eye, air (oxygen and wind) is something apparently invisible and immaterial (although a chemical element) yet required for biological life. In the Hebrew Bible (Kaplan, 1981), both spirit and soul are linked to air and breathing (*Ruach*/wind, *neshama*/soul, and *neshima*/breath). *Ruach* or wind/spirit is like a fragrance (*Reach*) that can be sensed despite its invisibility. Spirit as wind also points to movement within stillness (of the mind). In addition, soul is also spoken in terms of *nefesh* that comes from the root *nafash*, meaning to rest, as in the Sabbath. These words point to a signifying chain linking the breath to a state of rest or calmness.

Emptiness is also linked to space in the sense of the empty space that exists within the cavities, orifices, and channels of the body. Air circulates through the empty pipes that run between the nostrils, the throat, the lungs, the stomach, and the mouth. Air also has a function of connecting or linking the inside and the outside between people and between people and their environment.

I propose that breath can be considered what Lacan called an *objet a*. Dolto (1987), who was a follower and colleague of Lacan, called the breath an unconscious image of the body. The breath as an unconscious image of the body differs from the specular image as a total image of the body reflected in a clear mirror. If anything, the breath as an *objet a* is represented by the mouth and the nostrils as part-objects. However, the notion of the part-object in this context appears as a "holon". A holon is something that is simultaneously both a whole and a part (Koestler, 1967). The holon is similar to the synecdoche as a figure of rhetoric or language where the part of something is used to refer to the whole thing (for example, a sail for a boat). However, in my opinion, a holon also evokes a part that not only contains the totality but also contains a hole or emptiness in it.

As the breast is to the mouth, the breath is to the nostrils. The breath is an imageless image or an empty image, and for this reason alone perhaps it can be called unconscious. In addition, the breath circulates within the tubes of the body much like the mamilla, the urine, faeces, gaze, voice, and no-thing that Lacan (1966a, p. 303) also considered forms of the *objet a*. Finally, the breath, like the *objet a*, is a something that is a nothing or a no-thing.

The *objet a* is what the Other lost and continues to be present as an absence or a no-thing within the Other. The breath circulates between the emptiness of the other and the emptiness of the subject. Within the subject, the *objet a* remains in the form of the transformations of *jouissance* precipitated by grieving the loss of the object. The subject cannot be the *a* for the Other nor can the Other give this object to the subject. Yet the Other remains within the subject as a no-thing or as the presence of an absence. Air like the *objet a* is what unconsciously circulates between the subject and the Other.

In addition, within the Other of language, as well as within the subject, air lives between words and within the silences between words. The subject has to breathe between words, and Lacan says that the subject inhabits the space or gaps within discourse. Thus, I link breathing with the subject of the Real, and the latter is also linked to the subject of *jouissance*. Breathing can be both cause and effect of *jouissance*. Voluntary breathing awareness can produce the relaxation response and phallic *jouissance*, or sexual arousal and excitation, can lead to an increase of the breathing rate within the autonomic nervous system.

In addition, a subject can represent a split or a division between two signifiers ($) as in the example of the flight or fight response between two opposing subjects/signifiers. Such a split can manifest intra- or inter-subjectively, as shown below. The division and duality is a result of homeostasis as a defence and of aggressiveness in the name of the survival of the individual.

$$\frac{S_1}{S_2(\$)} \quad \text{or} \quad S_1 \leftrightarrows S_2$$

The division between S_1 and S_2 represents a relationship of contradiction. Either the unconscious subject causes the fading of the ego or the ego causes the division of the subject (by repressing the subject/object of the unconscious). In the first case, the Symbolic prevails over the Imaginary and a symbolic order is sustained. In the second case, the Imaginary prevails over the Symbolic, leading to a division in the subject and the order itself.

Usually S_2 is the story that is told about a signifier or a subject (S_1). However, in the narrative and discursive process a story or S_2 supplants/suppresses or causes the disappearance of the signifier or the subject (S_1) that contradicts or could be the basis for other possible censored stories that could have been told about the same subject.

The subject becomes the split between two dominant and suppressed parental stories/imaginary signifiers. What is missing from the dominant story, or what can be found in the gaps in the dominant story, are three things: the suppressed story/signifiers, the subject, and the void itself. The balance between conflicting stories is restored by suppressing one of the terms involved and subordinating the suppressed term to the dominant one. Both the subject and the void/lack are suppressed in the process.

The notion of homeostasis or balance in the case of psychical defences is similar yet differs from the function of homeostasis at work within natural systems (not identical).

The function of high or low defensiveness is related to the double meaning of stasis and homeostasis. Homeostasis keeps stress/desire at a certain high level for both excitation under sexual arousal and the fight/flight response (sympathetic) or at a low level for a calming and relaxing response (parasympathetic). In both cases, homeostasis is a necessary and positive natural regulating mechanism.

However, within the mind and psychosocial phenomena, either form of homeostasis can be detrimental or beneficial, defensive or non-defensive. In addition, there is the further question if there is such a thing as healthy and unhealthy defences in the psychical realm.

In biological homeostasis, the tension or intensity has to be kept constant either at a high or low level, but in either case tension is a beneficial event. In the phenomena of psychical defences, the tension in desire or arousal can be detrimental or beneficial. Desire can be defensive (to produce the lack in the Other) and the defence can also produce a form of desire or *jouissance*. The high tension in the case of sexual arousal or exercise, for example, can be beneficial for the subject and the body, although they both could be psychically defensive and detrimental. Both instances could represent aggressive forms of bolstering the ego of narcissism and a denial of the lack or vulnerability of the subject.

High tension and low tension need to be distinguished from the presence or absence of defensiveness. Either high or low tension could be defensive and non-defensive. Low tension could be non-defensive in cases where lowering tension leads to the ability to examine conflicts or problems. Conversely, lowering the tension and anxiety, for example, could strengthen the defences against addressing the causes and circumstances of anxiety because anxiety is no longer there. In such cases, the defences could be beneficial in the short run but detrimental in the long run.

Perhaps this distinction between short-term versus long-term outcomes is enough to account for the question of healthy versus unhealthy defences. Again, the same dialectical logic is at play: healthy can be unhealthy (in the long run) and unhealthy can be healthy (in the short run). High tension and conflict could be detrimental and unpleasant in the moment but beneficial in the long run. Low tension could be pleasant and beneficial in the moment but detrimental in the long run.

The critical difference depends on the capacity for observation, reflection, and retrospection, all of which are associated with insight or what Buddhism calls wisdom beyond wisdom. It is the latter that will regulate whether high or low tension will be detrimental or beneficent in the near or long-term future. Finally, Zen meditation, as a body—mind practice, incorporates high tension and low tension at the same time. In zazen, there is high tension or intensity in the body while the mind is at rest. In this sense, zazen resolves the contradiction between the sympathetic and the parasympathetic subsystems.

Being able to relax calms the anxiety but also serves the defences that produce the anxiety by lowering the anxiety but keeping the objects/ causes of anxiety out of awareness.

Awareness of breathing can be brought to bear to support the integrity of the organism but also of the dominant position. Automatic or autonomous breathing, like unconscious defences, aim at restoring homeostasis, self-preservation, and the *status quo* of the subject of the statement. The subject of the statement is linked to the ego, the ego-ideal, and the Jungian persona, because the ego is trying to put his/her best foot forward.

On the other hand, in Reichian psychotherapy, intentionally increasing the breathing rate was an integral part of working through the character and bodily armour. Voluntary breathing and speaking about family history, relationships, sexuality, or aggressiveness were used successively within a session.

Breath awareness can be used to increase the space for the subject of the enunciation that lives within the gap between signifiers. The subject of the enunciation is the subject of the unconscious, and therefore the subject in its true sense. In the process, some space can be created between the subject and his/her identifications. This can be of value to both participants in the analytic process.

On the side of the analyst, breathing can be used to support the free-floating attention that is necessary for analytic listening. On the side of the analysand, the analyst, who is not a medical doctor, can use breath awareness to intervene in cases of frequent and severe panic attacks. Breathing is less harmful than depending on anti-anxiety medications that cause dependence and require higher doses (build tolerance) over time.

CHAPTER EIGHT

Consciousness, awareness, the unconscious, and the three dimensions of experience

In this chapter, I will explore the concept of experience as understood in philosophy, psychoanalysis, and Zen Buddhism. I propose that the Lacanian theory of the Borromean knot provides a multidimensional framework that illuminates how the mentioned disciplines and the different notions and dimensions of experience (Real, Symbolic, Imaginary) interact and intersect one another.

The concept of experience is a good example of how different theorists approach a term from different, and sometimes opposing, perspectives that in fact need to be understood as interrelated within a multidimensional perspective such as that of the Borromean knot.

Phenomenology can be described as the study of the structures of consciousness as experienced from the first-person point of view. According to phenomenology, the central feature of an experience is its intentionality, its being directed towards something, since it is an experience of or about some object (Smith, 2007).

An experience is supposed to be directed towards an object by virtue of its content or meaning (which represents the object) and not necessarily by the so-called independent or objective quality of the object. However, this notion of intentionality can be seen from different perspectives. Is the conscious ego of a particular individual the agent of intentionality and signification, or is the agency of intentionality rather given by the unconscious or the ongoing dynamic and singular permutations of the unconscious structure of language and relationships? R. D. Laing (1964) in his book on Sartre addressed his critique of psychoanalysis in the following way:

> If a certain type of psycho-analytical thinking would reduce the complex realities of behavior and experience to such "pseudo-irreducibles" as an unsurpassable constitutional datum, an innate proportion of, say, life and death instinct, then existential criticism must set it on the correct course and help it to discover the intelligible choice of self, the fundamental project of becoming a certain sort of personal being. If we see personal life in Sartre's terms as constituted-constituting, as a synthetic unity of what we make of what we are made of, of moulding ourselves out of how we have been moulded, we must conclude that psychoanalytic theory in its weaker aspects ignores the active constituting, making moment of personal unity, thereby reducing the person to a resultant of instinctual vector/abstractions which leave no place for intentionality in each life.

(p. 23)

The target of Laing's critique was Kleinian rather than Lacanian psychoanalysis. We know that Lacan (1966a) wrote "The Instancy of the Letter in the Freudian Unconscious". The word "instancy" can also be referred to as agency, although instancy points to the fleeting quality of the experience rather than to a reified permanent or static structure. The way we experience phenomena or things is mediated by the agency/instancy of the letter/signifier more than by the pressure of biological instincts. The Other mediates the intentions of the subject.

If I want to read a book, do exercise, practise the guitar, or meditate, all of these projects/intentions/choices and resultant activities are the activities of a subject mediated by the cultural and linguistic factors associated with reading, athletic culture, music, and meditation, to name only a few. Purposes and intentions are embedded within language and require a subject to appropriate them. However, if one thinks of experiences with a particular aim/objective/gain in mind, this can only be an introductory approach to experience. The aim of gaining/constructing a self or a social ego and recognition eventually gets in the way of realisation. Realisation or actualisation is mediated by approaching an activity with what Zen teacher Shunryo Suzuki Roshi (1971) called a non-gaining beginners' mind. Ultimately, artists/scientists have to let go of themselves or their ego in the creative process, while at the same time being careful not to construct the letting-go process as yet another ego-making project.

Intentions are the subject matter of the ego-ideal that parents pass on to their children but that children have to embody in relationship to their own Life drive and narcissism. Intentions are first incarnate and personified in the Other, which here represents another flesh-and-blood human being that loves/desires the subject and on whom the subject's own self-love depends. Eventually, the relationship to the Other is replicated within the subject's own self. All of these are structural symbolic conditions and considerations that supersede any concern with the role of individual consciousness in intentionality. Although consciousness is found conditioned by the object and the place the subject has in the structure, awareness has the function of witnessing the effect the structure has in subjectivity. In contrast to consciousness, Real awareness as witness is ultimately unconditioned by either the subject or the object. I will discuss this feature of awareness further on.

The subject's first intention is to love and be loved/recognised by the Other. This relationship between the subject and the Other is the same as that between signifiers: $S_1 \rightarrow S_2$ and $S_2 \rightarrow S_1$. S_1 and S_2 are like the relationship between Lover and Beloved that represents Jack and Jill to one another. Lover is what represents Jack for the signifier beloved that also represents Jill for the signifier lover, otherwise known as Jack the subject.

Words and signifiers reveal not only wishes and desires but also the binding of ethical and rational intentions that do not conform to the aims of pleasure-seeking, or object-seeking for that matter. The ability to withstand pain, and postpone gratification, and make efforts that go beyond the obstacles of resistance is also an important dimension of intention and purposive action. In fact, it is this latter dimension of intentionality that has the greatest effect in the shaping of character and the meaning that experience has for a subject. We construct our selves, and transform our energetic intensities, via performing and re-presenting the intentions/practices of the Other.

It is this principle of enacting or practising the projects of others that make intentions our own and render them experiential. This is how

Heidegger (1953) thought of being as *Dasein*, or being-in-the-world. The world is as much outside as it is inside and, more often than not, the world inside is unconscious to us. We are not aware of the conditions that determine our experience to the same degree that we may notice the weather, for example.

Our very bodies are the product of evolution and the experiences of the species over long periods of time. We only know these experiences through the faculties and bodies that have evolved over time. Experience includes both learning and repetition. The word "nail", for example, can mean either the nail of a finger or a nail that binds or fastens two pieces of wood together. Both are the product of past experience that determines present experience and how we use fingers and hammers.

All experience requires a socially constructed subject that embodies and confirms the laws and regularities found in that culture. Cultures represent a set of principles and purposes or intentions aimed at modifying the experience of the subject in its natural environment. By using the Other and the reality principle of the society, the subject may learn to accept, work with, and transform/critique the problematic aspects of their experience.

Knowledge as wisdom is directed towards the quality of life of the subject of experience and is not solely dedicated to the explanation of phenomena and/or the discovery of the laws of nature.

Although an ego-psychology of consciousness or of intentionality and Freudian psychoanalysis both emphasise "consciousness-raising" or making conscious the unconscious, these traditions differ with respect to the emphasis given to the unconscious mind. The traditions also differ with respect to how the unconscious is understood. Freudian psychoanalysis critiques consciousness for the link that consciousness has with the ego and the ego's belief of being the master of his or her own house or the apex of creation. This critique also applies to the use of the practice of Buddhist mindfulness that has become popular and marketable in the United States as a way of building the sense of mastery that the ego individual has over experience.

For Zen, awareness is something both natural and hard won (as the capacity to live in the present moment) and the result of an in-depth exploration and practice of the body—mind and subjectivity. Awareness in Zen is a consciousness beyond consciousness, and therefore a consciousness that includes the unconscious or an unconscious awareness, in the sense of a themeless awareness without a subject or an object, or at least where the object of awareness may be something as intangible as the breath. The suchness/emptiness of breathing as an act is indivisible from its object: air or the invisible molecular form of matter that Shakespeare called the "airy nothing of heaven". Who is aware and about what? Who, What? These questions point to awareness as a mystery.

According to Freud (1920), awareness receives perceptions but retains no trace of them, so that it can react as a clean sheet or blank screen to every new perception. In my opinion, awareness is distinct from ego-consciousness (Cs.) because, for example, it receives the internal perception of a unary trait such as the person's name, yet remains distinct from the name. An example of this can be seen in the phenomena of name change. Awareness can establish a new link between the person and the new name, thus showing the difference between the unary trait as a memory value and awareness as a unary trace equivalent to zero.

Traits are organised within what Freud called the unconscious-perceptual system (Ucs.-Pcs.). Perception and the preconscious are unconscious in a descriptive sense. In this sense, perception can be said to be unconscious. Perceptual stimuli pass through awareness but are not processed there. They are processed in the Ucs.-Pcs., and only after having passed through a fresh evaluation/censorship can they emerge into Cs. as a recognition and interpretation of experience. Unentangled information is the kind that we perceive with consciousness once it emerges in a particular place of a structure or system.

The unconscious may contain what quantum theory (Deutsch, 1997) calls entangled or condensed information (Q'bits) that we do not perceive. Awareness receives momentary Q'bits or traces that are not perceived/retained as traits and thus remain entangled/condensed. According to quantum theory, entangled particles can share information with other entangled particles regardless of space—time. We do not have the capacity to perceive entangled particles, in the same way that, for example, we do not see the traces of birds flying in the air but other birds might.

Awareness itself might be such an entangled particle that we cannot see or understand because it does not retain a stable trait of its own. In this sense, there can be an unconscious awareness, however paradoxical this notion may sound. Awareness, or A, is a zero while Cs.

is a one. However, one cannot be One without a zero (Moncayo, 2012). Cs. cannot be awareness without the function of zero as a traceless trace that can receive traits without being totally defined by them. Awareness remains entangled and capable of experience but beyond our understanding and perception.

Awareness is a subjective faculty that differs from fantasies/ impulses or the prejudices of the ego-Cs. It is also based on direct experience rather than discursive argumentation or statistical analysis. Nonetheless, when awareness turns towards the subject or the object, the subject and the object arise together as intrinsic aspects of language and logic that are co-extensive with the material organisation of natural phenomena. Natural phenomena include the instinctual nature that gives rise to the imagined or fantasised constructions/interpretations of subject and object, as well as the actual interdependent symbolic relationships between the subject and object of a sentence, for example.

In addition, the contrast between reason and the experience of the senses is not absolute. Not only does instrumental rationality link cognitive interests with economic interests and the development of objects of use and consumption, but explanations can also have an impact on experience and subjectivity. Often, explanation can help someone feel understood. An example of this can be found in the treatment of anxiety disorders. Often, explaining to a person that they are having a panic attack, and that this is a well-known symptom/syndrome that will eventually pass, can alleviate the subjective feeling and belief that the person has that they are dying from a heart attack.

However, from a Lacanian perspective, the reason this explanation works is that the doctor is functioning on the basis of the transference to the subject supposed to know. Through knowledge, the person feels loved, reassured, and understood. This effect points to the connection between knowledge and love, a connection that is not entirely rational in terms of how we commonly understand rationality. The connection between love and knowledge highlights the link between knowing and the unconscious. There are unconscious ways of knowing about things if only because we choose to ignore what we know, or because we do not even know that we know or not know. In the latter case, we may experience something that is inconceivable in words or remains otherwise unformulated.

Interpretations deepen our experience because of the link between unknown knowing (Q'bits?) contained in the interpretation and the unknown knowing contained within the analysand's unconscious. Lacan's renewed practice of interpretation focuses on the relationship between the unknown knowing in the analyst and the unknown knowing in the analysand, rather than in the analyst using reason to make conscious the irrational unconscious of the analysand. The latter inevitably leads in the direction of using logic to correct the irrational beliefs of a patient (a cognitive-behavioural perspective).

Unconscious knowing is a knowing about lack/emptiness and desire. Knowledge in this sense is the knowing or disclosure of being and the lack/emptiness of being. Self-knowledge, or knowledge about subjectivity, rather than objective knowledge about natural phenomena, represents the study of the self. However, the study of the self has several dimensions. It includes the knowledge of mental and personality factors, but ultimately the study of the self is the study of Being or the reality of no-self. A subject that cannot find himself/herself will seek their self in the object or in the Other. However, as Lacan has pointed out, the Other cannot give the subject his or her own being.

The Other does not have the object that the subject thinks the other has to give and that the subject wants/lacks. All the Other and the subject have is their own emptiness. Wondrous emptiness is the agalma that the subject is seeking and that the Other appears to have. The agalma is the empty dimension of the *objet a* within the Real. Desire or the lack of being is seeking for the agalma in the object. The *objet a* is only a semblance of the phallus, the breast (etc.). The imaginary aspect of the *objet a* cannot give the subject his/her Being.

The revealing of Being has to do with revealing the emptiness of the Other and of the subject. This emptiness is also something that is neither subject nor object but rather a form of *jouissance*. Lacan says that the *objet a* is a semblance of *jouissance*. The subject has to find the *jouissance* of the Other as an Other *jouissance* within himself/herself. It is this *jouissance* that can serve as the basis of sublimation and a direct satisfaction of the drive that does not repress either phallic or feminine *jouissance*.

As we see, deconstruction of the subject or of the object, or of the ego's master's discourse, does not eliminate experience or the experience of *jouissance*. Analysis or deconstruction only deepens/transforms rather than eliminates experience. The subject is not only an effect of imaginary (ego) or symbolic forces but also embodies the agency of

Real unborn or infinite Life. The subject of the Real occupies the place of what is lacking within the Other of society and constitutes the place of transformation of the social/symbolic structure.

The subject of the Real is the no-place or the cause that is a-causal, or at least not a cause in the traditional sense of the word. Ordinarily, S_1 is a cause of S_2 (the constituted causing the constituting), the other causes the self, but self is also a cause of the other, or S_2 is a cause of S_1 (the constituting causing the constituted), a cause produces an effect, and the effect can be a cause for another effect, or the cause can function as an effect and the effect can function as a cause. Psychosocially, the ego and/or the master are causes in the traditional sense of the term. When the a-causal no-self is replaced by the ego, ego-representation leads to a closure of Being that wrecks havoc on society, the individual, and the environment.

When causality resides in the unconscious rather than in the ego, people often think that intentions or human activity become the effect of instinctual impulses ("I was not thinking", or "what was I thinking?!"). But another way to look at unconscious causality is that causality itself has become invisible or has disappeared. The cause is not invisible; rather, there is no cause: true being is non-being and true self is no-self.

Although causes disappear once an event has taken place (as a flashing into the phenomenal world), and their disappearance leads to a search for lost or hidden causes, none of these causes, when revealed or realised, will give us our Being or freedom. Instead, Being and freedom are realised by bringing causality to a halt (a-causality or the place where the privative a stops the search for the object).

According to Thompson (2003), Heidegger (1950) followed Hegel in understanding experience as something that befalls, affects, surprises, and transforms the subject. However, a change of form can represent either an involution or an evolution, something positive and progressive or something negative and regressive. The shock is by no means solely transcendental. Both the id, or the sexual and aggressive drives, life or death, and the sublime can have mind-altering effects. This distinction also parallels the difference between forbearance of suffering as a virtue and suffering that is nihilistic or masochistic and has no constructive or elevating/edifying purpose. Only sublimation represents a form of repetition with a difference, or new realisations/revelations that renew the old or the previously experienced and make the new different from the old. The slime or the viscosity of the id only looks like something new, but in reality it is a wolf in sheep's clothing.

If the conventional or so-called normal ego is presumed to be the ordinary state of mind of the individual in society, then both libidinal/aggressive excess and virtuous sublimation can produce a similar effect in opposite directions. This formulation is consistent with Freud's definition of sublimation (paraphrased above) as a direct satisfaction of the drive not involving repression.

The use of instrumental reason to further the socially accepted enjoyment of the senses or to satisfy the basic needs for food, clothing, and shelter would not qualify as experience according to Heidegger's definition. It is often the experience with hedonism and the road of excess that leads to the palace of wisdom (Blake, 1790, *The Proverbs of Hell*) and sublimation. This was certainly the case with the historical Buddha. In his father's palace, all his desires were indulged while once he left the palace and became an ascetic he denied himself all the impulses that he had previously enjoyed, and more. Eventually, and based on his lived experience with the norm and the extremes, he found the teaching of the middle way and his own personal enlightenment. Following Buddha's teaching and practice, at the turn of the Common Era, Mahayana Buddhism, as formulated by Nagarjuna and Vasubhandu in India, took the further step of linking enlightenment with a person's ordinary activities in the world as well as the enlightenment of all beings.

To avoid metaphysical or conceptual reification, the subject of the Real or the Real subject must be seen as a mode of *jouissance* and as a form of Being-in-between-worlds more than a Being-in-the-world. The Being-in-between-worlds is what allows the subject to consider each world as the One world, although there is more than one world. The signification of words emerges from a Real world of suchness beyond words and the world of language. Signification and words go back and forth between these two worlds, just like a bodhisattva (enlightening being) goes back and forth between the world of suffering or Samsara, and the world of liberation or Nirvana. However, what I call the subject *of* the Real, and the subject as metaphor (being in language and in the word) also needs to be distinguished from the pre-conceptual being or the not-thinking associated with pre-verbal or pre-linguistic drives and intensities (the subject *in* the Real). The former represents the essence of Being as non-being, or being as wondrous emptiness.

Experience cannot be completely understood through language because language filters experience through something other than itself. On the other hand, experience is also the point of articulation of symbolic structures. Experience is the moment in time when speech appears as a flashing into the phenomenal world and disappears in an instant or just as quickly as it arrived. Once spoken, words vanish into thin air or into an extra-linguistic world beyond words. The use of language and speech is included within experience, although not all experience is included in language.

A different manifestation of language that Lacan called lalangue is required to reveal a dimension beyond words within words. The Real is the empty Bell or the emptiness of any musical instrument as the potential for the sound that is carried over into the essence of the sound itself. The Real is the sound that was already there before the word was uttered (the Zen sound of one hand clapping) and that continues in the echo of the word once it has been uttered. The sound or acoustic image in speech is the dimension of the Real within language or the Symbolic. When one word sounds like another word (homophony), this indicates similitude rather than similarity. Similitude points to the Real (unconscious) in the sound rather than to resemblance in the Imaginary or Symbolic (Moncayo, 2012).

Rather than the ego, it is emptiness or the reality of no-self as the essence of Being that awards the subject the experience of the world/word as being his/her own. As Dogen (1231–1253) says in the Genjo koan: the ten thousand dharmas (phenomena) advance and realise the self. Birds, the sky, flowers, mountains, and grasses all advance and realise the self. A mountain manifests the being of the mountain, and at the same time a mountain confers the subject of the Real his or her own being. It is not that a human being thinks he/she is a mountain as an object, but that thanks to the emptiness of being the subject finds the mountain as-if in himself/herself. At the same time, the subject can also be a mountain as a metaphor or a signifier. Both of my patronymics Moncayo and de Bremont refer to mountains. The signifier mountain represents the subject for another subject/signifier (Claude or cloud, for example). In the emptiness of the subject *qua* nothing, the subject finds the signifier (Claude/cloud) as-if in himself/herself.

The world is personal and intimate not because the subject perceives the world in terms of his own ego, as the measure of all things, or because he/she finds in the world the signifiers that he/she has disowned in himself, but because the empty essence of being is confirmed by the empty luminosity and transparency of things. The vacuity of the Other confirms the vacuity of the subject. In contrast to idealism, things exist without the ego that perceives/recognises them, and yet the empty space within the atoms that constitute things is made up of the same "mind" as the quantum subatomic empty mind of the subject. The subject *qua* nothing and the substance/matter *qua* subject or mind amount to the same thing. The object or transcendent reality, and the transcendental concepts or ideas, are both empty (the substance as subject, rather than the classical/philosophical other way around) because an absolutely empty subject (not substantial) is presupposing them.

The core of being is not a strong personal ego, because the ego is an unconscious formation rather than the essence of a human being. I argue that the being of the subject (*son être du sujet*) has to be found in non-being and beyond being and not being. But what about the deliberations and choices that a subject makes *vis-à-vis* the intentions of the Other? When the subject appropriates an intention of the Other as his/her own and takes responsibility for it, who is this agent, or what is the agency that can now be made responsible for those choices? A subject/signifier is re-issued or re-generated, as a result of the sexual and psychical union of two human beings, and the pre-existing battery of signifiers and subjects.

A subject is drawn to or seeks particular discourses/subjects and by appropriating them constructs his/her own subjectivity along the way. Another way of saying this is that the ego seeks an Other to identify with and close the gap/lack in being. A subject affirms one idea and negates another idea that he/she disagrees with. A self is built out of a series of preferences and negations, and in the process something is gained but something is also lost. What is lost is not only a content that could be used to construct a different identity but the very vacuity of the subject's being (subject of the Real). In addition, what is also lost is the awareness of the appropriation and the truth that the self or the ego is derived from the Other.

In this sense, and to stay with Heideggerian concepts, authenticity and appropriation are interrelated; or to use Lacanian concepts, separation runs counter to alienation. We have to speak with our own voice, and yet at the same time recognise the desire for recognition and identification and do something different with it. I am Lacanian but Lacan is not without lack and so am I. Moncayo does not complete Lacan nor does Lacan complete Moncayo. Moncayo is what represents me for the signifier Lacan. I appropriate Lacan and make Moncayo speak in Lacan's voice, yet the two can also be differentiated. Although I am Moncayo, I am more Lacanian than a follower of Moncayo. I find Lacan or "this awareness" finds Lacan as if in-myself or in the emptiness of my own being. Lacan as the signifier of a lack or of the emptiness of being is what draws me to Lacan and makes this movement possible. Because Lacan is empty, I don't have to always agree with him nor get upset if somebody criticises him. The same goes for me. Because I am empty or this awareness is empty, I don't have to get upset if somebody criticises or ignores me, and I am not obliged to always agree with myself. I reserve the right to change my mind. This infinite right is inherent to the impermanent and changing nature of Being.

My agency is limited to emptying myself out so that I can recognise Lacan's or Buddha's influence on me and at the same time find myself in the emptiness of Buddha and Lacan. When I recognise the emptiness of Buddha and Lacan, I become myself or I recognise this emptiness as more me than myself. Along the Way the subject acquires the capacity to permutate or re-arrange the internal workings of the discourses known as Buddha and Lacan. Buddha, Lacan, and Moncayo are divested of their imaginary ego-identifications, and in the process the Imaginary is transformed into a symbolic Imagination capable of revisioning the symbolic structure.

Finally, and to conclude, the approach to Real being, wondrous emptiness and the subject of the Real, also has important consequences for the practice of analysis and the function of the analyst. Usually, the personal qualities of the analyst (being personable, warm, or understanding) that facilitate the transference relationship and the analytic process are considered in contrast, if not opposition, to the workings of the neutrality, objectivity, and abstinence that are also considered essential ingredients of psychoanalysis as a treatment method. The former can lead to suggestive treatments, the repression of the negative transference, or enactments due to excessive gratification or indulgence within the analytic relationship. The latter can lead to excessive frustrations, negative therapeutic reactions, and abandonment of the treatment and the therapeutic relationship.

In either case, the important point is that warmth/kindness or equanimity and neutrality be something more than personality traits. It is important not to collapse a distinction between the personality traits of an analyst and the traceless traces of the analyst's Being. It is the analyst's being that is important, not the personality characteristic. What is important are the traces of Buddha rather than the personality of the teacher/analyst. The analyst's personality consists of the conditioned habit-patterns, the narcissistic traits that constitute compromise formations between defences and fantasies, between defences that conceal fantasies and fantasies that have defensive purposes.

This would even be true for the areas of ego-autonomy achieved by the transformation of id quantities into qualities of the ego or ego-traits (vices into virtues): from greed to generosity, from hate into kindness, envy into gratitude, and so on. In these dual instances, dual qualities can always reveal their opposites (altruism can be egoistic and egoism altruistic). Disclosure can be a form of false honesty or modesty, and deception can be used for strategic altruistic purposes.

It is the non-dual traceless traces of wondrous empty Being that utterly reveal the common origins of vice and virtue, the It within the id and the It as id. Here, the analyst can be his/her own self in the form of desire (of the analyst) or that of the (symbolic) Law. True kindness and composure are direct qualities of "It" rather than lukewarm or second-ary reaction-formations.

CHAPTER NINE

Zen practice and the practice of Lacanian psychoanalysis

Freud (1926e) conceived of psychoanalytic practice as different from that of priests and pastoral or educational counsellors. The analyst, in order to function as such, has to renounce being in the position of an ideal leader, moral educator, or pastoral counsellor, who will teach or guide the subject.

Freud differentiated psychoanalysis from pastoral counselling within the context of his general psychological critique of religion. It is well known that Freud (1907b) labelled religion the obsessive neurosis of humanity and that he was inclined to interpret spirituality as a defence against sexual and aggressive drives. Freud's materialistic stance follows from the eighteenth-century scientific paradigm that had predicted the demise of religion and spirituality. Freud (1927c) dismissed the consolations provided by religion as either infantile symbiosis with the mother or infantile dependence on a providential father.

However, as already mentioned earlier, it is likewise important to remember that trends aiming at the reformation of religion have co-existed for two centuries in the West alongside the rejection of religion advocated by the scientific paradigm.

Science secularised religious knowledge and replaced the advice of priests for the advice of psychiatrists and psychotherapists. However,

Freud had gone one step further than this by not only simply secularising authority and leaving things otherwise unchanged. Freud scrutinised the superego itself as the internalised voice of authority, whether religious or secular.

Modern so-called scientific forms of psychotherapy have simply regressed to providing non-self-reflective forms of secular advice. In this, they don't differ very much from the pastoral counselling field that is making ample use of secular forms of psychotherapeutic knowledge. In fact, there is an entire new field that is seeking to integrate forms of spiritual counselling with "evidence-based" psychotherapy practices.

In addition, the spiritual traditions themselves made ample use of psychoanalysis to cleanse their own traditions of prejudice, intolerance, dogma, and bigotry. Once these elements have been removed from spirituality, then this brings the pastoral counselling field much closer to contemporary evidence-based forms of psychotherapy. Both spirituality and psychotherapy can be seen as forms of prescriptive and preventive medical advice for healthy living. This includes such things as relaxation, meditation, mindfulness, exercise, and so on.

In addition, the trend towards integrating psychoanalysis and pastoral counselling runs through the works of Jung (1958), Tillich (1952), and is currently best represented by Kung (1979), the existentialist therapies of Frankl (1962) and May (1957a), and the psychoanalytic revisions of Meissner (1984), Jones (1991), and Spero (1992).

Although I agree that the Freudian view of religion is relevant for only the defensive and pathological aspects of spiritual experience, and I also agree with the project of expanding the conceptual and experiential horizons of psychoanalysis (to include non-defensive and healthy spirituality), this work does not endorse an integrative framework for exploring the similarities between spiritual practice and the practice of analysis.

Such mentioned integrative endeavour risks blurring the difference between psychoanalysis and pastoral counselling, between psychoanalysis and psychotherapy, and between psychoanalysis and Buddhism. The many contradictions between spiritual practice and modern psychotherapy should not be reconciled, in my view, by appealing to a need to introduce explicit spiritual values, a moral order, or a search for meaning in life into the practice of psychoanalysis and psychotherapy.

The pages henceforth will outline a perspective on the relationship between the practice of analysis and meditation practice which steers away from the pitfall of viewing analysis as a form of explicit moral treatment (in the narrow sense of the term). This is despite the fact that, as mentioned in the previous chapter, psychoanalysis itself may contain secular forms of non-theistic spirituality.

Psychoanalysis may be better described as secularising forms of non-theistic spirituality that also hold critical perspectives towards religious authority and authority in general, while remaining distinct from a rebelliousness towards authority that still remains caught within the very authority that it is rebelling against.

Along these lines, spiritual practices such as petitionary prayer, contemplative prayer, and meditation may also need to be differentiated. Zen meditation will be used as an example of meditation, and the spiritual practice most similar to the analytic attitude. Petitionary prayer is the spiritual practice that lies at the point of maximum conflict with the analytic and scientific attitude. The worshipper petitions a deity just like a child petitions a parent. Contemplative prayer falls somewhere in between petitionary prayer and meditation. The function of contemplative prayer is evocative rather than supplicate, and while petitioning always presupposes a theistic (whether monotheistic or polytheistic) spirituality, meditation and contemplation can be non-theistic.

According to Kung (1979), psychoanalytic treatment should not only be oriented to the past but also help the subject with the future meaning of the good life or the purpose of a life well lived. Kung advises to give people a value-orientation that guides them away from hedonism, addictions, narcissism, and conformism. In this view, psychotherapy is equivalent to pastoral counselling or to a reorientation of consciences. According to Kung, restating a case made by Jung long before, the healing, redemptive, and renewing forces of religion may be more powerful than pure psychological analysis. This may be so, but, in my opinion, and that of many others, these forces are not best exemplified by moral counselling or telling others what to believe and how to behave or live.

Within the pastoral counselling or the religious existentialist perspective, meaning is usually dualistically posited against lack of meaning, theism against atheism, being against non-being, nothingness, or emptiness, and so on. From a dialectical perspective, dualism describes either/or views which give predominance to one term or the other but do not arrive at a dialectical position wherein opposite terms may contain each other (non-duality).

Beyond the first steps of Erich Fromm (1960), Lacan's work contains the seeds of a positive and intrinsically psychoanalytic conception of emptiness and "senselessness" or meaninglessness. In a non-dual sense, senselessness includes both meaning and no meaning. No meaning points to a meaning beyond ego-ideals and moral purposes. By way of example, I offer the following Zen dialogue cited by D. T. Suzuki (1949):

> Yung asked Huang: "I am told that your reverence frequently enters Samadhi. At the time of such entry, is it supposed that your consciousness still continues, or that you are in a state of unconsciousness? If your consciousness still continues, all sentient beings are endowed with consciousness and can enter into Samadhi like yourself. If, on the other hand, you are in a state of unconsciousness, plants and rocks can enter into Samadhi."
>
> Huang replied: "When I enter into Samadhi, I am not conscious of either condition."
>
> Yung said: "If you are not conscious of either condition, this is abiding in eternal Samadhi, and there can be neither entering into Samadhi nor rising out of it."
>
> Huang made no reply. He asked: "You say you come from Neng, the great master. What instruction did you have under him?"
>
> Yung answered: "According to his instruction, no tranquillization, no disturbance, no-sitting, no-meditation—this is the Tathagata's Dhyana (Buddha's meditation)."
>
> This said, Huang at once realized the meaning of it and sighed: "These thirty years I have sat to no purpose."
>
> (Suzuki, 1949, p. 35, the brackets are mine)

Sitting to no purpose can be considered a useless and failed activity or as precisely the point, and the purpose of no purpose. What we are trying to achieve was there all along, although we did not know it or we knew it without knowing it. We are trying to realise what we already are, not what we will be in the future, although the present moment may not be fully realised until the future.

For the most part, the existentialist school does not appropriate a positive view of emptiness as the Real beyond meaningful or purposeful representation. As already mentioned, Lacan defines human experience as organised by three dimensions: the Real, Symbolic, and Imaginary. The Real refers to that aspect of experience that lies beyond language, image, and logic and yet constitutes their very foundation.

The positive approach to emptiness appears not only in the Zen Buddhist and Taoist tradition but also in the sophisticated Christianity of Meister Eckhart and classical Jewish Kabbalah. Existentialist religious thinkers, as in the case of Tillich, are guided by a moral aim to overcome the threat of non-existence and non-being. Sometimes, the traditions mentioned are considered to be forms of mysticism, as Lacan did; however, mysticism implies an opposition to or a duality with reality. Mysticism is Other-worldly while Zen is right here and now in ordinary life: form is emptiness and emptiness form.

Non-being is not a threat to existence because existence is always arising out of non-existence and disappearing into a state that cannot be defined by what we call existence or non-existence. According to Zen Buddhism, the dual categories of being and non-being, meaning and meaninglessness, existence and non-existence, are not applicable descriptions of the spirit of non-duality or the non-dual spirit.

Similarly, while there are important metavalues transmitted through the psychoanalytic situation, these values do not emanate from the place of the moral will. The latter is always caught in dualistic views of good and evil. From a metalevel and dialectical perspective, what is believed evil contains some good and, vice versa, what is believed good contains some evil. When some idea of evil is too ardently despised, then the mind in general will not be at peace with itself and thus still under the influence of evil. In psychoanalytic terms, moral will is to be located at the level of the superego.

The superego derives from primitive sources and its judgements operate with the energy of aggressiveness and destruction. It divides rather than unifies the subject. Spanish Jewish Kabbalist Moses Cordovero (1981) noted that the demonic forces contained within the function of judgement are always associated with the tree of good and evil (the Torah of *Malchut*), rather than with the non-dual values of the tree of life (the Torah of *Chochma* and *Keter*).

Following the biblical metaphor from the Book of Genesis, it can be asserted that the values emanating from the level of the tree of life correspond to those associated with the practice of analysis: values connected with a sublimated death drive or with a death drive that in the end crosses over to the other side, the side of love, Eros, and infinite Life.

The aim of analysing and transforming the superego in the direction of the subject, points to a psychoanalytic ethic. Ethics here can be distinguished from morality in a number of ways. Ethics are subjective and follow the transformations in one's character (ethos), as opposed to morality which follows the customs and opinions/sayings of those with social authority. This definition of ethics is consistent with how Lacan defined psychoanalysis as an ethics of desire. In analysis, the subject has to re-appropriate desire from the desire of the Other. An ethics of desire consists of the imperative to act in awareness of one's desire rather than in conscious or unconscious denial of it. Thompson (2004) has defined psychoanalysis as an ethic of honesty, after the model of free association and of speaking freely in the analytic situation without holding anything back.

However, once the ego is transformed and depersonalised, the Symbolic order does not dissipate along with the ego or superego. Since language and the Symbolic order are already empty and non-substantial, yet effective, they do not represent a problem or obstacle. At the end of analysis, character remains under what I have called the unary trace (Moncayo, 2012). The end result of psychoanalysis does not amount to a liberal, fun, lively, and playful character as opposed to a serious, stoic, or disciplined character. This distinction still remains within the scope of a hysterical versus an obsessive orientation to ethics and character formation.

A subjective destitution or benevolent depersonalisation at the end of analysis goes beyond the distinction between liberal and conservative, extroverted and introverted, hysterical and obsessive characters, although it may preserve positive traits (in the form of traces) and characteristics of both.

The question of renouncing the position of authority or of suggestive treatment has been critiqued and rejected on a number of fronts. Within North American relational psychoanalysis, analysts don't like the negative principle associated with frustration, renunciation, or castration. They tend to see such concepts as associated with Old Europe and traditional religious points of view.

Anglo-Americans view frustration as optional and would rather concentrate their efforts towards positive psychologies and the creation of non-frustrating and gratifying environments. Such efforts, of course, fit perfectly well with consumer capitalism. For the latter, there is nothing better than buffering the raw edge of consumerism with some form of humanistic ideological varnish.

Humanism typically confuses and collapses the distinction between imaginary and symbolic, unnecessary and necessary, forms of alienation. The frustrations/renunciations imposed by the environment are perceived as unnecessary evils that could be overcome with the dream-like project of a wish-fulfilling consumer society. These are the dreams that can be wished upon Hollywood stars. Such dreams serve to cover the disasters in the personal lives of the wealthy icons that are the focus (and envy) of the media and the popular imagination.

Most anthropologists study cultures from a quite different perspective, and most seem to agree that renunciation is a very basic definition of culture. To become a social human being signifies to become a subject to the rules of the culture. To receive the gifts that the culture has to give requires that the individual also give something of his/her own body and mind. In other words, loss and separation are an integral aspect of individuality within culture.

At the same time, psychoanalysis, and Lacanian psychoanalysis in particular, contains a very precise and fine distinction between sacrifice and renunciation. Sacrifice represents an unnecessary and imaginary form of renunciation.

Sacrifice requires an idealisation of the Other to whom the sacrifice is being offered. In other words, a sacrifice is performed for the purpose of building a perfect Other without lack or inconsistencies. Then perhaps such Other may fulfil all of the ego's wishes and fantasies.

This is not unlike a mother who plays the victim and reproaches her children for all of the things she has done for them while complaining that they do nothing to fulfil her narcissistic expectations.

Such a mother sacrifices for her children but only because they represent her own imaginary phallus or narcissistic extension. Sacrifice, especially when it is openly advertised and flaunted, is only pretend renunciation. The sacrifice is offered in the hope or expectation that the idealised narcissistic object will give the sacrificed object back to the ego. True renunciation requires the acceptance of the lack both in the subject and in the Other and even the renunciation of renunciation. Ego power is renounced and apparently stays with or completes the Other. However, the Other is empty and does not need the power of the ego, and after all is said and done, the subject does not gain the power of the Other but rather the Other's emptiness.

Elsewhere (Moncayo, 1997), I postulated a distinction between two types of life and death, binding and unbinding, one type of attachment and detachment linked to the primary process and the pleasure principle and another to the secondary process and the constancy or Nirvana principles as defined in the text.

However, in Chapter Two, I have also proposed that primary and secondary processes in Freud also need to be understood in terms of Lacan's band of Möbius and Bion's notions of reversible perspectives.

These latter notions point to a contradiction between Freud's and Breuer's ideas. For Breuer, binding quiescent energy was associated to a primary function of the brain and linked to homeostasis. For Breuer, Freud's primary process represented a degraded form of energy. Freud had a negative view of the primary process (collapsing the distinction between ancient and archaic) and a positive view of the secondary process (collapsing the distinction between civilisation and homeostasis). In fact, as argued in the previous chapter, both can be either/or and both/and.

The life drive or Eros (the One as the later Lacan calls it), which produces lasting connections and unifying ties between people, needs to be distinguished from the binding or attachment under the pleasure principle (seeking pleasure and avoiding pain). The latter produces temporary unions that turn into divorces and separations, once the tie turns from one of love to one of hate or aversion. This is a life drive at the service of death, or a case where, as Freud put it, the aim of life is death.

Lacan's concept of *jouissance*, describing the interpenetration of life and death, pleasure and pain, describes particular combinations or configurations of life and death, pleasure and pain, under the pleasure principle or the Nirvana principle, respectively. This concept has clinical significance given that *jouissance* is what is at stake in the production of symptomatology and psychical pleasure/pain such as fear, anxiety, and depression. The later Lacan spoke of three different types of *jouissance* (of the Other, phallic, and the Other *jouissance*), and the third *jouissance* also came in three subtypes (feminine, of the mystic, of meaning).

The reality principle is like the constancy or Nirvana principle given that in the reality principle, the search for pleasure includes the postponement of gratification and the acceptance of pain. Pleasure and the tolerance of pain can go together. This also differs from masochism, because in masochism there is a search for pain as a precondition of pleasure. Nonetheless, there is also a point in which forbearance stops being a virtue and can turn into masochism.

The Eros or life drive that would be before and beyond the pleasure principle (the early Lacan's inconvenient *jouissance* of the Other), defined herein, is the Eros linked to the One and to the binding or condensing function of quiescent energy. Lacan considers *jouissance* to be beyond the pleasure principle because he defines the pleasure principle as a principle of homeostasis.

However, Lacan collapses the distinction between the pleasure principle, the reality principle, and the Nirvana principle. Homeostasis can come in high or low tension, which is similar to the constancy principle or the Nirvana principle defined as an equanimity principle (equality in pleasure and pain). Freud also explains the pleasure principle in terms of hallucinatory wish fulfilment. The pleasure principle in Freud is a principle of both defences and drives, including the death drive.

The constancy or Nirvana principle is more fundamental than the pleasure principle, although both can be considered as going beyond one another. Nirvana, in contrast to the pleasure principle, becomes indistinguishable from an Eros that produces more lasting bonds and attachments by unbinding or detaching the libido from archaic love and hate objects and thus transforming free energy into a bound or quiescent kind(ness).

If the formula for the relationship between the two drives under the pleasure principle is "the aim of life is death", the reverse is true under the Nirvana principle. The relationship between life and death under the Nirvana principle is a case where the aim of death is life. Pleasure, in this instance, as the pleasure of the good, rather than the good of pleasure, is defined more by a principle of constancy, of lasting connections, and of seeing things through to the end.

Such metaethics of the tree of life (which constitute both an ethic and a theory) also need to be distinguished not only from a moral or pastoral orientation but also from a purely rationalist or secularist perspective such as that of ego-psychology. Ego-psychologists, following Freud, distinguish between a repressive morality of the superego and traditional religion and the more flexible and rational restraints emanating from the ego as Freud defined it. In this view, psychoanalysis is guided by the therapeutic imperative of replacing the pathologically repressive constraints of the superego with the flexible, conscious, rational, and voluntary restraints of the ego.

Ego-psychologists find secular health values in the rational treatment collaboration between analyst and analysand as described in the concept of a therapeutic alliance. Higher ethics require the rational ego-functions of objective criticism and reflection. However, with the ego-psychology model, we arrive at a modern, secular, and rational ethic but not yet to a transrational or Real dimension of experience. Thus, although the mystic and the scientist share a non-moralistic approach to reality, the abstention of moral judgement, as an analytic practice of superego deconstruction and reconstruction, in and of itself, does not lead to the discovery of the Being of the subject.

Both psychoanalysis and meditation practice can be conceived as vehicles for accessing a larger non-dual mind. In the case of Zen Buddhism, the phenomena/noumena of a larger mind coincide with the nature of wondrous Being and with a spiritual register of experience. In both models and practices, the evocation of "Big mind" does not occur primarily through the observance of moral or rational guidelines for behaviour.

Meditation entails an observation of the mind within the mind while abstaining from discriminating between good and bad or subjective and objective mental contents, whereas free association in psychoanalysis suggests a different form of ideation not under the control of the ego.

The ego, as the agency of defence and of rationalising explanations, tends to become a hindrance to the analytic process. Thus, in contrast to how many critics would have it, within this line of analysis, it becomes possible to consider psychoanalysis as being more than a purely intellectual process. In other words, psychoanalysis also conceives of ego-rationality as a defensive operation in need of therapeutic modification or deconstruction.

Thus, it is possible to argue that the defensive egos and superegos of both analysand and analyst have to be set aside in order to evoke a larger dimension of experience. The process of self-transformation in psychoanalysis and meditation experience can be understood, following Zen and Lacan (1960), not as an ego-function, but rather as a process of shedding imaginary ego-representations and revealing benevolent depersonalisations and creative subjective destitutions.

I agree with Meissner (1984) when he stresses that so-called mystical experience "does not undermine or destroy identity but in fact has a powerful capacity to stabilize, sustain, and enrich identity" (p. 151).

The meaning of this statement is contained within the etymological sense of the word "mystical". Mystical is associated with mist, with something unsubstantial.

Meditation experience destroys identity in the sense that it destroys the illusory or imaginary ego-identifications. It is a necessary symbolic death that dialectically affirms a larger and more ultimate form of psychical identity beyond ego-identifications. Thus, following Lacan, it becomes possible to argue that mystical experience and psychoanalysis share a practice of subjective destitution and benevolent depersonalisation. What is destroyed or deconstructed in such a process are not the ego-functions *per se* but the imaginary construct of a substantial ego-entity.

In this regard, Loewald (1978) has also called for understanding the so-called "higher psychical functions", not with ego-psychology constructs, but rather with positively defined metapsychological concepts. He regarded the primary process and unconscious desire as sources of creativity, renewal, and timeless forms of intuitive knowing.

I have mentioned that Buddhism, unlike psychoanalysis, is not interested in deconstructing and tracing back the sources of ego-identifications or of desires to the familiar and symbolic history of a subject. Here, I have agreed with Rubin when he observes an absence of a psycho-historical dimension within Buddhism.

But from a Lacanian perspective, the presence of a psycho-historical dimension does not necessarily provide evidence and support for the actual existence of a substantial self or ego. Beyond the Imaginary, and within the Symbolic, the subject is a metaphor and a name for a series of functions and processes that occur within language and discourse (Moncayo, 2012).

The Buddhist notion of no-self does not conflict with the Lacanian paradigm given that this is precisely a point where both traditions coincide to a significant degree. Both could be said to converge on the Zen formula that "true self is no-self", or the Lacanian-informed formulation that "true subject is no-ego". Both formulations illustrate the realisation that the true subject requires the symbolic death or deconstruction of imaginary ego-identifications/representations.

It is the experience of no-self, of the subject as metaphor, emptiness, quiescent energy, or an Other *jouissance* which grounds and constitutes what has been called the analytic attitude, the therapeutic stance, or what Lacan calls the subjective position of the analyst. As such, the latter point in the direction of the evocation of a different state of mind than that associated with ordinary ego-experience. Thus, the practice of what Lacan calls benevolent depersonalisation applied to both analyst and analysand constitutes a near friend to the experience of meditation and the awakened state in Zen and Buddhism in general.

The direction of the treatment and the subject and power of the unconscious

Lacan outlined some of his clinical notions in "The direction of the treatment and the principles of its power" (1979). In Lacanian psychoanalysis, the two elements of direction and power are correlated: for there to be a direction to the treatment, the analyst has to renounce the ego-power granted to him/her by the analysand's transference and the therapeutic alliance between them. Rather than the analyst, it is the unconscious of the analysand who "knows" the truth manifesting through the symptom, but due to repression and concomitant disguises, the subject appears to ignore it. From this place of ignorance, the analysand searches for an ideal "master" in the analyst.

Freud (1921c) described the wish of people to look for leaders and leading ideas to hold authority over them. The analysand comes into analysis wanting the analyst to wield a curative power over him/her. Because of this, Lacan always insisted upon differentiating psychoanalysis from the direction of souls or pastoral counselling or any other variety of counselling.

I have mentioned that Lacan finds antecedents for the position of the analyst in the Stoics and the Socratic mayeutics. Like Socrates, the analyst engages people in conversation appearing to know nothing and being willing to listen to anyone who professes to know or who wants to know something about themselves.

Like Socrates, the analyst eventually makes profession of no knowledge except of that of his/her own non-knowing. I say eventually because in the pre-treatment phase or in the early treatment, the analyst engages the analysand via the transference to the subject supposed to know and uses explanation as a rudimentary form of interpretation. Analysands know both less and more than what they think they do. To those who appear to know, the analyst shows them that there is something they actually don't consciously know about themselves; to those who appear to ignore their own self, the analyst shows them that in fact they do (unconsciously) know.

In the example of psychotherapy or the practice of analysis, a patient comes either positively or negatively predisposed to a therapeutic encounter/interaction. Entering the psychotherapeutic field already requires a certain ego-deflation or symbolic castration on the part of the patient. He/she has to be willing to acknowledge a certain degree of suffering and inability to help himself/herself on his/her own. From this place of suffering, stagnation, and helplessness, the patient reaches out to the therapist/analyst. This is the place of not knowing, of the subject of the unconscious, and of expecting and sometimes demanding that the analyst know something and wields a curative power.

When negatively predisposed, the ego of the analysand will display resistance and a devaluation of the knowledge of the analyst: "I know who I am, and nobody knows more about myself than me, and I do not think you can help me, and actually I am not doing so bad after all." Using Lacanian theory, one can distinguish between the ego and the subject. The ego is the small mind of Zen Buddhism that already knows it all and has nothing to learn from anybody. The "I" is at the centre of all statements. The ego says, "I know, I have attained".

The subject corresponds to the empty Big mind of the beginner which is innocent, does not claim to know, and is open and ready for surprises and new possibilities. But the key point is that access to the larger subject requires an ego-death. Although the ego claims to know, in reality it does not know, because it is the subject that in truth knows. Conversely, although the ego claims not to know, in reality it does know because the subject knows.

At this juncture, it becomes all-important that analysts not respond to the patient from the place of the ego. If the analysand, in the transference, asks for a master of knowledge, the analyst should act from the place of not knowing, the equivalent of Socrates showing people that in fact they did know. But it is the unconscious subject of the patient who knows, not the ego. In the analytic situation, this truth is brought forth by a renunciation on the part of the analyst. If the analysand claims to know and that the analyst does not, the analyst still responds without self-consciousness from the place of a knowing that does not know that it knows. The analyst needs to acknowledge that the individual knows but point in the direction of unconscious knowing by the subject and not the ego.

By speaking of a form of knowing that does not know that it knows, Lacan intended to combine knowing and non-knowing into a single statement or state. The analyst has to both know and not know or non-know. In order to develop a therapeutic relationship, the analyst has to occupy the position of the subject supposed to know(ing) and at the same time demonstrate the humility and honesty that comes from unconscious knowing or from the ego being de-centred by the unconscious Big mind. With this formulation, Lacan brings to bear Freud's insight into the group mind to elucidate the relationship between the leader and the group at work in the analytical or therapeutic relationship.

Freud's view of the relationship between leaders and groups or people is more traditional than modern although it contains elements of the two. It is well known that in his group psychology paper (Freud, 1921c), he made ample use of the social ideas of Le Bon and McDougall. Group psychology debases the psychology of the individual, and groups need leaders and heroes in order to raise them to higher and better levels of cultural and psychological development. On the other hand, not only does the Other need the One in the form of the leader, but every subject needs the Other in order to become a subject within the culture.

A leader can have the function of either raising or lowering the functioning and desires of a group. The ringleader of a gang or a group is an example of how an individual in a group can challenge legitimate or benevolent authority and influence the group in a negative direction. On the other hand, a hero is the individual who aims to restore group leadership to its original or proper legitimate status and to challenge the illegitimate or unjust power of a tyrant, a system of government, or an organisation.

Either the group or the leader can be good or bad, depending on the situation. This paradox is reflected in the relationship between two of Freud's favourite myths: Oedipus, and the primal horde. In the more primitive myth of the primal horde, the sons kill a vicious and abusive father and then renounce violence themselves; while in Oedipus, the son kills the father after the father had earlier tried to kill the son due to being told/prophesied that the son would grow up to kill him (a self-fulfilling prophecy).

Group life is characterised by a continuous paradoxical struggle between the group and the leader. It is never completely clear whether the group's effort to unseat or challenge the leader is unjustified and based on primitive impulses and fantasies or whether the leader is using or abusing leadership in improper or irrational ways.

The position of the analyst is a response to the two horns of this dilemma. The so-called position does not so much mean that the analyst has rank over the analysand (position in a hierarchical structure) but how the analyst relates or positions himself/herself in relation to the questions and conflict posed by the relationship to authority. Here Freud's work may also reflect the views of leadership stemming from the Hassidic movement and its cultural influence on European Jewry, including Freud's father.

According to Hassidut (Dresner, 1974), humility is the necessary qualification for the leader to receive the support of the higher powers available in the world. The *tzaddik* or saintly person is aware of his/her shortcomings or lack and is not proud of "having arrived" at a higher station in life. On the other hand, there is also false humility and there are wholesome forms of self-confidence.

The wise man learns from all people, and this is certainly reflected in the psychoanalyst who learns about and from his analysands by listening to them more than speaking at them. The position of the analyst is an aspect of providing a mental health service, although analysts are being paid for it. Correspondingly, analysts have to pay with their egos in order to be of service to the analysand. The analyst brings the analysand back to their own Other, or to the Other within themselves, "Who" is actually their true desire and subjectivity.

Prior to helping others, however, analysts have to be analysands before they can be analysts. This is an aspect of the position of the analyst that comes from below rather than from above. The analyst has to descend first into their own subjectivity before he/she can help others do the same and together ascend to a new place within subjectivity (including an ascent in professional status for the analyst). The leader has a covenant with both day and night: to turn the light of the ego and defences into the darkness of the unconscious, and the darkness of the unconscious into the light of a new I, self, or "It".

The analyst does not rule but simply listens, watches, and bears witness. Out of this awareness without content emerges a capacity to use and permutate the words of the analysand. The analyst also has to bear the attacks of the analysand and of the people against psychoanalysis. To be strong in the midst of opposition, the leader has to exude a certain degree of self-confidence. This certainty or self-confidence comes from the emptiness at the core of Being. The head has to be bowed down but also lifted towards the heavens. This reflects the alternation in Buddhist practice between zazen and the practice of bowing during service and formal greetings. Bowing teaches humility while zazen breeds self-confidence.

The leader may display what may appear as the wholesome and wordless self-assurance of a tiger or an elephant standing or walk-ing in the jungle. "It" does not mean the tiger/elephant will initiate an attack, but that the animal has the strength and courage to survive one. Occasionally, even a saintly leader has to display the silent dignity of true personal authority and not let others trample them, although to others this may look like the way of pride or arrogance. Otherwise, humility can easily turn into self-abasement, inaction, or weakness.

It is this capacity to survive the positive or negative transference, the poise and composure of analytic listening, as well as the level of com-fort with human nature and nature in general, that lends the analyst and the analytic situation its therapeutic effectiveness.

Finally, to carry out the analytical function and be able to work with the power attributed to the analyst in the transference relationship, the analyst must make three payments: with his/her person, with words, and with the core of his/her being. Such payments describe the Being and the spiritual/psychical or benevolent depersonalisation of the ana-lyst and will be considered one at a time.

Payment with one's person

To let go of the social ego requires a form of subjective destitution, at least a partial retreat from social behaviours and conditions, and a letting-go of what Jung called the social mask or persona, our favour-ite ego-images and verbal platitudes. The analytic or therapeutic rela-tionship is not a social relationship because it differs from professional work relations with peers, superiors, and subordinates, and it differs from relationships with lovers, teachers, family, and friends. It also dif-fers from relationships with priests in that the analyst is not a moral guide or a guru. The analyst, like the Buddha, is no more than an arrow pointing inwards to the patient's own intrinsic mind as the locus of truth and liberation.

In work relations, a certain measure of success, of goals and objec-tives, is expected from the ego. The ego is expected to know something under the performance requirements governing work relations. Nothing of this sort is expected in analytical practice. Analysis is the place where the ego can fail miserably, and all ego-ideals are suspect and subject to deconstruction. Even the most ungrammatical form of language will be accepted in analysis.

Moreover, psychoanalysis thrives on mistakes as access points or gateways to the unconscious. A Zen saying describes the life history of a Zen teacher as that of one continuous mistake or of one mistake after another. In addition, for the analysand, the suspension of a social relationship also suspends the mental defences operative through social discourse and results in openness to inner experience.

In social, sexual, and familiar relations, the ego desires, expects, and even demands things from others. The analyst pays with his person when giving up those dispositions in relation to the analysand. The analyst must ultimately disregard even the desire to cure or provide a successful treatment to the patient. The reverse only intensifies the ego-resistance of the patient to the treatment.

But then, what are the gratifications "permitted" to the analyst? Money and livelihood for one thing. But this should not lead one to think that greediness towards money on the part of the analyst could not become a hindrance to the treatment and the therapeutic relationship. Ultimately, the practice of analysis is a spiritual satisfaction.

Paying with one's person also requires equanimity with respect to personal values. Does this mean that there are no values implied in the therapy situation? The abstention of judgement implies values of a different order, or metavalues. "Metavalues" implies that values are there, and we should not ignore them or be value-blind, but we need to go beyond and not act on them. We suspend values in order to achieve values on a different level.This point about metavalues will be elaborated and expounded further on.

For example, whenever a therapist encounters homophobia or dislike for homosexuality, or heterophobia or dislike for heterosexuality, sexism or dislike for men or women, addiction to prostitution, or racism and anti-Semitism, it is not fruitful to try to reform the analysand into adopting the correct values. This will only engender argument, ego battles, and wreck the therapeutic relationship. Rather, abstaining from preaching one's values will facilitate an exploration of the themes and conflicts that lie at the root of such ethical failures. In the long run, such method stands a much better chance of preventing problematic social attitudes and values.

I am not advocating a value-free or "objective" scientific approach. As established elsewhere (1998a), subjectivity is always implicit in any relationship between a knower and a known. It is not possible to avoid a subjective position. The question becomes one of how to work with our subjectivity in order to realise subjectivity without a subject and affect a subjective or spiritual destitution.

Truth is rectified error within the context of a permutation of subjective experience. As aforementioned, psychoanalysis thrives on mistakes as gateways to unconscious truths, and the life of a Zen teacher is that of one mistake after another. Ego-ideas/ideals, in the sense of ideological false views, must be let go moment to moment, one piece at a time. To acknowledge being wrong and give up ego-attachments to erroneous beliefs and assumptions requires a certain humility and sobriety of mind which is common to both the spiritual and scientific attitudes. It is this attitude that clears and prepares the mind for new insights to arise.

To pay with words, the language of the unconscious and of non-duality

The second payment is to pay with words. Another aspect wherein the therapeutic relationship differs from a social relationship is the type of dialogue that characterises the use of language in analysis. This aspect of analysis coincides with what in Zen Buddhism Dogen (*Hachi Dainingaku*, 1231–1253) calls one of the eight awarenesses of an enlightened subject: avoiding idle speech. In contrast to a symmetrical dialogue whereby somebody talks and somebody responds, an interpretation, in the analytic sense of the term, means that somebody speaks more and somebody speaks less.

In addition, the analyst not only has to speak less but has to speak in a different manner. Within the psychoanalytic situation dreams and unconventional linguistic formations, such as slips, puns, jokes, etc., are matched by the use of interpretative speech on the part of the analyst. As Harari (1985) has pointed out, interpretation requires fine-tuning and a skillful use of words meant to evoke something different from conventional or ordinary speech.

Moreover, interpretative speech is not the speech of ordinary life in two significant respects:

1. In analysis, the analyst needs to allow what is equivocal, paradoxical, and ambiguous instead of expecting and utilising forms of linear directive speech; and

2. As aforementioned, an interpretation should not be a move whose goal is to obtain something. In other words, interpretative speech like poetical language needs to be distinguished from any form of instrumental or communicative discourse. Interpretation does not aim at communication as a means for something else or to ask someone to do something, but rather simply to evoke and invoke a particular signification.

According to Lacan, *lalangue*, as the text or language of the unconscious, escapes the grammatical or formal logical organisation of discourse. The signifying chain is composed of key signifiers which are polyvocal and equivocal in nature. Moreover, what is evoked by a paralogical use of language is the experience of the unconscious that for our purposes has a certain similarity with a Zen definition of experience.

Within Zen Buddhism, the realm of a non-dual reality is revealed by a non-dualistic or unconventional use of conventional language. Metaphorical intuitive utterance transgresses and elevates the ordinary meaning of words. Our thesis here is that because the reality of the Zen Buddhist Big mind includes a core experience beyond language and symbolisation, its manifestation within the symbolic requires a different use of language from that of formal social/logical language and the language of science.

For example, a student asks Zen ancestor Joshu "what is spirituality?" Joshu responds, "a puddle of urine in the Buddha land (or holy land)". The student then asks, "Could you show it to me?", and Joshu responds: "do not tempt me". In another case, the student asks, "What is Buddha?", and the teacher responds, "ten pounds of flax (or cloth symbolising the four layers of robes worn by a Zen priest)".

Far from simply constituting heretical statements, such senseless or nonsensical enunciations are aimed at dislodging the student from ego-ideals, from imaginary, dualistic conceptions of Buddha and spirituality. Spirituality is not something sacred and pompous opposed to something mundane or ordinary.

A deviant, innovative, and surprising utterance plays with the binary structure of formal language to make it say something that escapes the determining duality of the symbolic in terms of social language. But from a purely social conventional point of view, such speech constitutes a payment with one's person because it risks being perceived as unusual, peculiar, foolish and even downright deviant.

Lacan also made a distinction between empty and full speech. The analysand often wastes time by focusing on trivialities or rationalisations that remain far removed from the causal core of the subject's suffering. Thus, analysis as the discourse of the unconscious is concerned with unfolding not so much the well-known story line, but rather the unknown dreams and unconscious core themes and fantasies.

In the early Lacan, the terms "empty" and "full" had opposite and dual meaning, while the later Lacan came around to consider them on the same side, as Zen does. Emptiness is not the absence of something and fullness could also be full of shit. Full in the latter sense could represent an excess of meaning that comes to mean the same thing as idle speech. Empty speech in the later Lacan (Seminar 24) points to a senseless solitary signifier or S_1.

In listening, the analyst needs to localise in the flux of speech the capital elements or signifiers, the signifying diamonds and nuggets within the coal and dross of ordinary speech. Thus, to pay with words is to elevate the use of words as done by the dream-work. It implies a conversion of being to a more truthful and essential state. But just as the dream-work is constructed or woven by a larger unconscious subjectivity than the ego, so in interpretative speech, the speaking ego or enunciator should be cancelled as much as possible in favour of the enunciation from the place of non-self.

In order to raise the analytical function, the analyst needs to speak from the place of no-self (the unknown knowing subject), while the ego as the enunciator is cancelled as much as possible in favour of allowing the power of the signifier to transform and illuminate the subject. The aphanisis (disappearance) of the ego results in the epiphany (appearance) of the subject (true subject is no ego). Thus, the cognitive ego is not the agent of insight, but rather it is the subject who bears witness to the lightening of wit and knowing contained within the treasure chest of the signifier.

Creativity here comes from the play of the signifier rather than from the ego. Lacan invents a post-Cartesian form of linguistics that goes some way in explaining why Chomsky ignored Lacan (and called him a charlatan) despite the former's interest in Cartesian and French linguistics. Chomsky was also more interested in cognitive-behaviourism than psychoanalysis.

Chomsky (1966) follows Descartes in considering animals as mechanical instinctual organisms ruled by conditioning and responses to external stimuli. Humans instead can think and this capacity gives them a creative edge over animals and the rest of nature. Thus, Descartes proclaimed: "I think, therefore I am." As mentioned in prior chapters Lacan permutated Descartes proclamation into "I think where I am not". The human mind is doing the thinking and the talking without the conscious control of the ego, while the ego vainly imagines itself as the origin of thought.

Paradoxically, creativity comes from restoring the automatism to language by releasing it from the conscious control of the ego (in this case, the instrumental communicative function). This is what nowadays is called "being in the flow" or a form of state-dependent manifestation of creativity. An enunciation has to come from a mind larger than the ego. We become true human beings when we can voluntarily accede to the functioning of nature and bring the humanity of thought into concourse with its origins in Being writ large.

In analysis, the interpretative saying should be brief, concise with less emphasis on grammatical syntaxes and conjunction. Sayings are fresh and adorned with an element of surprise. Defined in this way, the use of language in psychoanalytic practice acquires a remarkable similarity with the proverbial use of language in spiritual discourse. Both imply an enunciation from the place of non-self and the corresponding aphanisis or disappearance of the ego.

Thus, the fact that the Lacanian dimension of the Real exists outside language does not mean that we are left in a position of not being able to say anything about the core of our experience. Silence does not necessarily possess more truth-value to express the Real although sometimes it may. As stated in the previous chapter, the evocation and manifestation of the Real requires a different use of language. *Lalangue* thrives on the homophonic or metaphorical rather than grammatical or syntactic elements of language. Most importantly *lalangue* points to a form of *jouissance*.

Herewith are presented two vignettes as examples of *lalangue*. An analysand, whom I will call J., had been struggling over not wanting to have "two sessions a week." He was also in conflict with seeing his struggle as having anything to do with the analyst. At the beginning of the next session he made a comment regarding the waiting room saying: "your waiting room is 'too weak." I have said that *lalangue* appears as a deviant or peculiar predication. Somebody could say, this must be a grammatical mistake; no English speaker would say your waiting room is too weak!

And yet the fact remains that this was an educated native English speaker. The analyst responded by saying "two a week is too weak." Again, a deviant predication is matched by a peculiar interpretation. This analysand represented here by the letter J. (the signifier is what represents the subject for another signifier: the analyst) and who was marked and effected/affected by being named after an Aunt whom his father envied (the subject appears first in the Other), was caught in an imaginary ego-struggle with the analyst.

To the resistance of his imaginary ego, two sessions a week represented an imaginary form of castration. I say imaginary, because he was not ready for a symbolic renunciation (castration) of his ego-resistance. Thus, he wanted to tell me in some way that it was not he but I that was weak. He chose the small size and poor taste of the waiting room to say this. On the other hand, the unconscious text chose a word or signifier (weak) that was homophonically linked to the two signifiers that represented castration in his mind (two a week). The analysand was making an imaginary or ego-defensive use of the symbolic link, while the analyst appeals to the aphanisis or disappearance of the imaginary ego and the appearance or epiphany of the metaphoric subject as an effect of the signifier. Once the text of *lalangue* becomes linked via the act of interpretation, it is no longer a question of an imaginary ego-to-ego relationship: the signifier and the laws of the Symbolic represent the subject.

The second vignette is personal and I offer it in the spirit of the work with (and the concept of) the *sinthome*. Lacan always said that his work, however abstract and difficult, was about the practice of analysis. Yet it was difficult for him to speak about his analyses and his own personal analysis because of the institutional and personal relationships involved.

This is a problem of psychoanalytic organisations in general, but it was particularly true for Lacan due to his problems with the International Psychoanalytic Association and because many of his analysands attended his seminar. In the case of the IPA or the APA, a relationship of dependence is created when the status in the hierarchy of the organisation, and the associated economic and social interests involved, are linked in some way to the personal experience of analysis. The organisation enforces conformity rather than the free manifestation of the unconscious.

This is partly due to the fact that the unconscious is conceived as primitive and in need to be controlled by ego-bureaucracies or what Lacan called "egocracies". The sense of Freud's descriptive unconscious is lost. This is not surprising given that, according to some historians, early on, Freud was already somewhat removed from the organisation that he helped to create and that supposedly had the task of ensuring the survival of his work and of the profession of psychoanalysis.

Lacan, for his part, attempted to come up with a new organisational device in which the personal experience with analysis could be discussed and studied. This is what came to be known as "the pass". However, the pass became mired in similar organisational dynamics, and Lacan soon abandoned it.

However, parallel to this attempt, and at a conceptual level, he was working on the notion of the *sinthome*. For the convenience of the reader, I will briefly mention that the *sinthome* was a way of explaining the symptom in terms of the Real and of what of the symptom remained after analysis and could therefore still be at work in organisational dynamics.

A characteristic of egocracy is to represent itself as a standard of normalcy or of normality not in the sense of health but in the sense of normative conformity. For this purpose, diagnostic labels can be used to attack and invalidate creative thinking that seems to deviate or threaten the powers that be. Jung, Lacan, and Bion were all called different things including being psychotic. At the same time, those individuals using labels as weapons never disclose their own psychopathological proclivities for fear of loosing their status or position within the hierarchy of the organisation. This was so much the case that Lacan finally proposed to settle the controversy about his diagnosis by publicly declaring himself a hysteric.

This is also true in Zen organisations. Zen teachers do not speak about their symptoms and the conflicts within the organisation are kept closely under wraps and not openly discussed. Part of the difficulty is that human beings do not handle conflict well and when conflict returns from suppression, it is in a primitive and destructive form, rather than something interesting and subtle.

The eruption of conflict is related to the problem of character traits and the fact that most people do not take responsibility for traits that seem to continue after analysis sometimes unchanged. So this is where the relevance of the *sinthome* comes in. The *sinthome* is a way to speak about a character trait as a symptom but also as a potential trace of *jouissance*, realisation, and enlightenment. Any character flaw or fault is a kind of gap, but a gap (*lacuna*), especially if it contains water or allows the free passage of light, also has a spark of moonlight in it.

The question of character is interesting because in Zen practice the flaws or shortcomings of a teacher are attributed to their character rather than to the enlightened aspect of their mind. The character of a teacher is supposed to be the part of their mind that would be most appropriately addressed by Western psychotherapy. However, from an analytic perspective character is the aspect of the mind that is most difficult to change via psychotherapeutic means. The latter is true because people mostly don't recognise their character as a problem/symptom that they want to change. So both Zen and psychoanalysis could expect that the other tradition be more effective with the problems of character, although in actuality character is something that both traditions may face difficulties changing. Psychoanalysis could be the more effective of the two so long as the subject recognises the character traits as their own and as something that they want to change. However, once an analytic intervention succeeds in transforming a trait into a trace or an ego-dystonic trait, such trace could also become a catalyst for more profound Zen realisations. This would be an example of a potential supplementary or cross-fertilising relationship between Zen and psychoanalysis.

I consider it healthy and a positive event that after analysis, analysts are able to speak to other peers about their *sinthome* and the personal experience of analysis. Such speech should not have a bearing on the person's status as a clinician or in the organisation, and does not in any way signify an evaluation of that person's analysis (successful or not). I will demonstrate what I mean by speaking to peers about the *sinthome* in the form of a personal vignette.

In a personal communication with a known and respected North American psychoanalyst (who shall remain anonymous for purposes of her own comfort), the following dialogue took place. She was writing to congratulate me for a forthcoming book (not this one) that had come to her attention. She said: "Like all your work, it sounds even from afar bristling with challenge and enlightenment."

As the reader may have surmised from my writing, I am not a native English speaker. English is literally my mother tongue, although my native tongue is Spanish. Accordingly, I did not know the meaning of the word "bristling". After looking it up in the dictionary, and to my surprise, I discovered that like the *sinthome*, the word "bristling" has antithetical meanings.

"Bristling" means both overflow (of *jouissance*) and an "aggressively defensive attitude". I say the meaning is antithetical because in this context I consider the word "overflow" as a positive description of an event (or a constructive form of *jouissance*). In addition, "bristling" here is functioning as a holophrase (a single word to describe complex antithetical ideas) or as a word that could represent the entire sentence (the part for the whole). In the sentence, the antithetical meaning of bristling is revealed in the expression "with challenge and enlightenment".

Suffice it to say that I have not been without an "aggressively defensive attitude" in my life, and my colleague's statement is a nice example of something that I work with in that book (Moncayo, 2012) and that has to do with the relationship and difference between a character trait and a trace and how analysis helps us go from one to the other. The transition from trait to trace is an important aspect of the *sinthome* and of the process of the resolution of the transference neurosis that continues after the end of analysis.

In an aggressively defensive attitude, the operative word is "defensive" because the aggressiveness may be covert rather than overt. This attitude may be operative even in the example or vignette I am discussing in that it includes a critique of bureaucracies. I critique them perhaps because I fantasise myself excluded from them, and perhaps even covertly envy their power and prestige, but more importantly, in my opinion, is my aspiration to continue the post-analytical relationship to the unconscious via the *sinthome* and the light that this relationship could shed on organisations, and analytical organisations in particular. We have to become friends with our own unconscious, as a condition for becoming analytical friends with one another. With friends like the unconscious, who needs enemies?!

Most likely, my analytical friend did not intend the statement as an interpretation, but what are we going to do, the unconscious is the unconscious, and we delight in our friendship to it, and one another.

The *sinthome* can be a letter and a word, a letter and a *jouissance*, a bristling and a glistening, and precisely indicates the place where the S_1-S_2 in speech and in the address to the Other becomes an S_1-S_0 relationship.

The third payment, the desire of the analyst, and the question of metavalues

The third payment required of the analyst is payment with the core of his/her being. Lacan invents the concept of the desire of the analyst and declares it to be the nodular point or hub around which the analysis turns. Why? Because Lacan believed that Freud not only created a new discursive situation but also invented a new subjective position or state: that of the analyst.

Lacan states that the desire of the analyst is something different from the other desire or the desire of the other as well as stating that it is neither the vocational desire to be an analyst nor the personal desire of each analyst: it is an impersonal desire for death, not of dying, but of death. The desire of death is not a death wish or a form of nihilism or self-destructiveness. Rather, the desire of the analyst is linked to a constructive function of the death drive.

A desire of death involves not doing what is customary with desire, which is to attempt to be desired. The analyst must first seek to be desired but then procure that the analysand directs this desire toward others. This is the most difficult payment to accept because it requires that the analyst relinquish the ideal (egoic) position in which the analysand has placed him/her. This is what is stoic about the analyst in the sense of auto-inducing or self-introducing a narcissistic wound. At this juncture the importance of termination can be clearly discerned.

There is something deadly both in the desire of the analyst and the termination of analysis in the sense of the cutting off and detachment associated with the death drive. This appears to be contrary to Eros that always leans towards union and synthesis. From this vantage point, one can understand why the analyst's desire is a special subjective destitution requiring a payment with the core of one's being. The analyst must work on something having to do with his/her own desire. This makes it the most decisive and fundamental of the three payments. It is only on the basis of such payment that one can tolerate paying with words and with one's person. Only if the analyst declines to put himself/herself in the privileged position of being desired for life can he/she attack his/her own ego-identity by leaving aside values, choices, and other narcissistic gratifications.

With the notion of the third payment with the core of one's being we return to the question of re-visioning the ethical structure and the intrinsic spirituality of the analytic situation. I mentioned earlier that the values emanating from the level of the tree of life of non-duality (of good and evil), correspond to those associated with the practice of analysis. Values related to a sublimated death drive or with a death drive that in the end (of aims/ends), crosses over to the other side, or the side of Eros.

Regarding so-called health values, the Buddha, like Freud, is known to have used the well-known parable of the surgeon. The doctor has to extract the arrow from the body, cutting and temporarily causing more pain, in order for the wound and the body to heal and live. The practice of cutting, separating, *desêtring* or non-being, discarding, letting go, and non-attachment are all the manifestations of a non-dual good connected with the symbolic register of the death drive. It is in this sense that Lacan linked the symbolic order to the function of the death drive. However, I am also linking a sublime reach of death or Nirvana with Eros that is something that Lacan did not explicitly do.

Thus, in unison with the Gospel and Genesis, I submit that there is a life which leads to death and a death which leads to life, or put dialectically and non-dualistically, there is life within death (under the Nirvana principle) and death within life (under the pleasure principle). I argue that the Eros which I associate with what Lacan called the second death under the Symbolic precisely refers to a distinction between the *jouissance* of the Other and an Other *jouissance* that others (Miller, 1997) have found implicit in Lacan's work.

The deadly aspect of mystical experience destroys identity in the sense that it destroys the illusory or imaginary notion of ego. Zen practice, for example, is commonly referred to as leading to an ego-death. It is a necessary symbolic death that dialectically affirms a larger and more ultimate form of psychical identity. Thus, I have stated that mystical experience and Lacanian psychoanalysis share a practice of what Lacan calls subjective or mental/psychical destitution and benevolent depersonalisation.

The same can be said with respect to paying with one's person as a form of renunciation or negation of personal values. I have argued that the abstention of judgement implies values of a different order or metavalues. In a way, I am using Maslow's (1968) concept of metavalues but conceive of them in the context of a Zen Buddhist concept of non-duality, the Freudian/Lacanian/Buddhist understanding of a symbolic death, and the Freudian/Nietzschean notion of a transvaluation of psychical values. It is well known that moral values or what I am calling superego values operate within a classical dual relationship to desire. In addition, superego values are often fervently desired and compel one to forbidden desire.

The dividing, aggressive component of superego judgements, although having a social utility, nevertheless need to be neutralised under the influence of a non-dual Eros which is not the opposite of hate and which is cultivated and evoked by the renunciation contained within the desire of the analyst. The life of desire, of dual love, quickly turns into hate and deadly aggressiveness, and hate, once socialised, quickly turns into dual morality and resentment.

Thus, both dual desire and morality end up on the shore of a death that is the end of life. I have also mentioned that the desire of the analyst, which is a desire for emptiness or for no particular object, can be seen as a desire for death, for Nirvana, for the serenity of a symbolic death that gives rather than ends life. It gives life because a desire for emptiness or the emptiness at the root of desire regenerates rather than negates or ends desire. A desire not to desire would still be just another desire. Emptiness as the end/aim of desire is not the end or extinction of desire.

The desire of the analyst is also Buddha's desire. And Buddha's desire or the desire of the analyst, although beginning from the condition of death and suffering produced by a dual life of desire and morality, generates a transvaluation of psychical values that illuminates the meaning of a second symbolic death at the service of life and "rebirth". In this latter shore, life and death, Eros and Nirvana, do not constitute polar elements but constitute two sides of the same ground.

Freud spoke of the transvaluation of psychical values in reference to the workings of repression: what was pleasant becomes unpleasant and vice versa. The moral good replaces the good of pleasure by turning the latter into something bad and the bad of frustration into something good. The practice of analysis reverses this process: the moral good or superego becomes suspect and the bad of desire becomes once again something good and acceptable to the analyst. But since psychoanalysis is not hedonism, this cannot be the end of the story. Becoming intimate with one's desire is not equivalent to the fulfilment of human desire, which is something impossible.

The dialectical reversal and transvaluation whereby the good becomes bad, the bad becomes good, life becomes death and death life, the crossing over to the other side, are classical examples not only of the workings of the psyche, of analysis as a therapeutic practice, but also of spiritual practices which seek the non-dual One by turning one term over its opposite.

In addition, this dialectical reversal also operates in intersubjective relations. For example, at first, the analysand comes representing the side of suffering, division, death, the "I am dying, I cannot live like this", and the analyst represents the possibility of life and true desire. At the end of analysis, a transvaluation of these values needs to take place. The analyst needs to move to the place of the second death, of a spiritual/psychical death that renews life by renouncing the desire to be desired and becoming dispensable to the analysand. The analysand needs to move from the place of death and suffering to the place of recovering the possibility of desire and of desiring someone else, not the analyst.

The place of the second death is that of the freeing the libido from archaic objects in the transference and therefore also eventually from the analyst/therapist. It is an experience equivalent to grief; grieving the lost objects as images that define the ego or with which the ego is identified, and therefore the second death also represents a loss at the level of the ego, a subjective permutation, and psychical destitution. Finally, the peace of Nirvana, of the second death, is associated with non-pathological grief because it represents freedom from clinging and an eventual return to the natural quiescence of the mind.

The relationship between a symbolic death and the desire of the analyst can also be observed in the forbearance of suffering associated with the position of the analyst as a support for the transference. To exercise the analytic position, the analyst needs to withstand the love and hate of the analysand as a function of transference and not as response to past or present behaviour of the analyst towards the analysand. The analyst takes on the problems of the analysand as if they were his/her own in so far as he/she will be perceived by the other as having done this or that to him/her, either literally or figuratively.

Moreover, by following the Kleinian school, or perhaps, more specifically, the work of Bion on the concept of projective identification, then the metaphor would be complete. The analyst gets to feel and experience mental states that are not his own in order to metabolise them and return them to the analysand in a more benevolent and favourable form. Moreover, if the analyst is hated and verbally attacked in the transference, the analyst is not to respond in kind but rather merely provide interpretations.

A parallel can be drawn between the position of the analyst and that of the archetypal Christ. According to Catholic dogma, Jesus took on the abuse of the world in order to enact the function of a huge recycling container for the thoughts, feelings, and actions of the human world. From this perspective, one can get another glimpse regarding the intrinsic spirituality of the analytical situation that does not require even a single mention of an ethical or religious counsel or teaching.

Finally, it can also be argued that the desire of the analyst produces what Maslow (1968) named a B-cognition or a knowing of being which is impersonal, without human desire, unmotivated, non-attached, and not ego-centred or ego-based. Maslow likened the B-cognition to what Krishnamurti called choiceless awareness. It is the latter that bestows the ability to perceive the ineffable, that which cannot be put into words. A choiceless awareness is another way of talking about paying with one's person in terms of renouncing personal choices and preferences and paying with the core of one's being in the sense of a desire not to be desired.

From this vantage point, it becomes possible to arrive at a different understanding of the meaning of the alleged consolations provided by both religion and psychoanalysis. The consolation provided by psychoanalysis needs to be included in the equation because, as a therapeutics, psychoanalysis encompasses a solution to the problem of suffering, even if only partially. Psychoanalysis prides itself on being able to tolerate absences or lacks: of perfection, religion, an ideal sexual relation, an ideal marriage or society, and so on.

Psychoanalysis denounces the imaginary crutches and consolations provided by religion as either a fusion with the mother or infantile dependence on a providential father. Both of these forms are intrinsic to the symbolic lies and imaginary deceptions of love. However, the psychoanalytic tolerance of absence is the cultural analogue to the spiritual function of renunciation, non-attachment, and the ability to be alone in the face of the Real. Analytic absence cannot be dualistically regarded as sheer absence. Such absence produces not a positive fetish, an imaginary phallic or religious object, but an ethical presence, a psychical and energetic awakened/adverted position/state within the analyst. For the analyst, it functions as a source of consolation in the sense of a core of being associated with self-control, equanimity, and a therapeutic stance.

REFERENCES

Abe, M. (1999). *Zen and Western Thought*. Honolulu: University of Hawaii Press.

Adorno, T. (1978). Subject and object. In: A. Arato & E. Gebhardt (Eds.), *The Essential Frankfurt School Reader*. New York: Urizen Books.

Adorno, T., Frenkel-Brunswik, E., Levinson, D. & Sanford, N. (1950). *The Authoritarian Personality*. New York: Harper.

Allport, G. W. (1950). *The Individual and His Religion*. New York: Macmillan.

Altemayer, B. (1988). *Enemies of Freedom; Understanding Right-Wing Authoritarianism*. San Francisco: Jossey-Bass.

Bachelard, G. (1975). *La formacion del espiritu cientifico*. Buenos Aires: Siglo Ventiuno Editores.

Bakan, D. (1958). *Sigmund Freud and the Jewish Mystical Tradition*. Boston: Beacon Press.

Baker, H. & Baker, M. (1987). Heinz Kohut's self psychology: An overview. *American Journal of Psychiatry, 144*: 1.

Barrat, B. (1993). *Psychoanalysis and the Postmodern Impulse*. Baltimore, MD: Johns Hopkins University Press.

Batson, C. D. & Ventis, W. L. (1982). *The Religious Experience: A Social-Psychological Perspective*. New York: Oxford University Press.

Baudrillard, J. (1981). *For a Critique of the Political Economy of the Sign*. St Louis: Telos.

Bellah, R. N. (1970). *Beyond Belief: Essays in a Post-Traditional World*. New York: Harper & Row.

Bielefeldt, C. (1988). *Dogen's Manuals of Zen Meditation*. Berkeley: University of California Press.

Bion, W. R. (1965). *Transformations*. London: Karnac, 1984.

Bion, W. R. (1995). *Attention and Interpretation*. New Jersey: Jason Aronson.

Blake, W. (1790). *The Marriage of Heaven and Hell*. New York: Dover, 1994.

Bobrow, J. (2010). *Zen and Psychotherapy: Partners in Liberation*. New York: Norton.

Bock, D. C. & Warren, N. C. (1972). Religious belief as a factor in obedience to destructive commands. *Review of Religious Research, 13*: 185–191.

Bollas, C. (1989). *Forces of Destiny*. London: Free Association Books.

Brand, C. (1981). *Personality and Political Attitudes*. Oxford: Pergamon Press.

Buber, M. (1923). *I and Thou*. London: Continuum, 2004.

Campbell, J. (1967). *The Hero with a Thousand Faces*. Cleveland: Meridian Books.

Campbell, J. (1968). *The Masks of God*, 4 vols. New York: Viking.

Cannon, W. (1932). *The Wisdom of the Body*. New York: Norton, 1963.

Chomsky, N. (1966). *Cartesian Linguistics: A Chapter in the History of Rationalist Thought*. New York: Harper & Row.

Cordovero, M. (1981). *The Palm of Deborah: Anthology of Jewish Mysticism*. New York: Judaica Press.

Derrida, J. (1992). Of an apocalyptic tone newly adopted in philosophy. In: *Derrida and Negative Theology*. New York: Suny Press.

Deutsch, D. (1997). *The Fabric of Reality*. London: Penguin.

Dilthey, W. (1894). *Descriptive Psychology and Historical Understanding*. The Hague: Martinus Nijhoff, 1977.

Dogen, Z. (1231–1253). *Moon in a Dew Drop*. San Francisco: North Point Press, 1985.

Dogen, Z. (1231–1253). *Shobogenzo: Treasury of the Eye of the True Dharma*. London: Windbell, 1994.

Dogen, Z. (1231–1253). *Hachi Dainin-gaku*. In: *The Hazy Moon of Enlightenment*. MA: Wisdom Books, 2007.

Dolto, F. (1979). *The Jesus of Psychoanalysis*. Trans. Helen R. Lane. London: Doubleday.

Dolto, F. & Nasio, J. D. (1987). El Niño del Espejo. Espana, Gedisa, 2a Edición, 1992. *Journal of European Psychoanalysis, n. 1*, 1995.

Dresner, S. H. (1974). *The Zaddik*. New York: Schocken.

Durkheim, É. (1954). *The Elementary Forms of the Religious Life*. London: Allen and Unwin, n.d.

Eigen, M. (1993). The area of faith in Winnicott, Lacan and Bion. In: *The Electrified Tightrope*. London: J. Aronson.

Eigen, M. (1998). *The Psychoanalytic Mystic*. London: Free Association Books.

Engler, J. H. (1981). Vicissitudes of the self according to psychoanalysis and Buddhism: A spectrum model of object relations development. *Psychoanalysis and Contemporary Thought, 6*: 29–72.

Engler, J. H. (2003). Being somebody and being nobody: a re-examination of the understanding of self in psychoanalysis and Buddhism. In: J. Safran (Ed.), *Psychoanalysis and Buddhism: An Unfolding Dialogue*. Somervilled, MA: Wisdom Books.

Epstein, M. (1995). *Thoughts without a Thinker*. New York: Basic Books.

Epstein, M. (2007). *Psychotherapy without the Self: A Buddhist Perspective*. New Haven: Yale University Press.

Erikson, E. (1977). *Toys and Reasons: Stages in the Ritualization of Experience*. New York: Norton.

Etchegoyen, H. (1991). *The Fundamentals of Psychoanalytic Technique*. London: Karnac.

Feagin, J. R. (1964). Prejudice and religious types. *Journal for the Scientific Study of Religion, 4*: 3–13.

Fink, B. (1995). *The Lacanian Subject*. New Jersey: Princeton University Press.

Fink, B. (1997). *A Clinical Introduction to Lacanian Psychoanalysis*. Cambridge, MA: Harvard University Press.

Flournoy, T. (1903). Les principes de la psychologie religieuse. *Archives de psychologie, 2*: 33–57.

Frankl, V. (1962). *Man's Search for Meaning*. Boston: Beacon Press.

Frankl, V. (1975). *The Unconscious God*. New York: Simon and Schuster.

Freud, S. (1900a). *The Interpretation of Dreams. Standard Edition, 4, 5*. London: Hogarth, 1953–1974.

Freud, S. (1905c). *The Psychopathology of Everyday Life. Standard Edition, 6*.

Freud, S. (1907b). Obsessive actions and religious practices. *Standard Edition, 9*.

Freud, S. (1910c). *Leonardo da Vinci and a Memory of His Childhood. Standard Edition, 11*: 59–137.

Freud, S. (1911). *Psycho-Analytic Notes on an Autobiographical Account of a Case of Paranoia (dementia paranoides). Standard Edition, 12*: 3–82.

Freud, S. (1912–1913). *Totem and Taboo. Standard Edition, 13*: 1–161.

Freud, S. (1912e). Recommendations to physicians practicing psycho-analysis. *Standard Edition, 12*: 109–120.

Freud, S. (1920g). *Beyond the Pleasure Principle. Standard Edition, 18*: 7–64.

Freud, S. (1921c). Group psychology and the analysis of the ego. *Standard Edition, 18*: 67–143.

Freud, S. (1923b). The ego and the id. *Standard Edition, 19*: 1, 3–66.

Freud, S. (1926e). The question of lay analysis. *Standard Edition, 20*: 179–258.

Freud, S. (1927c). *The Future of an Illusion. Standard Edition, 21*: 3–56.

Freud, S. (1928a). A religious experience. *Standard Edition, 21*.

Freud, S. (1939). *Moses and Monotheism. Standard Edition, 23*: 3–137.

Fromm, E. (1950). *Psychoanalysis and Religion*. New York: Bantam Books.

Fromm, E. (1960). *Psychoanalysis and Zen Buddhism*. San Francisco: Harper Colophon.

Fromm, E. (1966). *You Shall Be As Gods: A Radical Interpretation of the Old Testament and its Tradition*. New York: Holt, Rinehart, and Winston.

Fromm, E. (1976). *To Have or To Be?* New York: Harper & Row.

Gadamer, H. G. (1975). *Truth and Method*. London: Sheed & Ward.

Gorsuch, R. L. & Aleshire, D. (1974). Christian faith and ethnic prejudice. *Journal for the Scientific Study of Religion, 13*: 281–307.

Greeley, A. M. (1975). *The Sociology of the Paranormal*. Sage Research Paper in the Social Sciences. London and Beverly Hills, CA: Sage Publications.

Greenson, R. R. (1978). The working alliance and the transference neurosis. In: *Explorations in Psychoanalysis* (pp. 199–224). New York: International Universities Press.

Grotstein, J. (2003). Introduction: Bion, the navigator of the deep and formless infinite, overview. In: *Building on Bion: Branches, Contemporary Developments and Applications of Bion's Contributions to Theory and Practice*. London: Jessica Kingsley.

Habermas, J. (1968). *Knowledge and Human Interests*. Boston: Beacon Press.

Harari, R. (1990). *Discurrir el Psicoanalisis*. Buenos Aires: Nueva Vision.

Heidegger, M. (1949). *Existence and Being*. http://www.marxists.org/reference/subject/philosophy/works/ge/heidegg2.htm

Heidegger, M. (1950). *Hegel's Concept of Experience*. New York: Harper and Row, 1970.

Heidegger, M. (1953). *Being and Time*. Trans. Joan Stambaugh. New York: State University of New York Press, 1996.

Hoffman, E. (1981). *The Way of Splendor: Jewish Mysticism and Modern Psychology*. Boulder, CO, and London: Shambhala.

Homans, P. (1970). *Theology after Freud: An Interpretive Inquiry*. Indianapolis: Bobbs-Merrill.

Hopenhayn, M. (1997). *Despues del nihilismo: de Nietzsche a Foucault*. Santiago: Editorial Andres Bello.

Horkheimer, M. (1978). On the problem of truth. In: A. Arato & E. Gebhardt (Eds.), *The Essential Frankfurt School Reader*. New York: Urizen Books.

Husserl, E. (1900–1901). *Logical Investigations, Volumes One and Two*, Trans. J. N. Findlay. London: Routledge, 1976.

Idel, M. (1988). *Kabbalah: New Perspectives*. New Haven: Yale University Press.

Jakobson, R. (1975). *Ensayos de Linguistica General*. Barcelona: Seix Barral.

James, W. (1902). *The Varieties of Religious Experience*. Cambridge, MA: Harvard University Press, 1985.

Jones, J. W. (1991). *Contemporary Psychoanalysis and Religion*. New Haven: Yale University Press.

Joyce, J. (1916). *A Portrait of the Artist as a Young Man*. New York: Viking Press, 1964.

Jung, C. G. (1919). Archetypes and the collective unconscious. *Collected Works, 9*. New Jersey: Princeton University Press, 1981.

Jung, C. G. (1944). Psychology and alchemy. *Collected Works, 12*. New York: Bollingen Series XX.

Jung, C. G. (1958). Psychology and Western religion. *Collected Works, 11*. New York: Bollingen Series XX.

Jung, C. G. (1962). *Memories, Dreams, Reflections*. New York: Pantheon.

Jung, C. G. (1964). *Man and His Symbols*. New York: Basic Books.

Kant, I. (1788). *Critique of Practical Reason*. Chicago: Chicago University Press, 1949.

Kaplan, A. (1981). *Meditation and the Bible*. York Beach, ME: Samuel Weiser.

Katagiri, D. (1988). *Returning to Silence: Zen Practice in Daily Life*. Boston: Shambala.

Kim, J. H. (2007). *Dogen on Meditation and Thinking: A Reflection on His View of Zen*. New York: State University of New York Press.

Kochumuttom, T. A. (1982). *A Buddhist Doctrine of Experience*. Delhi: Motilal Banarsidass.

Koestler, A. (1967). *The Ghost in the Machine*. New York: Penguin, 1990.

Kohut, H. (1966). Forms and transformations of narcissism. *Journal of the American Psychoanalytic Association, 14*: 243–272.

Kohut, H. & Wolf, E. (1978). The disorders of the self and their treatment: An outline. *International Journal of Psycho-Analysis, 59*: 413–425.

Kristeva, J. (1987). *In the Beginning was Love*. New York: Columbia University Press.

Kung, H. (1979). *Freud and the Problem of God*. New Haven: Yale University Press.

Lacan, J. (1953). *The Function of Language in Psychoanalysis*. New York: Delta Books, 1975.

Lacan, J. (1959). *La Etica del Psicoanalisis*. Buenos Aires: Paidos, 1988.

Lacan, J. (1960). *Seminar 7, on the Ethic of Psychoanalysis*. New York: Norton, 1988.

Lacan, J. (1961). The direction of the treatment and the principles of its power. In: *Écrits*. New York: Norton, 1979.

Lacan, J. (1964). *The Four Fundamental Concepts of Psychoanalysis*. New York: Norton, 1981.

Lacan, J. (1966a). The instancy of the letter in the unconscious or reason after Freud. In: *Écrits*. Trans. Bruce Fink in collaboration Heloise Fink and Russell Grigg. New York: Norton, 2006.

Lacan, J. (1966b). The subversion of the subject and the dialectic of desire. In: *Écrits*. Trans. Bruce Fink. New York: Norton, 2002.

Lacan, J. (1966c). Posicion del inconsciente. In: *El Inconsciente, Coloquio de Bonneval*. Buenos Aires: Siglo XXI, 1975.

Lacan, J. (1966–1967). *Seminar XIV: The Logic of Fantasy*. Unpublished.

Lacan, J. (1968–1969). *El Seminario. Libro 16. De un Otro al otro*. Buenos Aires: Paidos, 2008.

Lacan, J. (1973). *The Four Fundamental Concepts of Psychoanalysis* (p. 53). New York: Norton, 1978.

Lacan, J. (1974). *"La Troisième"*, in *Lettres de l'Ecole Freudienne*, 16, Paris, 1975, pp. 178–203.

Lacan, J. (1977). *Seminar XXIV*, 8 March. Unpublished. (Quoted by P. Julien, *Jacques Lacan's Return to Freud*. New York: New York University Press, 1994.)

Lacan, J. (1991). *Séminaire le Transfert*, VIII. Paris: Seuil.

Laing, R. D. & Cooper, D. G. (1964). *Reason and Violence: A Decade of Sartre's Philosophy*. London: Routledge, 1999.

Laplanche, J. & Leclaire, S. (1966). El inconsciente: un estudio psicoanalitico. In: *El Inconsciente, Coloquio de Bonneval*. Buenos Aires: Siglo XXI, 1975.

Laplanche, J. & Leclaire, S. (1968). Fantasy and the origins of sexuality. *International Journal of Psychoanalysis, 49*: 1–18.

Leavy, S. (1990). Reality in religion and psychoanalysis. In: *Psychoanalysis and Religion*. Baltimore, MD: Johns Hopkins University Press.

Lefèvre, H. (1975). A social model of the unconscious. In: *El Inconsciente, Coloquio de Bonneval*. Buenos Aires: Siglo XXI. (Original work published 1966.)

Lévi-Strauss, C. (1958). The effectiveness of symbols. In: *Structural Anthropology*. New York: Basic Books, 1976.

Lévi-Strauss, C. (1968). On symbolic efficacy. In: *Structural Anthropology*. Harmondsworth: Penguin, 1972.

Loewald, H. (1978). *Psychoanalysis and the History of the Individual*. New Haven: Yale University Press.

Lyotard, J.-F. (1989). *The Postmodern Condition*. Minneapolis: University of Minnesota Press.

Magid, B. (2002). *Ordinary Mind: Exploring the Common Ground of Zen and Psychotherapy*. Boston: Wisdom.

Marini, M. (1992). *Jacques Lacan: The French Context*. New Jersey: Rutgers University Press.

Maslow, A. H. (1964). *Religions, Values, and Peak Experiences*. Columbus: Ohio State University Press.

Maslow, A. H. (1968). *Toward a Psychology of Being*. New York: Van Nostrand Reinhold.

Masterson, J. F. (1985). *The Real Self: A Developmental, Self, and Object Relations Approach*. New York: Brunner/Mazel.

May, R. (1957a). *Man's Search for Himself*. New York: Norton.

May, R. (1957b). The relation between psychotherapy and religion. In J. E. Fairchild (Ed.), *Personal Problems and Psychological Frontiers: A Cooper Union Forum* (pp. 168–187). New York: Sheridan House.

Meissner, W. W. (1984). *Psychoanalysis and Religious Experience*. New Haven: Yale University Press.

Meissner, W. W. (1996). The pathology of beliefs and the beliefs of pathology. In: Edward Shafranske (Ed.), *Religion and the Clinical Practice of Psychology*. Washington, DC: APA.

Miller, J. A. (1997). The drive is speech. *Umbr(a)*, #1, 1997. *Journal of the Center for the Study of Psychoanalysis and Culture*.

Molino, A. (Ed.) (1998). *The Couch and the Tree: Dialogues in Psychoanalysis and Buddhism*. New York: North Point Press.

Molino, A. (Ed.) (2010). *Tra Sogni Del Buddha E Risvegli Di Freud*. Milan: Arpanet.

Moncayo, R. (1997). Freud's concepts of drive, desire and nirvana. *Umbr(a)*, #1.

Moncayo, R. (1998a). Cultural diversity and the cultural and epistemological structure of psychoanalysis. *Psychoanalytic Psychology, 15(2)* 262–286.

Moncayo, R. (1998b). The Real and the Symbolic in Lacan, Zen and Kaballah. *International Journal for the Psychology of Religion, 8(3)*: 179–196.

Moncayo, R. (1998c). True subject is no-subject: The real, symbolic and imaginary in psychoanalysis and Zen Buddhism. *Psychoanalysis and Contemporary Thought*, Autumn.

Moncayo, R. (1998d). Psychoanalysis and postmodern spirituality. *Journal for the Psychoanalysis of Culture and Society, 3(2)*: 123–129. 123–129. Autumn.

Moncayo, R. (2008). *Evolving Lacanian Perspectives for Clinical Psychoanalysis: On Narcissism, Sexuation, and the Phases of Analysis in Contemporary Culture*. London: Karnac.

Moncayo, R. (2012). *The Emptiness of Oedipus: Identification and Non-Identification in Lacanian Psychoanalysis*. London: Routledge.

Moncayo, R. & Harari, R. (1997). Principles of Lacanian clinical practice. *Anamorphosis. Journal of the Lacanian School of Psychoanalysis, 1*: 13–28.

Nasio, J. D. (1992). The concept of the subject of the unconscious. In: D. Pettigrew & F. Raffoul, *Disseminating Lacan*. New York: State University of New York Press.

Neruda, P. (1924). *Poemas de Amor y una Cancion Desesperada*. New York: Vintage Espanol, 2010.

Otto, R. (1929). *The Idea of the Holy*. Oxford: Oxford University Press, 1949.

Patsalides, A. (1997). *Jouissance* in the cure. *Journal of the Lacanian School of Psychoanalysis, I, 1*.

Pfister, O. (1944). *Christianity and Fear: A Study in History and in the Psychology and Hygiene of Religion*. London: Allen and Unwin.

Piaget, J. (1932). *The Moral Judgment of the Child*. New York: Simon & Schuster, 1997.

Post, S. (1980). Origins, elements and functions of therapeutic empathy. *International Journal of Psycho-Analysis, 61*: part 3.

Prigogine, I. (1984). *Order Out of Chaos*. London: Shambhala.

Rahula, W. (1974). *What the Buddha Taught*. New York: Grove Press.

Rank, O. (1909). *The Myth of the Birth of the Hero*. Baltimore, MD: Johns Hopkins University Press, 2004.

Rassial, J.-J. (2001). *El sujeto en estado limite*. Buenos Aires: Nueva Vision.

Richardson, W. (1990). Lacan and theological discourse. In: J. Smith (Ed.), *Psychoanalysis and Religion*. Baltimore, MD: Johns Hopkins University Press.

Ricoeur, P. (1970). *Freud and Philosophy: An Essay on Interpretation*. New Haven: Yale University Press.

Ricoeur, P. (1991). *From Text to Action*. Evanston, IL: Northwestern University Press.

Roof, W. C., Carroll, J. & Roazen, D. (1995). *The Post War Generation and Establishment Religion—Cross-Cultural Perspectives*. Boulder, CO: Westview Press.

Rosenbaum, R. (1999). *Zen and the Heart of Psychotherapy*. Philadelphia: Brunner/Mazel.

Roudinesco, E. (1986). *Jacques Lacan & Co: A History of Psychoanalysis in France*. Chicago: University of Chicago Press, 1990.

Roudinesco, E. (1993). *Lacan*. Buenos Aires: Fondo de Cultura Economica, 1994.

Rubin, J. B. (1996). *Psychotherapy and Buddhism: Toward an Integration*. New York: Plenum Press.

Safran, J. (Ed.) (2003). *Psychoanalysis and Buddhism: An Unfolding Dialogue*. London: Wisdom.

Scholem, G. (1962). *On the Mystical Shape of the Godhead*. New York: Schocken Books.

Scholem, G. (1978). *Kabbalah*. New York: Meridian.

Shakespeare, W. (c. 1600). *A Midsummer Night's Dream*. New York: Penguin, 1982.

Shinert, G. & Ford, E. (1958). The relation of ethnocentric attitudes to intensity of religious practice. *Journal of Educational Sociology, 32*: 157–162.

Silva, P. (1979). *An Introduction to Buddhist Psychology*. New York: Barnes and Noble.

Smith, D. W. (2007). *Husserl*. London: Routledge.

Smith, J. (1990). On psychoanalysis and the question of nondefensive religion. In: *Psychoanalysis and Religion*. Baltimore, MD: Johns Hopkins University Press.

Smith, J. (Ed.) (1991). *Psychoanalysis and Religion*. Baltimore, MD: Johns Hopkins University Press.

Sokolowski, R. (1991). Religion and psychoanalysis: Some phenomenological contributions. In: *Psychoanalysis and Religion*. Baltimore, MD: Johns Hopkins University Press.

Spero, M. H. (1992). *Religious Objects as Psychological Structures*. Chicago: Chicago University Press.

Spezzano, C. (Ed.) (1997). *The Soul on the Couch*. New Jersey: Analytic Press.

Suler, J. R. (1993). *Contemporary Psychoanalysis and Eastern Thought*. New York: State University of New York Press.

Suzuki, D. T. (1930). *Studies in the Lankavatara Sutra*. Delhi: Motilal Banarsidass, 1999.

Suzuki, D. T. (Trans.) (1931). *The Lankavatara Sutra*. London: Routledge, 1932. http://lirs.ru/do/lanka_eng/lanka-nondiacritical.htm

Suzuki, D. T. (1949). *The Zen Doctrine of No-Mind*. London: Rider Books, 1969.

Suzuki, S. (1970). *Zen Mind, Beginners Mind*. New York: Weatherhill.

Tanahashi, K. (1984). *Penetrating Laughter: Hakuin's Zen and Art*. Woodstock: The Overlook Press.

Thich Nhat Hanh (1974). *Zen Keys*. New York: Anchor.

Thompson, M. G. (2003). The primacy of experience in R. D. Laing's approach to psychoanalysis. In: R. Frie (Ed.), *Understanding Experience: Psychotherapy, Philosophy, and Postmodernism*. New York and London: Routledge.

Thompson, M. G. (2004a). Happiness and chance: A reappraisal of the psychoanalytic conception of suffering. *Psychoanalytic Psychology, 1*: 134–153.

Thompson, M. G. (2004b). *The Ethic of Honesty: The Fundamental Rule of Psychoanalysis*. Amsterdam: Rodopi.

Tillich, P. (1952). *The Courage To Be*. New Haven: Yale University Press.

Trungpa, C. (1973). *Cutting Through Spiritual Materialism*. Boston, MA: Shambhala.

Vergote, A. (1990). Confrontation with neutrality in theory and praxis. In: *Psychoanalysis and Religion*. Baltimore, MD: Johns Hopkins University Press.

Verhaeghe, P. (1998). On the Lacanian subject. In: D. Nobus (Ed.), *Key Concepts of Lacanian Psychoanalysis* (pp. 164–189). London: Rebus Press.

Vetter, G. B. (1958). *Magic and Religion: Their Psychological Nature, Origin, and Function*. New York: Philosophical Library.

Vitz, P. (1988). *Sigmund Freud's Christian Unconscious*. New York: Guilford Press.

Welwood, J. (Ed.) (1979). *The Meeting of the Ways: Explorations in East/West Psychology*. New York: Schocken Books.

Wilber, K. (1984). *Eye to Eye: The Quest for the New Paradigm*. Boston: Shambhala, 2001.

Wilden, A. (1975). Lacan and the discourse of the Other. In: *The Language of the Self*. New York: Delta Books.

Winnicott, D. W. (1960). The theory of the parent–infant relationship. In: *The Maturational Processes and the Facilitating Environment*. London: Hogarth.

Wulff, D. (1991). *Psychology of Religion*. New York: Wiley.

Wuthnow, R. (1992). *Rediscovering the Sacred: Perspective on Religion in Contemporary Society*. Grand Rapids, MI: Eerdmans.

Žižek, S. (2005). The most sublime of hysterics: From Hegel to Lacan. In: *Interrogating the Real*. London: Continuum.

INDEX